Let Go & Heal

Recovery from Hurt
and
Emotional Pain

Mark Linden O'Meara

Let Go and Heal: Recovery from Hurt and Emotional Pain

© 2019 by Mark Linden O'Meara
All rights reserved. This book, or any parts thereof, may not be reproduced or transmitted in any manner whatsoever, transmitted electronically, or distributed by any means without the written permission of the publisher.

Library and Archives Canada Cataloguing in Publication

Title: Let go & heal: recovery from hurt and emotional pain / Mark Linden O'Meara.
Names: O'Meara, Mark Linden, author.
    Includes bibliographical references.
Subjects: LCSH: Life change events—Psychological aspects. | LCSH: Adjustment (Psychology) | LCSH:
    Self-actualization (Psychology) | LCSH: Emotions. | LCSH: Self-realization.
Classification: LCC BF637.L53 O34 2019 | DDC 158.1—dc23

Published by Soul Care Publishing, Vancouver, Canada.

Copy Edited by Meghan O'Meara

Lyrics to "Cry (If you want to)" reprinted with the permission of Casey Scott and Signal Songs/Tainjo Thang (ASCAP) All Rights Reserved/ Used by Permission

Excerpts from *It Will Never Happen to Me: Growing Up with Addiction as Youngsters, Adolescents, Adults* by Claudia Black reprinted with permission of M.A.C. Publishing, 1850 High St. Denver CO. USA.

About the Author

Mark Linden O'Meara has a Master of Education in Counselling Psychology from the University of British Columbia, a Master of Business Administration (MBA) from Aspen University, and a Teachers of Adults Certificate from Cambrian College. He is a member of the Canadian Psychological and Therapist Association and is a Certified Canadian Counsellor.

Having made a commitment to himself to heal, Mark began to search for a better way of dealing with life. Through the recollection of painful childhood memories and by challenging his self-limiting beliefs, Mark let go and found a new way of looking at himself and the world. He discovered ways to resolve and release emotional pain and experience a greater connection with joy and love.

Mark warms his audiences with his personal story, anecdotes, and unexpected wit. He is an insightful writer who inspires his readers through his journey of healing and change.

Mark is also the author of *Prayers and Meditations for Daily Inspiration, Kitten and Bear and The Big Tree, Let's Let Go: The Raindrop's Journey*, and is working on numerous new books. He is also a singer and a recording artist. He has two albums in progress – *Renewal* and *Run Like the Wind* – and more coming. He lives and lectures in Vancouver, Canada.

Acknowledgments

This book is dedicated to all the people who came into my life when I needed them to provide support and encouragement, to teach me a lesson I needed to learn, to tell me the name of a book I needed to read, or to provide guidance with a valuable life lesson. Without them, my healing process wouldn't have been possible, or the creation of this book.

Special thanks go to Jose, an angel I met only once, but who gave me a special message to rise up again from adversity. Thanks also for support from my friends Cecily, Brian, Steve, and Angelina. Kind remembrance goes to my late friends Bruce Messecar and David Schoon for their inspiration and kind encouraging words.

My appreciation goes out to Kelly Davidson for her constructive suggestions, proofreading, and feedback about structure through numerous versions and revisions of early drafts. Special thanks to Angela Knoll for the encouragement and editing of the first drafts of the introduction section.

I give very appreciative thanks to my niece, Meghan O'Meara, for meticulous editing, attention to detail, and providing valuable feedback and suggestions regarding readability and consistency.

Special thanks to Melba Burns for encouragement, emotional support, and understanding of the creative process and all I was going through while finishing this book. Special thanks to Leticia Sanchez for moral support and very constructive feedback and Tina Giannoukos for support, encouragement, and helping me understand the life of a writer.

Thanks to Sophia, my stepdaughter Samantha, and her husband Stan, and for the gift of two wonderful grandchildren Brady and Amber.

I also give special thanks to my parents, who gave me life.

Mark Linden O'Meara,
October 10th, 2019

Table of Contents

PART 1 – LEARNING ABOUT EMOTIONAL HEALTH 1

1. INTRODUCTION 1
   - Defining "Letting Go" 1
   - My First-Level Healing 2
   - My Deeper Healing 3
   - Why I Wrote This Book 6
2. MIND, BODY, AND EMOTIONS 10
   - The Benefits of Expression 10
   - Myths about Emotions 12
   - Do Thoughts Create Emotion? 13
   - Unresolved Events Become Triggers 14
   - The Healing Power of Tears 15
3. DEPRESSION – MANY MEANINGS, MANY CAUSES 22
   - The Nature of Depression 22
   - The Metaphors of Depression 24
   - Causes of Depression 25
   - The Secret Strength of Depression 28
   - It's Not All Bad News about Depression! 30
4. THE MASKS YOU WEAR 32
   - Smiler Mask 33
   - Pollyannaism or Pronoid Mask 33
   - The Neutral/Flat Mask 34
   - Defensive Mask 35
   - Victim Mask 35
   - Busy Mask 36
   - Intellectual/Rationalization Mask 36
   - Insensitivity Mask 37
   - Fatigue Mask 37
   - Joker/Clown Mask 38
   - Caretaker/Gossiper Mask 38
   - Listener Mask 39
   - Silent/Hiding Mask 39
   - New Age Healer Mask 40
   - Focusing on Other People Mask 40
   - Attention Seeking Mask 41
   - Superiority Mask 41
   - Imposed Masks – Scapegoat, Black Sheep, and Victim 41
   - Masks – Good or Bad? 42
   - Removing Masks 42

5. **HOW YOU AVOID YOUR FEELINGS** 44
   - Keeping Busy 44
   - Keeping the Focus on Others.. 44
   - Taking Drugs 44
   - Drinking Alcohol 45
   - Taking Legalized Drugs or Prescription Medicine..................... 45
   - Maintaining Denial 46
   - Maintaining Noise 46
   - Smoking and Other Compulsive Behaviors 46
   - Compulsive Shopping 46
   - Self-Abuse and Self-Harm... 47
   - The Racing Mind and Obsessing 47
   - Technology and the Internet 47
   - Comparing Yourself to Others 48
   - Dissociating... 48
   - Living Too Much in "The Now" 49

6. **HURTS OF THE HEART** 50
   - Dealing with Loss and Grief 50
   - Day-to-Day Events 53
   - Holidays and Christmas 54
   - Chronic Conditions 54
   - Living, Loving, and Learning.. 55
   - Rejection, Betrayal, and Letdowns 55
   - Jealousy 56
   - Parents Wanting "The Best" 57
   - Bullying, Teasing, and Humiliation 57
   - Creative Soul Wounding 58
   - Reality Can Hurt! 59
   - Shame and Guilt 61
   - Infidelity and Divorce 61
   - Betrayal and Loss.. 62
   - Keeping a Secret 63
   - Sexuality and Orientation 63
   - Becoming More Aware 64
   - Moral Trauma and Demoralizing Inaction................................ 65
   - Crimes of Personal Invasion 65
   - Instances of Injustice 66
   - Long Periods of Unpredictability 66
   - Perfectionism 66
   - Other People's Rules and Decisions 67
   - Experiencing Poverty 68
   - Ostracism, Isolation, and Humiliation 68
   - Dealing with a Sociopath 68
   - A Broken Heart and Unrequited Love 70
   - Revictimization 70

    Vicarious Traumatization 71
    Creative Constipation 71
    Classifying Human Suffering 72
7. ABUSE, TRAUMA, AND THE WOUNDED SOUL 74
    Defining Abuse and Trauma 74
    Recognizing Abuse 76
    Destructive Communication Styles 80
    Defining and Identifying Dysfunction 81
    The Rule of the Unspoken – Expected Collusion 84
    The Explosive or Low Resiliency Personality Types 85
    The Rule Book 86
    An Adverse Environment 87
    Commonalities of Dysfunctional Families 89
    You Are Not Your Abuse 90
8. MEMORIES – FACT OR FICTION? 91
    A Forgotten Past 91
    Emotional Memory Triggers 92
    The Recovered Memory Debate 93
    Facilitating Memory Recall 95

PART 2 – DEVELOPING INSIGHT AND GROWING 99

9. THE KEYS TO DEVELOPING INSIGHT 101
    Breaking Free of a Closed System 101
    Learning to Meditate 102
    Developing Inner Psychological Space 103
    Developing the Inner Observer 104
    Stop, Look, Listen 105
    Body Awareness through Chakras 107
    Invoking Your Insightful Higher Self 109
    Follow Your Intuition and Hunches 110
10. LEARNING ABOUT YOUR BELIEFS 113
    The Stages of Challenging a Belief 114
    Discovering Your Attitudes 115
    Attributions and Subtext 116
11. LEARNING THE LANGUAGE OF FEELINGS 120
    Our Emotional Habit Inventory 122
    So, What Am I Feeling? 124
12. BEGINNING TO FEEL AGAIN 127
    Opening Up to Emotions 127
    The Past Is in the Present 128
    Unthawing Frozen Feelings 129
13. THE EMOTIONAL LIFE CYCLE 133

>   The Event 133
>   Sensations 134
>   Expression or Repression 134
>   The Energy of Release 135
>   Achieving a New Emotional Baseline 136
> 14. FIVE STAGES OF DEEP RELEASE 137
>   Biting the Bullet 137
>   Burning through Exquisite Pain 137
>   Surrender 138
>   The Death of Pain 138
>   Completion and Awakening 139

PART 3 – HEALING THE INNER WOUNDS 141

15. DEFINING HEALING 143
>   Finding Your Undamaged Self 146
>   Awareness of Choice and Invoking New Reactions! 147
>   Silencing Shame, Guilt, and the Inner Critic 148
>   Breaking "Loop" and "Spiral" Thinking Patterns 149
>   Ending Defeatist Behaviors 150

16. THE PROCESS OF DEEP HEALING 153
>   Applying Your Learning, Insight, and Growth 153
>   The Key to Healing – Re-evaluating Your Beliefs 153
>   Healing Core Wounds and Triggers 159
>   Challenging Beliefs about Relationships and Purpose 160

17. GETTING UNSTUCK 162
>   The Self-Pity Trap 163
>   Holding On 165
>   Increasing Your Awareness 166
>   Facing the Truth 168
>   Reaching a Crisis Point 168
>   Working on the Real (and Deeper) Problem 169
>   Confusion Can Lead to Innovation 171
>   Creating Creativity 172
>   Invoking the Power of Hope 172

18. TO FORGIVE OR NOT FORGIVE? 177
>   Is Forgiveness Really Necessary? 177
>   Defining Forgiveness 178
>   Should I Confront? 180
>   The Mask of Pseudo-Forgiveness 180
>   Facilitating Forgiveness 181
>   Blocks and Catalysts to Forgiving 182
>   Seven Steps to Forgiveness 183
>   Making Amends 187

    Self-Forgiveness..188
19. RESOLVING ANGER AND RESENTMENT **190**
    The Nature of Anger..190
    Anger and Timing 191
    Developing Self-Control 192
    Needing a Voice for Your Needs...193
    The Need for an Apology..194
    Anger and "Who You Remind Me Of" 194
    Anger Expression Styles and the State-Trait Anger 194
    The Four Pillars of Undoing the Anger Habit....................................195
    Changing Your Expectations 198
    Healing Rage 198
    Anger Resolution Exercises 200
20. HEALING WITH CREATIVITY **205**
    Musical Expression 206
    Express Your Traits and Talents...208
    Discover Hidden Talents...209
    Artistic Expression 210
    Dance and Drama 210
    Keep a Diary or Journal 211
    Write Letters of Letting Go...211
    Write and Rewrite Your Story 212
    Create Poetry 214
    Read Fiction...214
    Write the Letter You Would Like to Receive 215
    Create a Vision Board 215
    Create Ceremonies of Completion and Letting Go 215
    Talk to an Empty Chair 215
    Graveyard Visits – When Someone Is No Longer with You 216
    Make Use of Emotional Movies and Other Media 216
    Visualize a Different Outcome...217
    The Birth Order Exercise..217
    Draw Your Life Timeline 217
    Cultural and Religious Healing Practices 218
    Research Your Family Tree 218
    Let Your Healing Be Personal 219

PART 4 – TRANSFORMING YOUR LIFE 221

21. INVOKING PERSONAL POWER **223**
    Developing a Healthy Attitude 223
    Accepting Personal Responsibility..224
    What Is Your Life Sentence?..226

  Giving Up the Victim Role 227
  The Art of Self-Evaluation 229
  Don't Feel Ashamed When Insight Comes 230
  Parenting Yourself and Healing the Inner Person 232

22. CHANGING DIRECTIONS 237
  Unloading Your Freight Train 237
  Focus on Gratitude, Kindness, and Compassion 237
  Look Outward with Empathy! 239
  Activation of the Love Voice 241

23. TRANSFORMATIVE LIVING 242
  Redefining Success 242
  Developing Self-Compassion 245
  The Key to Feeling Good – Developing Worthiness 246
  Who Can I Be? – Accepting the Fluid Personality 248

24. CONCLUSION 250

25. BIBLIOGRAPHY 253

Part 1 – Learning about Emotional Health

1. Introduction

Defining "Letting Go"

In your quest to heal, you may have heard time and time again that you should "let go and move on." Although the advice appears to be helpful, you may not know how to let go. In some way, you feel stuck, knowing what you want, but unsure how to proceed or what the true problem might be. You may have tried letting go, doing emotional work, or forgiving someone from your past, only to find the emotions rising again at a later time. You may find yourself imagining what your life could be like if not hampered by hurt, trauma, and fear, yet you are unsure about how to achieve this goal. You have been hurt and are surviving – yet there seems to be something missing from your life.

As we start this journey together, you may be asking, what is the definition of "Letting Go"? I have given this considerable thought and have concluded that it means:

> "Allowing any person (including yourself), place, thing, or organization to be what it is at this moment in time, without judgment or expectation of change."

Let this definition sink in for a moment. You can apply this definition to emotion, attitudes, people, yourself, and your workplace. Essentially, it says, "What is, is." Most emotional pain comes from not accepting reality. It is a definition to apply in the moment. If you are feeling pain, you accept that you are feeling pain. If you are experiencing joy, then you accept the joy.

You will learn that this definition brings about a powerful paradox. By letting people be who they are, you change yourself. By accepting the current situation, you switch to being an observer. By being an observer, you can study the situation without the fog of emotion or expectation and then plan to make changes within yourself. It allows you to perform courageous acts of growth and personal activism without being motivated by harmful anger, fear, or resentment.

The definition I have provided comes from many years of personal growth, learning to accept others, yet setting boundaries. In no way am I advocating that you roll over and accept difficult, unjust, or unfair situations. Letting go allows you to learn to live without expectations. You can be centered during difficult times, with a strong sense of self-control and wisdom.

In applying the principles in this book, you, too, can learn and experience the benefits of getting in touch with your emotional self and your associated thought processes. Just like learning to drive a car, you can develop the skill of releasing your emotions and managing your thoughts, attitudes, and behaviors. Expanding your rainbow of emotions, you may discover creative talents that you never knew existed within yourself. Your efforts to heal will affect your relationships and friendships on a deep level. You can rediscover a sense of childlike joy in adult living.

Indirectly, this book becomes a tool for better communication, closer relationships, greater joy, and an increased sense of connection with yourself and with others. By reading this book, you will find yourself developing an awareness of your emotions, patterns, thoughts, and behaviors. You will become aware of the parts of your past that you need to heal and how to heal them. You will then learn about uncovering and expressing emotions through various healing concepts, practices, and rituals. You will develop skills to challenge your thinking and integrate a new way of thinking into your life. Over time, you will realize you have created a greater sense of happiness. I hope that by learning to integrate the principles presented in this book, you will gain a sense of renewal and notice measurable changes in your life.

This book also has information about healing anger and rage, forgiveness, and getting unstuck, all of which were essential to my healing process. I am certain that these will be helpful in your healing process too!

My First-Level Healing

Before learning the concepts in this book, my life was seriously affected by a backlog of emotions fueled by negative underlying beliefs. Having learned to hide my pain at an early age, I developed numerous health and personal problems associated with emotional repression and dissociation. All of this led to a state of crisis, fatigue, and isolation, and problematic, distorted, negative thinking. A friend confided to me that no matter how hard I tried to have a good time, it seemed that something was always pulling me down. Despite being in considerable emotional pain, I was unable to communicate this to others, nor could I admit it to myself. Keeping myself very busy, at times compulsively, I realized I needed to slow down, but could not. Although emotionally wound up, I was also extremely numb to my feelings. Due to unresolved grief, I gave the impression to others to leave me alone even though my heart longed for companionship. Most of my obsession with projects and my irrational behavior were ways of avoiding my feelings. It is from this state that I eventually moved to a sense of serenity and connectedness with others. This change came about as I learned to deal with my emotions more effectively and challenge the underlying beliefs.

While the beginnings of this book came about after making a New Year's resolution to experience more joy, it was the facing of my emotional pain that brought about the achievement of my goal. In the three years following my New Year's resolution, I experienced a period of incredible change in my living accommodations, social life, career, and, ultimately, my level of self-knowledge. While some would call it a breakdown, I prefer to call it an opening of my heart. During this period, I searched for answers. I learned about the dynamics of releasing, letting go, and healing. Originally thinking that emotional expression was the sole key to my healing, in retrospect, I understand that healing occurred when I expressed emotions and when I challenged and changed my thoughts, beliefs, and behaviors. Emotions, thoughts, beliefs, and behaviors are clearly interconnected. Starting to change one of these can bring about change in the others. Releasing emotions can result in increased clarity of thinking. When thinking improves, emotions and behavior can more easily change.

My Deeper Healing

Learning about and healing my childhood traumas brought great improvements in my life, but significant difficulties lay ahead. While I continued to work on myself and felt a substantial level of healing, there came a period during which I experienced considerable adversity: health problems, fatigue, and burnout, as well as serious financial difficulties. I was exhausted, angry, and bitter, yet was the author of a book on healing.

I was no longer living the principles of what I had learned and written about.

These difficult times continued in the first three years after completing my master's degree. While helping a friend move, I was asked to help carry a heavy trunk of books. After lifting the rear end of the trunk, the other person holding the front of the trunk lost grip, and the trunk slammed to the ground, wrenching my already tensed neck and shoulders forward. I spent the next few days stuck in bed with a terrible whiplash headache. I lost my singing voice due to muscle tension. It took over fifteen years and tens of thousands of dollars to heal the daily headaches and damaged muscle tissue.

Furthermore, my master's program took much longer than planned: what was advertised as a two-year program took everyone three years to complete, myself included. The extra time needed to complete the program caused further financial problems. Furthermore, although my book sales were good (achieving National Best Seller status in Canada) and my marketing efforts resulted in a sustained momentum of sales, the one national book chain in Canada was experiencing financial difficulties, and my distributor stopped shipping books because of delayed payments. My book sales fell to almost nothing. Combined with only part-time work, the financial strains from my self-publishing, health costs, and student loan debt, I found myself declaring bankruptcy. I also had to deal with a botched hernia operation, a tick bite that led to Lyme disease, and a cancer scare that required surgery. At the time, it seemed my dreams of being a successful writer were in ruins. I had firmly believed that I could create my own destiny, but was greatly affected by things clearly beyond my control.

Despite having done a great deal of healing work, I realized that I was a mess, angry, bitter, resentful, and in severe physical and emotional pain. I seemed to have lost hope that things would get better. Instinct led me to challenge and overcome this state of mind. I knew that something was missing. A powerful dream provided the answer.

In my dream, I was trying to get to the top of a mountain. While driving my car up a hill to get to the park, the clutch began to slip, and the car slid back down the hill. I parked the car and got out. A bicycle was nearby, so I took a different route but found my chain broken. Carrying the bicycle up a path and joining a tour group, I came upon a sign that read, "Level eight to ten dangers exist on this path." People were coming down the hill on bicycles and nearly hitting me. Eventually, a clearing appeared where a sign pointed to an odd-looking tree stump about twelve feet around, with a sign that read, "Level Ten Danger!" Another member of our tour began jumping up and down on the stump, saying, "How could this be a level ten danger?" My dream was warning me that how I was dealing with my challenges of burnout, bankruptcy, and student loan issues were the greatest threat to my mental health.

The dream continued. Just then, the edge of the stump gave way, and the other member of our tour group began falling into the abyss in the middle of the stump. As he tried to free himself, he became more and more entangled, being swallowed up by the collapsed stump, its branches, and vines. By now, I could see that the hole was dark and went deep into the earth. I believe that the branches represented my circular and obsessive thinking about the issues I was trying to resolve in my life.

With everyone standing around in shock, I realized that this person would die if I did not help him. I took action and reached over, grabbing his hand and arm and pulling him over the lip of the abyss with all my body weight. Although he was still slightly tangled, it was obvious that the danger was over. He got up, and as he untangled himself from the branches, I joked, "Do you still think it's not a level ten danger?" The humor broke the sense of tension and relaxed everyone. As the group began to walk further up the path, I realized that I had saved this person's life through my actions, yet he seemed unaware of this and did not openly thank me. As we continued unencumbered on our journey, the man I had saved walked past me and touched me on the arm. It was his acknowledgment of thanks, his soul acknowledging mine. The event had shaken him, and thus me, at a very deep level.

In interpreting the latter part of this dream, I realized that the person who had fallen into the abyss was, in fact, me. I was depressed, discouraged, and had lost hope. What I took from the dream – and what my life has confirmed – was that if anyone were to pull me out of this depression, it would be me. I realized that I needed to help myself.

In dealing with my situation at that time, my understanding of how to recover from adversity was profoundly deepened. Recognizing that a rut is sometimes the highest mountain to climb, I developed a greater capacity for perseverance, hope, and self-guidance and asking for help. Reflecting on my previous lessons and developing a deeper understanding of the powers of forgiveness led me into a healthier state of hope, gratitude, self-care, and the ever-present power of choice.

Recovery involved learning to view my situation as temporary. I started to do things to take care of myself, one day at a time. Slowly I began to emerge from depression, learning to exercise my mind to be more positive, to be creative in my thoughts and to visualize a positive outcome, to meditate regularly, to exercise, and to eat better. Discovering that I had become disconnected spiritually, I began to pray and to trust that things would work out. Things started to clear up. My finances and health improved as soon as I began working on the real problem: namely, my attitude. Improvements became increasingly possible by taking concrete action to deepen my spirituality and learning about how I could help myself.

I understood at a deep level that I had, and continue to have, the power of choice – the choice to respond to thoughts, feelings, and emotions in a way that can benefit me rather than hinder me. I can choose to base my future projections on history or envision a completely new paradigm. I discovered that although I had learned to express and heal pain, I had yet to develop the skills to deal with resentment and anger. I began a journey to accomplish this, which was probably the greatest and deepest healing that I have experienced in my life thus far.

Why I Wrote This Book

Through my journey, I have learned a tremendous amount about the nature of emotions and what happens when they are suppressed. I have also read countless articles and papers regarding the effects of emotional, physical, and sexual abuse on the victim. The incidences of addiction, depression, and mental health problems are clearly linked to these distressing situations. However, I have also learned that it is not necessary to experience extreme traumatic events to end up being emotionally numb, out of touch with your feelings, and rationally impaired. Stressful life events, unsupportive family environments, or growing up in addictive or dependent families are just some of the factors that can lead to similar conditions.

I have experienced the reality that the effects of emotional distress and life challenges are not permanent, and that healing can take place. Through some trial and error, the support of others, seemingly chance meetings with people, and reading the right book at the right time, I experienced a major shift in my emotional, physical, and mental health. I worked diligently to get in touch with my emotions, thoughts, and feelings, releasing them to the universe, and experiencing the healing that will last for my lifetime. The work has paid off! I developed a much deeper understanding of myself, my past, and the emotions I was feeling in the present. With this work came new understanding and insight and a better way of being in the world. In my healing process, I established new friendships, changed careers, developed a greater degree of self-compassion, and improved my decision-making. The combination of these factors led to a healthier outlook. I have less disappointment and recognize what I have to offer other people. My self-esteem has improved. I am more assertive, and I experience a greater measure of joy in my life.

Over time, I learned that it is possible to express and resolve emotions safely and to heal emotional hurt. In the process, I experienced a sense of renewal and revitalization. I no longer have a lingering sense of dread and weariness about me. When problems arise, I am dealing primarily with the current situation rather than my emotional history. When issues come up in a relationship, I can deal with them more effectively, having resolved the burdens of my past. Of course, I still have difficult days, but I have successfully resolved a great deal of what is commonly referred to as "emotional baggage." I have begun to live my life in a way that I believe is a dream come true. Simply reminding myself of these improvements makes my day better!

The events that brought about the creation of this book seem humorous now that I look back. Originally, I started to write a "how-to" book on buying a house! My friend Stephanie kindly lent me her laptop to do some writing at my brother's isolated rural cottage. During the daytime,

Mark Linden O'Meara

I worked on a few projects around the cottage and wrote during the quiet evening hours. One of the projects I took on was to make improvements to the property. My father had dug a well years before, with only a shovel, resulting in two hernias! Each spring, however, pine needles and other debris would find their way into the well. The well required a thorough cleaning at the beginning of each cottage season. As I began this project, I noticed that my father had taken several shortcuts in building the foundation of rocks that lined the well walls. I ended up removing all the original work and rebuilding it from the bottom with a new and stronger foundation. As I recognized this as an analogy for my own life, I wrote a short essay on the subject. Then I wrote another and another and so on. As I read the words I had written back to myself, I found a new calling to write, finding myself totally immersed in a different direction.

With my new goal of writing a book about a different subject, and having experienced a great deal of positive change, I wanted to ensure that I fully understood the process through which I had moved. I also wanted to identify the key elements that facilitated my healing process. I believed that I could pass on valuable knowledge to others. And so I began writing, which in itself was positive and cathartic. Spending considerable time collecting information on the topics of healing, health, and resolving emotions, I searched for articles on the effects of emotional release. Collections of notes scribbled onto napkins, scraps of paper, match covers, and concert programs were transformed into a manuscript and, eventually, this book. What you have before you is the result of my healing process. It describes what I have learned and my ongoing desire to change and grow. I hope the information and techniques in this book will help you in your goal of emotional healing.

I would like you to keep in mind that there is no right or wrong way to go about healing and to let go. You are unique, and therefore, the techniques or solutions that you choose may be different from those someone else would find helpful. The images and experiences you relate to will also be unique. As a result, I have not included case studies in this book, as it would not be possible to include the depth and subtleties of any one individual's experience. I have, however, included my personal experiences and examples wherever possible. While reading about the ideas and techniques I present, I suggest that you examine your own life to see how they apply to you. Try to apply them in your unique way to your situation. I hope that you create your own experience from reading these pages. I hope this book will help you learn to safely and successfully heal the pains of adversity, growing up, entering into adulthood, and the various losses and challenges that you have encountered. There are great joys in life, but they are often clouded over with layers of blocked emotion, hindering the free expressive ability with which you were born.

Letting go is a process you can learn, practice, and improve. If you have not experienced the process of letting go, I will show you how through my own stories. I will describe the ideas, techniques, and attitudes that facilitate letting go and help you to move into a person who can better evaluate your emotions, to discover their underlying cause, and to use your emotional intelligence to change your life for the better.

I believe that letting go will allow you to feel more joy and to unlock your creativity and spontaneity, as it did for me. One of the most profound challenges to which you can rise is healing yourself. The ideas in this book have helped me tremendously. I hope that by sharing these insights, you and others may benefit from what I have learned and experienced.

Letting go, healing, and learning to be happy is a lifelong process. If your healing journey resembles mine in any way, you will experience profound effects in your life, now and in the future. Every bit of healing that occurs moves us closer to a healthier society! I believe anything is possible!

The answer to the question of "Why did I write this book?" is to help you through learning from my experiences. Take what you like and leave the rest, but remember that what you don't like may actually be what you need to do!

2. Mind, Body, and Emotions

Before the start of my healing journey, I was actually very numb emotionally. I rarely smiled and seemed to be surrounded by depression. There were a few triggers that brought about tears, and I noticed that after crying, my facial muscles relaxed, and I was able to smile and laugh more easily. In writing this book, I sought out research that validated the idea that emotional release brought about positive change. I found there was plenty! I also started to look at my own emotional myths regarding expression.

The Benefits of Expression

As many before me have learned, tears are a natural response to a loss or emotional injury. When you laugh or cry, a great number of chemicals and hormones are released through your tears. Even talking about your fears and anxiety can help in improving your outlook and coping. A study of women with breast cancer found that those who articulated their feelings decreased their anguish and experienced increased optimism. In *It's Never Too Late to Have a Happy Childhood*, author Claudia Black writes: "Where there is loss there are tears; tears are the elixir of recovery."

As with any expressive therapy, it is important to balance your thinking and behavior and avoid the pitfall of indulging in and hiding in the expression rather than moving on. With breast cancer patients, those who continually used this coping strategy of emotional expression increased their anguish later in the treatment program. It is with a word of caution that we examine emotional expression as a singular healing tool. As discussed in this book, you need to make sure that you focus on all aspects of healing: emotional expression, behavior modification, and re-evaluating your beliefs and thinking habits. You need to focus on all these aspects!

I'm sure you have observed that babies have an unrepressed ability to express their emotions. Babies as young as twelve months can read and respond to actors' emotions on TV. Babies also respond to emotions in the voices they hear around them, recognizing sadness at the age of only three months. The human body seems wired to recognize emotions.

Depending on your upbringing or due to events in your life, you may have developed a conditioned response of ignoring your emotions and trying to avoid your pain. In his book *The Six Pillars of Self-Esteem*, Nathaniel Branden says that to deny your emotions usually results in a loss of self-esteem. The loss of self-esteem occurs whether you are a child or an adult. Denying your emotions causes you to lose contact with your inner self and your ability to care for your soul. It is your soul that makes you human, and you are most human when you find a deep connection with your soul. I have since learned that denying how I was feeling about my troubles obscured my sense of self, which I have now recovered and continue to explore.

In *Care of the Soul*, Thomas Moore writes: "Soul is not a thing, but a quality or a dimension of experiencing life and ourselves." Your soul is that which holds your values, beliefs, and center of being. In caring for your soul, you must know how your soul expresses itself, and you must be able to observe and be connected with it. Moore also writes: "We cannot care for the soul unless we are familiar with its ways." To be familiar with your soul involves fully experiencing life and observing your reactions to it.

Life is a process of encounters often viewed as either positive or negative. Often you try to avoid the negative issues and feelings in your life, but in doing so, you miss valuable lessons to learn. Moore writes: "When people observe the ways in which the soul is manifesting itself, they are enriched rather than impoverished." To listen to your soul, especially in times of trouble, brings great rewards. Facing the part of yourself that you fear the most is what you must do to free yourself of pain and sadness. Being open to the pain of the soul brings awareness of yourself and helps you eventually form solutions to your problems. Solving those problems brings about an internal strength that you can carry forward with you. Moore continues: "When you regard the soul with an open mind, you begin to find the messages that lie within the illness, the corrections that can be found in remorse and other uncomfortable feelings, and the necessary changes requested by depression and anxiety."

Myths about Emotions

Typically, emotions have been labeled as either positive (such as joy and happiness) or negative (such as sadness and anger). Love and contentment have been viewed as the opposites of anger and rage, while joy and happiness have been viewed as opposites of sadness and depression. I think that this language needs to be re-evaluated. You need to view emotions as neither positive nor negative but simply as a reflection of your response to the events and internal processes that are occurring in your life. In Traditional Chinese Medicine (TCM), emotions are not categorized as positive or negative. The TCM view is that all emotions are considered normal, but that problems often arise when the emotions are suppressed, are in excess, or are at times insufficient. The key to TCM is to restore the balance of emotions, body, and mind.

Also included in the framework of ideas in TCM is the concept of stagnation. Getting the energy of emotions moving is a helpful notion. Each pleasant and unpleasant emotion has its own unique value in your life as a warning sign of needed personal work or an acknowledgment that you can find happiness.

Another myth about emotions is that the raw expression or venting of anger is healthy. Unless the underlying thoughts are examined, and the cause of the anger dealt with, venting does not bring about healing. Current thinking by most Buddhist leaders is that venting of anger only reinforces anger. Anger can only be resolved by examining the underlying thinking and hurt. In a later chapter, you will learn about the nature of anger and rage and how to deal with these difficult emotions.

Another common myth about emotions is that you believe you have the ability to selectively block out certain emotions. You tend to believe that you can avoid anger, yet still feel love. You think you can block out sadness and still feel joy. While you can adjust the contour of sound on your stereo by increasing the bass or treble controls, your ability to experience positive emotions is lessened when you suppress your negatively labeled emotions.

Do Thoughts Create Emotion?

I have searched far and wide for proof that only thoughts create emotions and have found none. Thoughts will impact your mood, but I believe the thinking and emotion systems are separate and far more complex than a two-way system. We may read a word that triggers a memory, which in turn brings up emotion. Sometimes we have feelings, and our inner voice begins to observe and wonder why we have those feelings.

It also is truly a myth that you can completely control your thoughts and feelings. As you are reading this, please do not think of a pink elephant. What did you just visualize? A pink elephant! The idea of trying not to think of something is called the "White Bear" effect. The harder you try not to think of something, the more often you end up thinking about it. It is very difficult to control your thoughts unless, of course, you have practiced meditation. With meditation, though, it is possible to tame or train your mind to respond more calmly and have fewer intrusive thoughts and images. Training, however, is different from controlling in that training provides a set of learned, acceptable behaviors while controlling attempts to force a condition onto an untrained mind.

A common analogy is that the mind is like twelve or more monkeys all attached by leashes to a pole. If the monkeys run free, there is chaos, confusion, and entanglement, but if you can teach the monkeys to sit still, there is calm, serenity, and order. While it is next to impossible to maintain total control over your mind, increasing your ability from a negligible degree of control to a slightly higher degree of mental self-discipline can greatly improve your daily living habits. The saying "Practice makes perfect" should be replaced with "Practice brings permanence"!

For a long time, I believed that I could control my feelings. The price I paid was high. There are certain behaviors and things you can do for yourself to improve your emotional state, but this is different from accepting the thoughts and feelings that come into your consciousness. By attempting to control your thoughts and emotions selectively, you block access to your soul. You need to let your soul be free to express itself. What you can control is your behavior around these emotions and thoughts.

Currently, there are many techniques and seminars aimed at providing a quick fix for emotional problems. While some of these techniques seem to provide a reprieve, many are not long-lasting, as the original problem is not resolved. In *The Power of Positive Thinking*, Norman Vincent Peale states: "It is important to discover why you have these feelings... That requires analysis and will take time. We must approach the maladies of our emotional life as a physician probes to find something wrong physically. This cannot be done immediately."

I have personally warmed to the concept that life challenges are very much like a meal. We take in food, process it, and discharge what we do not need, while at the same time, nourishment feeds the body. Life challenges are similar in that there is pain that you need to express through tears and other forms of expression, but there is also nourishment in new understanding and wisdom gained from your challenges.

Unresolved Events Become Triggers

By definition, a trigger is an event or experience that consciously or unconsciously reminds you of an experience in the past, and you react with the feelings or body sensations that you felt in the past. Triggers can bring about either a sense of happiness or a sense of dread and fear.

When you encounter a similar experience, the original or similar reaction is triggered. If you are fully aware of your emotions, then it is easy to discern what is going on internally. However, if you are like most people, the emotion may be felt as a sense of irritation, a threat, and a fight, flight, or freeze reaction is triggered.

The mention of Christmas, birthdays, relationships, a meeting with an authority figure, watching a movie with a scene similar to what you experienced, a conversation topic, a song, a picture, or smells can all be triggers. Often triggers are felt as an unexplained gut feeling that may be confused with intuition.

In my family, it took a great deal of courage to ask for the most basic things. Since the reaction of my mother would be inconsistent, approaching her with a request or sharing something usually resulted in a feeling of apprehension and fear. As learning theory would predict, I developed a fear of approaching people or bringing up my own needs.

Carl Jung talked much about the shadow, which is the part of you that you have hidden away from yourself and others. It is not always a negative thing. It could also be hidden talents. In *Meeting the Shadow*, Marie-Louise von Franz writes, "If you feel an overwhelming rage coming up in you when a friend reproaches you about a fault, you can be fairly sure that at this point you will find a part of your shadow, of which you are unconscious of." A Buddhist lesson that has helped me is to acknowledge I am suffering and that I do not understand why someone has done something, and that I can ask for help from people I trust will help. A beautiful analogy that helps me is that people are like water, and some are saltwater. If I can separate the salt from the water, I can see the pureness in each person and treat the salt as pain, delusions, and being misguided.

Realizing that rage is rising, I ask myself, "Why am I not reacting calmly?" The fact that I am reacting so strongly indicates that there is work for me to do. Perhaps your water contains some salt. While it is common to say that "It's not about you," it may actually be about you, or at the very least, your reaction may be about you!

The Healing Power of Tears

Shakespeare understood the power of tears when he wrote, "To weep is to make less the depth of grief." In recent years, scientists have been proving that tears are beneficial to our health and well-being. My own personal experience has proven this time and time again. Scientists have known for over fifty years that emotional tears are different from tears produced as a result of peeling an onion. Tears released on account of emotions contain more protein as well as one of the body's most powerful pain killers – beta-endorphin.

Dr. William Frey of the Dry Eye and Tear Research Center states that people who cry "may be removing, in their tears, chemicals that build up during emotional stress." Dr. Alan Wolfelt of the University of Colorado Medical School states: "In my clinical experience with thousands of mourners, I have observed physical changes following the expression of tears. Not only do people feel better after crying [sic], they also look better."

In "The Brain as a Health Maintenance Organization," authors Robert Ornstein and David S. Sobel respond to the question of why people cry.

The authors state that recent evidence suggests that crying "may be a way in which the body disposes of toxic substances." Many people believe that crying helps them to reduce tension. In the long run, a good cry makes them feel better.

Researchers have also found that crying is common among emotionally healthy adults and that crying is not necessarily a symptom of depression. In a study of people in their late sixties, researchers found that the adults had a good cry every two or three weeks. The main reasons for crying were to reduce feelings of stress. Other studies have found a strong link between stress-related illness and a reluctance to cry.

Tears have also been known to bring about changes in the behavior of people, even children, with seemingly disturbing behavior patterns. An article in the *International Review of Psycho-Analysis* describes how a child, completely withdrawn and with a destructive behavior pattern, broke out into a weeping fit in one of her therapy sessions. These weeping fits, which contained feelings of rage, despair, and sorrow, continued for several sessions, during which a change in the character of her appearance as well as in her behavior began. The article suggests that the release of tears was the first phase in deriving benefits from her psychotherapy.

Over two thousand years ago, Aristotle believed that crying could cleanse the mind through a process of catharsis. Catharsis is a means by which to reduce emotional stress through the expression of emotion. Many others have echoed Aristotle's thoughts. A variety of sources suggest clear benefits of catharsis – from aboriginal literature to the writings of Freud. Aristotle believed that theater and drama serve a useful purpose in catharsis. Sobel and Ornstein write: "Many people attend movies and plays that they know beforehand are, shall we say, elicitors of psychogenic lacrimation, or tearjerkers." People may often feel comfortable crying during a movie and do not experience any embarrassment or regret, knowing that the tears bring benefits.

In addition to releasing tears, crying results in several physical changes. For example, although a person in the stages of grief may show less facial expression and muscle tone, facial tension is increased. A study examining these factors noted that facial tension increases in the forehead, pulling the eyebrows together. Increased tension also occurs in the mouth and jaw, which results in a pulling down of the corners of the mouth. Your body releases a great deal of muscular tension when you cry. Sobbing with tears will cause a reflex that reduces and resolves the muscle tension associated with grief.

In a literal sense, crying and sobbing may be cleansing the mind, thus validating the original theory of catharsis. Perhaps tears and crying are the body's mechanism for releasing emotional tension, restoring the body to a state of equilibrium, and resulting in feeling calm and soothed.

Crying can also be a call for help, a signal that you are hurting, or an indication that you regret actions you have taken. Alternatively, crying may be a signal that you now feel safe with another person. In many cases, the shedding of tears can communicate what words alone cannot say. With the emotions released, you can feel a sense of clarity that can lead to change.

Crying with someone can also communicate both sympathy and empathy. Sympathy is understanding someone else's feelings, while empathy arises from not only understanding their feelings, but being able to sense what it is like to be in their shoes, to understand their situation including the emotions, circumstances, the impact of what they have experienced, and the difficult choices they have had to or are about to make.

While crying may be a natural response to hurt, for many of us, it does not feel natural at all. Not all of us have been taught to feel comfortable with crying. In your childhood, you may have been punished for crying rather than being rewarded. Most of us are unaware of the healing power of tears. Crying is the main action that helps you to release your suppressed emotions and heal. Although you may not be comfortable admitting to crying, it is a natural response to hurt. To control or block your tears is to deny your body's natural method of releasing and healing. Although we know that tears release chemicals, no one knows what happens to those chemicals if you do not cry. During my own process of catharsis and healing, I kept thinking that the tears I was releasing were somehow cleansing my body of the stresses that I had accumulated.

Many of you, however, are afraid of your tears. You may fear that if you start to cry, you will be unable to stop. I, too, felt a fear of losing control. However, I reminded myself that for years, I had exercised the discipline of keeping things under control and that I still had those skills.

I also found that as a wave of emotion was approaching, it seemed much larger compared to the view I had of its size once it had passed! To give myself the courage to face it, I constantly reminded myself of the benefits that expression would bring.

Most of us need to relearn that crying brings about healing when followed by change or communication. Initially fearful of tears, I began to learn and trust that crying soothes and brings about a reduction in stress. I discovered that when I was willing to let go and express my emotions, the stressful energy contained in them would dissipate and pass. The more I expressed my emotions and examined the underlying ideas, each day's events were less clouded by past events that I had not resolved.

Crying is a natural process by which you can release the energy in your emotions. It restores your mind and body to a more natural balance. It is also a powerful call for social support. When you suppress your tears, you end up using a great deal of energy to hold down or keep that energy at bay. You may feel as though you have stopped the tears, but what you have done is pushed the tears and hurt into your subconscious. The feelings are not resolved. The suppression ends up blocking your ability to feel joy and companionship. Several studies show that suppression leads to decreased positive emotions but not decreased negative emotions. Suppression, therefore, accomplishes the exact opposite of the expected result. When suppressing anger, the other person senses subtle cues, and the blood pressure of the other person rises. Suppression also has dramatic effects on willpower. When not allowed to show emotion while watching a video, a group of students showed a significant decrease in task performance compared to the group that was allowed to express their emotions. Suppression has been known to reduce being liked by social partners. People who repress emotions choose friends who are similarly challenged and resist becoming emotionally close.

In *The Power of Positive Thinking*, author Norman Vincent Peale importantly states: "An excellent and normal release from heartache is to give way to grief. In many cultures, the expression and showing of grief are seen as embarrassing and is discouraged. It may be considered foolish to express yourself through the expression of tears or sobbing. This, however, is a violation of your natural mechanism for the release of emotional tension and pain." As Peale says: "This is a denial of the law of nature. It is natural to cry when pain or sorrow comes. It is a relief mechanism provided in the body by Almighty God and should be used." To restrain emotion, to suppress it, or to inhibit it is to rob yourself of your natural means for eliminating the pressure of life. To deny your emotions is similar to denying that you must eat and drink to nourish yourself. As with other needs, you must not indulge in them, but you must not deny them altogether. Peale states: "A good cry by either man or woman is a release from heartache."

Often though, you may not be ready for tears and may develop your own crying substitutes. Adults will learn whole repertoires to substitute for crying. The simple act of talking and sharing in a support group may be one of the first stages in allowing the release to occur. If your tension level lowers, and you experience enough self-acceptance, then tears will likely follow.

Or it may be that your body is ready for tears – you experience tension in the chest and throat area, and the tears well up – but you do not give yourself permission to cry, and so you do not.

It is often easier to stifle the tears and continue with your tasks rather than express your feelings. If you pay attention to these signals and give yourself permission to cry and let go, then crying will usually follow. Noticing your breath at these times can also help you let the tears flow.

While the earliest tears will usually be experienced with tension in the upper chest and throat, a deeper type of release is possible. Crying can often lead to a deeper sobbing if you accept the pain you are feeling and allow the tears to flow fully. This type of release is centered more in the stomach area and will involve more of the body, particularly the abdomen and shoulders. A deep body sob promotes healing and is a more profound release of emotional tension. Sobbing with the whole body can be quite exhausting, and a period of rest afterward is a good idea.

With the release of chemicals through tears, your body heals, and you become more emotionally healthy. Having resolved the emotional tension, you tend to be less isolated since you no longer need to keep others at a distance, fearing that you will break down. Being able to tolerate emotions in others, you can express yourself more openly and listen to others without fear of old injuries being restimulated.

You may feel that you need to develop the courage to face your feelings. Upon reflection, you will realize that you have had the strength and courage all along. You survived the original event, and have had the strength to suppress your pain. You can learn to be more conscious of everything that is happening in the moment and not run from your emotions. You can heal the fragments of your life that need to be brought into the wholeness of your being and begin to feel alive again! When did you last cry? When did you last laugh? Think of a time you felt safe when it was OK to cry. If you have never had this feeling, you have the power to create it now!

There are still many things to be learned about the various balances that occur in the body. It is certain, though, that suppressing your emotions stops the natural healing process of your body. Repressing your emotions can lead to isolation, a reduction in clarity of thought, and diminished tolerance for emotions in others. Grief is a very isolating emotion. Fortunately, these symptoms are not permanent, and you can restore yourself through emotional expression and the healing power of tears. Keep in mind that while crying is helpful, true growth occurs when you receive social support, challenge your beliefs, create a new understanding of events, and achieve resolution.

Let Go and Heal

CRY (IF YOU WANT TO)

Cry if you want to I won't tell you not to
I won't try to cheer you up I'll just be here if you want me
It's no use in keeping a stiff upper lip
You can weep you can sleep you can loosen your grip
You can frown you can drown, and go down with the ship
You can cry if you want to
Don't even apologize for venting your pain
It's something that to me you don't need to explain
I don't need to know why.
I don't think it's insane
You can cry if you want to
The windows are closed.
The neighbors aren't home
If it's better with me than to do it alone
I can draw all the curtains and unplug the phone
You can cry if you want to
You can stare at the ceiling and tear at your hair
You can swallow your feelings and swagger and swear
You can throw things and show things and I wouldn't care
You can cry if you want to
I won't make fun of you I won't tell anyone
I won't analyze what you do or you should've done
I won't advise you to go and have fun
You can cry if you want to.
I can't make it all go away
I don't have any answers I've nothing to say
But I'm not going to lie to you and say it's okay
You can cry if you want to
Cry if you want to
I won't tell you not to
I won't try to cheer you up
I'll just be here if you want me to be near you
Maybe I'll cry too!

Written by Casey Scott, Copyright 1993 Signal Songs/Tainjo Thang (ASCAP) All Rights Reserved/Used by Permission

3. Depression – Many Meanings, Many Causes

The Nature of Depression

First of all, if you have not healed from abuse or adversity, you likely suffer from depression. Hence, it is important to gain an understanding of what depression is and what it isn't.

One of the main problems of discussing depression is that it is a vague term used to describe a very wide range of life situations and symptoms. While everyone gets depressed at some time or another, and I believe that depression can be a normal reaction to various events that occur in your life, I never felt great when someone labeled me or told me I was depressed. I have to admit that I felt embarrassed to admit that I was depressed, and I felt that it meant I had failed in some way. Self-care and self-compassion led me to accept that depression hits everyone at some time in their life, and sometimes when you least expect it. Whether you know the cause or not, going through depression is a difficult and challenging period.

It is important to stress the fact that depression is a natural response to these negative life events and is normally a transient mental state that will resolve if you do the right things to take care of yourself. Even though I have written this book, I accept that I might still go through periods of depression. While some people expect me to be happy and completely healed because I wrote this book, being honest requires me to admit and acknowledge that I still face life challenges, and my state of happiness varies. This is normal for any human being.

Fortunately, because I have this book as my guide, I am less likely to experience long-term depression because I have the tools to take care of myself and lift myself out of any rut that I encounter. I usually find that these periods of depression lead to a deepening of understanding and substantial growth if I am willing to accept the feelings I am having and open up to new beliefs and ideas about who I am. I do what I can to heal my depression and restore my health.

In surveying discussion groups on the Internet, I found that one of the busiest newsgroups was the support group for depression. On my old website for my first book, which provided information on a variety of mental health topics, depression was the most frequently accessed topic. In the newsgroup, people exchanged information on medication, side effects, signs of depression, and things that facilitated the resolution of depression. Many encouraged others, and for some, it was a chance to express themselves. The number of postings to this group indicates the number of people who are affected at the same time by depression. These individuals report lowered spirits, a loss of self-esteem, difficulty sleeping, and a difference in their everyday perspective. Other symptoms may include a loss of energy, weight loss or gain, changes in appetite, and physical complaints without any medical basis. Depressed people have also been shown to differ in the processing and anticipation of pain: they often demonstrate a hyper-vigilant response to anticipated pain and an inhibited ability to modulate the experience of pain.

Make no mistake – depression can be severe and challenging. Andrew Solomon writes: "Depression is a condition that is almost unimaginable to anyone who has not known it. A sequence of metaphors–vines, trees, cliffs, etc.–is the only way to talk about the experience. Its diagnosis often depends on metaphors, and the metaphors one patient chooses are different from those selected by another patient." Unfortunately, those who have never experienced it often suggest that "You should snap out of it!" Those of us who have experienced depression know that is not how it works.

Depression is different from usual mood fluctuations and short-lived emotional responses to challenges in everyday life. Especially when long-lasting and of moderate or severe intensity, depression may cause you to suffer greatly and function poorly at work, at school, and in family and other social situations.

In a recent Twitter campaign, Twitter users describe the worst part of depression. Here are some of the tweets:
- Feeling an overwhelming pressure to mask it, to pretend it isn't debilitating. It is exhausting.
- The waiting… waiting inside my broken head for it to go away and not knowing if it will outlast me.
- Feeling like a prisoner in your own mind, while the world thinks you're "a little bummed out."

- My mind is telling me that I'm lazy and pathetic because I have no motivation to do anything.
- The physical pain that most people don't talk about. Depression HURTS.

Coming out of depression can be a reawakening, but the corridors of depression can seem long, dark, and empty. Like others, when depressed, I was withdrawn and felt that I had a reduced ability to cope with and learn from life.

In her TED talk, violinist Ji-Hae Park describes the deep feeling of despair: "Although many people tried to comfort and encourage me, their words sounded like meaningless noise." I encourage you to go to YouTube and watch her inspiring video in which she describes how the power of music gave her comfort amid her hardship and restored her soul.

The Metaphors of Depression

As I mentioned above, talking about and describing depression is often done through the use of metaphors. In Chinese culture, the symbol of two trees making up a forest is used to represent depression. From within a thick forest, you can feel the sense of darkness, being unable to see a path, a canopy of growth blocking the light, and an inability to move freely because of the thick growth. While visiting a temple in Beijing, I met researcher Sonya Pritzker, who was conducting a survey on depression in China. In her article, "The Role of Metaphor in Culture, Consciousness, and Medicine," she describes many metaphors for depression including falling down, darkness, and lack of control. Sonya writes:

> "The concepts of darkness, lack of movement, and falling down can all be subsumed under the conceptual metaphor 'Depression is Down.' Being down is associated with sleep or darkness, and when we are down, as in for sleep or rest, we are not moving. The journey that is life is restricted when we do not, or cannot, move... Depression in the English language has many meanings. The *American Heritage Dictionary* (1992) lists nine definitions of depression, only one of which is the formal

psychological definition. Another describes a similar condition of 'sadness or despair.' Others include 'an area that is sunk below its surroundings; a hollow,' 'a reduction in physiological vigor or activity'; and 'a period of drastic decline in national or international economy', among others. Clearly, the metaphorical implications in these definitions point to the understanding in English-speaking culture of depression as a lack of activity, a state of being below or less than normal."

While we often think of depression as "feeling down," it can also manifest itself in a raised state of energy. Sonya writes: "[T]he clinical definition also includes symptoms one might not expect to see if metaphorical thinking were restricted to the notion of being 'down.' The symptoms are more restless and include a possible increase in appetite, insomnia, psychomotor agitation, and suicidal plans or thoughts. These symptoms point more towards the 'lack of control' metaphor."

One of the concerns about diagnosing clinical depression lies with the diagnostic guidelines. The earlier guidelines stated that an individual must be suffering from five or more of nine symptoms for two weeks. Keep in mind that a person suffering from less than five symptoms may be feeling challenged energy-wise, emotionally, and cognitively. Fortunately, the guidelines are evolving, and a new category of "depressive episode" has been added that allows for diagnosis during a stressful life challenge.

Causes of Depression

Just as there are many definitions of depression, it seems that depression can result from many factors. Any process of change (such as growing up) involves transformation and transition. Depression can occur as a result of a loss, a success, achieving a goal, a physical injury, a personal trauma, or simply as a result of a buildup of daily events. Change of any type, be it geographical location, lifestyle, work, daily routine, or contact with others can be a contributing factor in depression. Any loss of someone or something of value can be a catalyst for depression.

Other causes of depression can include:
- A process of transition
- Poor thinking patterns
- Lack of direction in life
- Achieving adulthood
- Discovering that life isn't measuring up to what you would like
- Unresolved grief
- A sense of helplessness
- An unfulfilling job
- Beliefs you hold about yourself that keep limiting your self-esteem

Feeling disconnected from your past self can also be a cause of and consequence of depression. Going through a period of upheaval, changing jobs, moving, making new friends, or realizing a major goal can result in this feeling of disconnect. Your familiar patterns are gone, your social circle may have changed, or you are now living in a different environment. This type of disconnect is called "derailment." All of these changes lead to an unstable sense of self. A stable sense of self is needed to maintain well-being.

Another cause of depression is a sense of learned helplessness. You may have grown up in a family in which you did not have any power to effect change in your situation. For years it seemed as though I had to accept the decisions and behaviors of others, and that nothing I did mattered. This ongoing situation instilled a sense of helplessness later in life. One of the ways out of depression for me was to identify areas in which I can make changes. Fortunately, the helplessness was only a learned behavior. Through some personal work, I gained my sense of agency and starting making changes. At twenty-three, I was inspired by a friend who quit her job and went back to school. I was in a dead-end mailroom job and could not even apply for positions as I did not have the required education. I thought that if my friend Laurie could do it, perhaps I had the courage to do it as well. I also learned that I could improve how I talked to myself and give myself encouragement. I've never regretted that decision. I had moved from stagnation to action. A saying from a "Dear Abby" column galvanized my efforts: "How old will you be in seven years if you don't go back to college?"

As mentioned earlier, stagnation is a key concept in Traditional Chinese Medicine (TCM). In TCM, depression is referred to as a form of stagnation – a restricted flow or obstruction. Symptoms of this stagnation include overattachment, preoccupation with fears, being unable to let go, and somatic symptoms arising from challenging emotions. I think the definition described me at various times!

It is also true that depressed people may also experience heightened awareness and uneasiness that manifest as inhibited facial expressions, emotion, and movement. I can also relate to this definition. In my early twenties, I experienced a profound depression. Each time I cried, I found that my facial expression increased, and I felt freer. Others noticed that I was smiling more often and was more expressive.

Depression may also result from a lack of short-term goals. There is an Irish proverb that says: "You don't plow a field by turning it over in your mind!" While some evaluation is necessary, too much rumination can lead you into a spiral of self-absorption rather than being able to see the world around you.

Do our thoughts create depression? They may or may not be the cause of depression, but the depression can be lessened by healthy thought, or it can be worsened by rumination. Often a feeling of sadness or hurt will be created by repeatedly reviewing feelings of hurt from the past without an increase in knowledge or understanding.

Long-term depression can be the result of problems in a person's thinking and attitudes. Unresolved issues and trauma can prolong sadness resulting from a stressful event. People who have avoided feelings or who are suffering from a significant loss may be characterized as depressed, yet it is grieving work that the individual may need to complete to resolve the sadness. In some cases, the events may be difficult to identify because the person has avoided their feelings and has not become appropriately and sufficiently upset by the events. A chronic feeling of sadness may also be indicative of the fact that certain areas of a person's life need changing. Some people may have an unsatisfying job or difficulties relating to others. Without resolution or positive change, sadness will be an ongoing component of their lives. In the cases of earlier abuse, the depression may be the result of a wound to the individual's character or soul, which requires a process of grieving, self-acceptance, and healing to resolve the depression.

From the above, we can conclude that the causes of depression are numerous. As well, there are some generalities about depression that should be examined. Depression has sometimes been described as anger turned inwards, but it is not fair to say that all depressions are the result of unexpressed anger. In labeling the depression as a disease, some may feel powerless to resolve the depression, but there is much that can be done. As research continues to explore and demonstrate through the use of "healthy pleasures" such as singing, meditation, yoga, and physical exercise, it is possible to naturally restore the brain to its optimal level of physiological health.

The Secret Strength of Depression

Whenever I have experienced depression, I have tried to look upon it as an opportunity to re-evaluate my beliefs and values. Perhaps you can do the same. Each transition or change involves letting go of something and accepting something new. In *The Secret Strength of Depression*, Dr. Frederic Flach writes: "In order to move successfully from one phase to the next, a person must be able to experience depression in a direct and meaningful way." There was a period after completing my master's degree that I entered a very deep depression. I felt overwhelmed by the level of student debt I was carrying, and the financial difficulties that came with it, while at the same time re-establishing my social life. Through the process of feeling and working through my depression, I learned how shaky my faith was in trusting that things would work out, and realized that despite feeling lonely, I had several friends who cared deeply about me. I also let go of some friendships that were not healthy. It became a time of cleaning house. I was having a recurring dream of kittens being discovered in the basement who had gone undetected for some time. As I moved through my depression and made sense of the fact that I had some new lessons to learn, the kittens became healthier and healthier in my dream each time I rediscovered them. While it took some time to work through this, I made great progress in learning that I needed to help myself.

Although depression reduces vitality and makes it difficult to find solutions to problems, there are benefits to depression. Often, creative people will attribute the creation of their work to an episode of depression. Many individuals who have made significant life changes also attribute the changes they made to periods of depression. As Dr. Flach writes: "To experience acute depression is an opportunity for a person not just to learn more about himself, but to become more whole than he was. Not only does depression afford a chance for insight, but 'falling apart' can accelerate the process of reordering one's life after serious stress."

Often these people will emerge from depression with a new and exciting view of life. Similar to the idea of the phoenix that crashes into the fire yet emerges as a beautiful new bird, a depression that is experienced and resolved allows us to rebound to new levels of understanding and meaning. Dr. Flach writes: "To be creative in any sense, a person must be able to relinquish old and fixed assumptions that block a fresh appraisal of a situation." Perhaps to be creative also involves being open to the experience of moving through depression.

Although hard to envision when depressed, according to Buddhist teacher Chögyam Trungpa Rinpoche:

> "Depression is the most dignified energy of all... Depression is one of the very powerful energies, one of the most common energies that we have. It is energy. Depression is like an oxygen tank that wants to burst but is still bottled. It is a fantastic bank of energies, much more so than aggression and passion which are kind of developed and then let out... Depression is not just a blank, it has all kinds of intelligent things happening within it. I mean, basically, depression is extraordinarily interesting and a highly intelligent state of being. That is why you are depressed. Depression is an unsatisfied state of mind in which you feel that you have no outlet. So work with the dissatisfaction of that depression. Whatever is in it is extraordinarily powerful. It has all

kinds of answers in it, but the answers are hidden. It is extraordinarily awake energy, although you might feel sleepy..."

It's Not All Bad News about Depression!

Perhaps as a society, we need to challenge our view of mental health and depression. Society has generally viewed the happy-go-lucky person as the well-adjusted person. Now we are gaining the understanding that episodes of depression are a natural part of life and growth. Perhaps the person who gets angry, cries, laughs, or gets embarrassed, and who works through depression, is the well-adjusted person. One article I read suggested that the outcome of trying to eliminate the symptoms of depression was to pathologize normal adaptive responses to stress. In an Internet posting on the topic of depression, an individual posed the question, "When will I be normal again?" Perhaps a better line of reasoning might be, "I am depressed. I am normal. How long will this last? What can I do to take care of myself?"

There is also no need to be gloomy about depression. An article in Mental Health states: "The 'gloomy' view of depression is relatively recent... Just a generation or two ago, conventional wisdom held that depression was the opposite – transient and self-limiting. ... This omission, and the field's lack of focus on good outcomes after depression more broadly, virtually guarantees an unduly pessimistic impression of depression's course."

The article goes on to state that "Research on depression... often focuses on the chronicity and recurrence. Also, people with recurrent depression are highly likely to be overrepresented in depression studies simply because, when researchers put a call out for subjects with depression, these people are statistically more likely to be suffering at the time, and so to be recruited."

There is a group of people who actually thrive after major depression. The article and the authors of the study state the public deserve to know that, as depression has often been labeled as a chronic recurrent condition, the researchers identified a group of people who were High Functioning After Depression (HFAD). The authors of the study suggest that the advice given to people about depression does not need to be gloomy.

An average of 40 to 50 percent of people who suffer an episode of depression do not go on to experience another. Be creative and increase your self-knowledge. Find growth and the lesson in your depression.

Recent research has shown that simply believing that you can change can lessen depression. In one study, students who expressed the desire to change a personality trait achieved a demonstrably more significant change in that trait than those who did not express such a desire. The more strongly people believe they can change, the more likely they will take responsibility for mistakes, which in turn leads to personal improvement!

4. The Masks You Wear

In my childhood, I became very skilled at hiding my hurt from others. It was a defense mechanism that saved me from additional shame and ridicule and that I carried into my adult life. I could not admit to myself how much pain I was in and how depressed I was, so I tried to paint a picture of being happy by smiling all the time. Unfortunately, I wasn't a very good actor, and people could see through my acting, and sometimes, some unkind classmates mocked me. At a later time, as I worked through my pain, I was able to finally be more genuine, and the people who mimicked me felt very embarrassed when they realized that I knew they were mimicking me. Being more genuine led to making more genuine friends after having removed my emotional mask.

Just as I did, you probably have become a skilled actor or actress in maintaining a front to others. You may try to appear to others as happy-go-lucky, yet you are hurting inside and too afraid to let others know what you are really thinking and feeling.

In most cases, it is not because you wish to deceive anyone that you wear these masks, but simply because it is the best coping mechanism you have learned. An emotional mask may also serve as a form of denial until you are ready to face the issues that have brought about emotional pain. While "denial" has often been thought of as a negative term, I truly believe that denial is simply a form of self-preservation since challenging one's beliefs and ideas can bring about confusion and instability in one's self-concept.

At times your masks were necessary to protect you, and they may have been an appropriate defense at some time. These masks may no longer be effective tools for daily living and may now be harming or detracting from your enjoyment of life and sharing with others. To open up to another requires trust and courage, especially if you have been emotionally abused or humiliated by others who were in a position of authority or trust. To become an emotionally healthy person involves identifying your masks and beginning to come out from behind the mask with yourself and those you trust. Peeking out from behind the mask allows others to see you more openly. The more you work at removing the mask, the more genuine you become. You are then able to form deeper connections with yourself and others. Which of the following masks do you use, and which do you recognize as others' masks?

Smiler Mask

A smiler is a person who always seems to greet you with a happy face. They seem to be consistently up when you greet them, but their smiles really mask their true feelings. When with closer friends, the smiler may let down their guard and confide some of their true feelings. With the appearance of an outsider, the mask will usually quickly reappear. While able to trust close friends, the smiler will maintain a front among most people. If asked how they are truly feeling, they might begin to honestly tell you, but would not likely be willing to face any pain they are feeling. Underneath the smiler is a sad person, who is likely ashamed or afraid to show they are depressed. They are afraid to be authentic out of fear of being rejected for not being happy.

Pollyannaism or Pronoid Mask

Pollyannaism refers to people who always seem extremely happy. They go around saying how wonderful all the rain is! Sometimes their excessively positive attitudes will begin to bother others. They never seem to get depressed, and nothing seems to bother them. They may try to force their happiness onto others. In truth, they may be hurting deeply yet cannot show this side of themselves to others. Their behavior serves as a form of denial of the real pain that they cannot yet face.

Truly, it would be wonderful if you could maintain a life that would generate such a state of happiness, but life has its "ups and downs" and therefore most people, like yourself, have ups and downs too. There is a difference between a compensating positive outlook to avoid pain and a genuinely positive outlook born out of a sense of freedom and choice. Life contains many issues that need to be worked on and resolved. Someone who is always up is not likely connected with their own feelings and issues. They are probably in a state of denial. The important question is whether their joy is genuine or a mask. Does this type of person have the ability to express and experience a wide range of emotions, or do they deny a side of their emotional spectrum and self?

As a form of denial, the pronoid will often mask pain by focusing on others. The pronoid will act in a manner that gives an impression of great concern for friends and co-workers. At times, however, when challenged emotionally, this mask of concern will show its cracks.

As the opposite of the paranoid, the pronoid often lives in a fantasy in which they overvalue themselves and overestimate their control of events in their lives. They may make statements about controlling their own destiny and will attribute circumstantial occurrences to their well-developed sense of willpower.

In an article in the *Journal of Medical Ethics*, psychologist Richard P. Bentall argues that happiness syndrome is a mood disturbance. Dr. Bentall suggests that the pronoid is really out of touch with reality. The pronoid lives a tinted view in which, as Dr. Bentall states: "Mere acquaintances are seen as close friends. Politeness and pleasantries are interpreted as deep friendships." The pronoid has difficulty expressing their true feelings about others and might be masking anger as well.

The Neutral/Flat Mask

An emotionally neutral person is someone who never seems to express any emotions at all. Their facial expression will remain mostly flat, with little smiling or expression of joy in their eyes. It is difficult to tell whether the emotionally neutral or flat person is up or down or anywhere in between, and rarely, if ever, does the neutral mask allow anger to be shown. They have become very good at masking their emotions, even if it is no longer intentional. This mask makes it difficult for them to experience closeness with others. A friend once told me that I was a repressed bundle of joy. I remember times when others in my family did not express joy, and their faces seemed disconnected from their hearts. At the age of sixteen, I got a phone call from my paper route supervisor informing me I had won a trip! I ran into the dining room and jumped up and down, yelling, "I won a trip to Florida! I won a trip to Florida!" I felt a sense of embarrassment when none of my brothers or even parents showed any reaction. I was greeted with absolute silence and absolutely no reaction or response. I learned at a subconscious level that showing joy was embarrassing and that there was no sharing of joy and started wearing this mask.

Defensive Mask

Defensiveness is something you likely display when your beliefs or behavior are challenged. In some cases, you may even become defensive when someone tries to help you. While it usually results in frustration for the other party, a defensive mask serves the purpose of protecting you from hurt. The defensive person keeps others at a safe distance, thus preventing emotions and pain from surfacing. Often considered a form of denial, defensiveness is a way of communicating that the mask wearer is not ready to deal with the pain. To remove the mask requires a degree of trust and willingness to face some pain. Defensiveness often means "I don't want to get hurt again."

Victim Mask

The person wearing the victim mask is someone who often talks about his or her problems but does not achieve resolution of the emotional content and continually blames others for their misfortune. They assume the role of victimization in most of their interactions. The victim mask usually develops from a sense of hopelessness and a lack of power to effect change in their childhood. They likely have been victimized at one time, and have experienced trauma and hardship. Instead of breaking out of the victim mold, they will continue to blame others for their misfortunes, claiming what someone did has ruined their life. To heal and let go of the victim mask, you can learn to accept that, at times, you are being victimized but do not have to play the role of victim. The victim role encourages powerlessness and learned helplessness. You can acknowledge the pain and horror of what you went through, but you learn to give that incident less and less space in your life and become empowered to exert more control and action with regard to your life from now on. Often the solution to the victim mask is to develop an awareness of family roles, set boundaries, and to realize that you have choices other than suffering or being a scapegoat.

Busy Mask

One of the common techniques used to avoid feeling is keeping extremely busy. The busy mask wearers take on extra work and volunteer for causes that take up a great deal of time. They do not know how to relax and have difficulty slowing down from a hectic schedule that many people would have trouble keeping up with. If not busy with some task, they will find something to fill their empty time slot.

Although they give the impression that they really enjoy what they are doing, and perhaps they do, the busy mask is really a defense against facing themselves and their emotions. They are so busy that they do not afford themselves the time to be with themselves. They also likely fear time in which they have nothing to do. While it can be invigorating to be around this person, it can be next to impossible to relax with a busy type, as they will find some extra tasks to do.

The trap that the busy mask generates is that the person may burn out over time and may be forced to slow down. The busy mask usually results in a Catch-22 situation where it is painful to keep so busy, but slowing down also means facing emotional pain. The person wearing the busy mask will need to slow down gradually, giving up the need for frivolous tasks and new interests. Slowing down abruptly can be a tremendous shock. Slamming on the brakes of a car causes a skid and possibly an accident. A slower controlled stop is far more desirable. As with all illnesses and problems, prevention is the best cure!

Intellectual/Rationalization Mask

A very important idea to consider is that emotions are not logical and that it is impossible to focus on thinking and on your emotions at the same time. By keeping all of your concerns on an intellectual basis, you can effectively avoid your emotional side and keep the emotions at bay. The cost of staying in your intellectual side is that your relationships suffer due to a lack of emotional content and connection. A person wearing the intellectual mask will be able to discuss ideas at length with great intensity but will have difficulty sharing feelings.

The intellectual mask may also be manifested in a rationalization of events. By thinking rather than feeling, the intellectual will rationalize events and behavior to the point that their feelings are dismissed. In both cases, however, the removal or dropping of the mask will bring back the associated feelings.

Insensitivity Mask

With all the television and movie violence and the negative events reported in the newspapers, it is very easy to become desensitized to the problems of others and to begin to even be insensitive to oneself. It can become difficult to notice the good in the world when bombarded with negative stories and images. A minister at our local church suggested that the worst thing you can do before going to bed is to watch the news because of the negative images that would be planted in your mind before going to sleep! Imagine if someone told you about murders, car accidents, and deaths over coffee. You'd probably have concerns about their mental health, as this would be a sign of suicidal tendencies. Yet for these stories to be reported to us on the radio when we wake up is considered "normal." We can become so accustomed to the negativity in the world that we become insensitive. I've also seen this mask in other people when they say things like, "I had it hard, so it's their turn to feel what it's like" or "I put in my dues so they should too." All that it takes to remove this mask is to remind yourself of your humanity, and your common goal to make this world a better place than when you arrived. Two wrongs do not make a right.

Fatigue Mask

Being tired most of the time can be the result of stress or a medical condition, but it can also be a method of avoiding life's issues. By staying in bed or by avoiding participation, you can also avoid dealing with the issues of the day. Chronic sleeping in can often be a sign of emotional tension and depression.

The person with the fatigue mask can often drop the mask if some event truly interests them. Once that event passes, they will likely revert to old habits of avoiding social activities in favor of what they may call rest. In fact, sleeping in late does not usually result in a feeling of being more rested but simply perpetuates a feeling of listlessness, hopelessness, and little accomplishment.

With the fatigue mask, you can shorten the number of active hours, which in turn reduces the number of hours in contact with the subtleties of your pain. Again, be careful in judging yourself. You may be tired, which rest will cure, but too much rest is considered harmful.

Joker/Clown Mask

Many of us have been around someone who knows all the latest jokes and can come up with a funny or witty line at a moment's notice. Joker masks can be fun to have around, but this behavior turns into a mask when you use jokes to keep people at a distance or to hide your pain. Especially with jokes, it is important to be balanced and appropriate. Can you tell a joke but also share something personal about yourself?

It can be much easier to be flippant than to show a deeper understanding and caring attitude. Humor is often used as a way of masking serious issues. Also, the joker or clown so often pulls jokes that when they actually open up or disclose something, the disclosure may be misunderstood or discounted. This occurs simply because people are expecting a punch line.

To lose the joker mask, you need to convince others of your serious side. It may involve some personal publicity work in trying to change others' image of you. As a person with a witty sense of humor who does stand-up comedy from time to time, I like to share my new material. I can walk up to friends and, without cracking a smile, deliver a setup to a joke and the punch line. Of course, people laugh, but they begin to expect a punch line each time I start a conversation. I've had to learn to say, "Here's my new joke." Like myself, the joker often finds that others welcome genuine and true friendship with a little bit of humor thrown in too.

Caretaker/Gossiper Mask

It would seem strange to classify these two masks together, but both really share the same basis or foundation. The caretaker mask appears on someone who spends the majority of their time looking after others rather than themselves. The caretaker shows sincere concern for others while ignoring their own needs. The gossiper will expend a great deal of energy talking about others and may often focus on solving other people's problems rather than their own. In both cases, the mask wearer focuses on others to avoid any attention being directed towards him or herself. Their focus on others is based on a need to avoid their own feelings and needs.

While it is a desirable trait to help others, this mask wearer defines his or her self-esteem through the gratitude received and the validation of self that comes with being seen as "being good." The mask may preclude the opportunity to discover your inherent goodness and worthiness independent of your utility to others.

Listener Mask

The listener is someone who devotes all of his or her time to listen to other people's problems, desires, and goals. Unfortunately, although they may have needs and goals of their own, they hide from expressing these by giving all of their attention to others. Although they would like to be listened to, they are reluctant to expose their own values and beliefs for fear of ridicule. The wearer of the listener mask has lost the ability to express their inner voice.

Silent/Hiding Mask

By being silent about your own needs and feelings, you can often avoid confrontation with others. A common characteristic of those who wear this mask is that they experienced rejection and ridicule earlier in life when they expressed their needs and wants to others. They may have been punished for being assertive and, therefore, have remained safe by learning to forego communicating their needs. They fear being rejected for requesting help from others.

Ironically, another way of hiding is to draw attention to yourself as an authority, by coming up with better answers, or by being different. These attitudes or behaviors keep you from being "just one of the gang" and save you from the feelings you might experience if you feel you aren't fitting in.

In each case, the mask protects you from rejection, but you do not fully participate with others, nor are you communicative. While longing for closeness, the silent and hiding mask prevents you from developing the intimacy that you desire.

New Age Healer Mask

Over my years of involvement in counseling and various self-help workshops, I have observed a condition that many new age people develop as an avoidance technique. As a public speaker and trainer, I have observed that, ironically, the best place to hide is at the center of the stage. By assuming the role of teacher, the New Age Healer sets up an authoritarian, hierarchical relationship. I have come into contact with some new age people who possess charm and charisma that help them keep people at a distance. While I'm sure the intention of their loving charm is to be kind, the ability of these people to let you get close is limited. The focus of their interest is always in maintaining the roles of you as one of their clients and themselves as the healer. The healer mask can be taken to extremes of persuasiveness. Healer mask types can remove their mask by showing that they can open up and build friendships rather than healer/client relationships. When at a post office to send one of my earlier manuscripts to a publisher for consideration, I began a conversation with a woman in line. After discussing my book, she asked, "Oh! Are you a healer?" I replied, "We are all healers – healers of our own souls, emotions, thoughts, and behaviors." While it is good to have a mentor and teacher, be careful if your mentor needs to be the center of attention, needs to be in complete control, charges exorbitant amounts for workshops, or always deflects accountability by claiming some problem between the two of you is exclusively your issue. Choose your mentors wisely.

Focusing on Other People Mask

One of the principles of self-help groups is to keep the focus on yourself. Focusing on yourself requires some practice as it's easier to focus on how others are behaving, acting out, or doing things that annoy us. By focusing on others, we distract ourselves and others from our own issues and needs. Focusing on others comes from a place of not being valued. It is sometimes a way to deny our problems, but it can also be a habit arising from being called selfish as a child, when in fact, all we needed was the normal encouragement and interest of our parents. If you find yourself focusing on other people, try to start making "I" statements rather than saying "other people" or "they." For example: "I believe...", "I feel...", "I would like it if..."

Attention Seeking Mask

By seeking attention, people are drawn into the attention seeker's drama. The attention seeker attempts to get validation and praise. While receiving and giving validation and praise are healthy in some situations, it may become a behavior that diminishes the validation and praise of others. There is no place for two attention seekers in a room. Attention seeking usually arises from the pain of being neglected and overlooked. To remove this mask, try to be quieter in a social situation, allowing others to be at the center of attention and be happy for their accomplishments.

Superiority Mask

The person with the superiority mask ensures that others know that they operate with full integrity, honesty, openness, and fairness as core values. However, the mask is actually a defense mechanism. It helps them to make themselves feel different from people in their life who have acted without these core values. The mask helps them avoid feeling shame about some situation, family, or group of people they have been associated with. By claiming they are superior in their core values, they can avoid their vulnerability and the reality that they likely have hurt someone at some time. Instead of acknowledging their weaknesses and forgiving themselves, they maintain an air of being slightly superior. They claim they are just like anyone else, but they put themselves on a pedestal while still claiming to be modest. Quite often, these people do behave with integrity and value, but at their core, they are afraid of their own insecurity.

Imposed Masks – Scapegoat, Black Sheep, and Victim

In some cases, we may find that our family imposes masks on us from a very early age. Each individual family member experiences stress. How they deal with it can have an impact on the children in the family. Quite often, a family will pick one member of the family to be the focus of their stress and inability to communicate with other family members.

You may find yourself in situations where you find it difficult to stand up for yourself, believe erroneously that things are your fault, or believe that you are "the black sheep of the family" when, in fact, these are just masks that your family imposed over your good nature. Unhealthy family members may feel threatened by your insight and desire to grow and therefore try to convince you that you are the black sheep of the family. A healthy family would welcome your insight and empathy. Hopefully, you will discover as I did, that the things you were criticized for are valuable traits in healthy families.

Masks – Good or Bad?
Keep in mind that none of the above descriptions of masks are meant to be judgmental. Masks are simply the result of habits you may have developed to hide your emotions and to protect yourself. At one time, these mechanisms may have been necessary and appropriate tools for self-defense. Unfortunately, they may no longer be serving you. You are living under different circumstances, and the threat may no longer be present, yet by habit, you continue to use them. You need to find a way to change your habits to achieve emotional health.

Many of you may wear one or more of the above masks at varying times. There are situations when wearing a mask may be appropriate. Sometimes you will meet individuals whom you may not trust and, therefore, may prefer to keep certain things close to your heart and hidden. You may also find that certain aspects of work require a friendly smile or demeanor that must be maintained, independent of your actual emotional state.

The key problem for many mask wearers is the inability to remove or lose the mask at times when sharing may be appropriate or when there really is no threat. Often you may miss opportunities for closeness because you are so accustomed to maintaining the mask. The mask can be helpful, but it can work against you if your habit and fear prevent you from removing it. If the latter is the case, you need to accept and feel comfortable with your emotions. This is the key to removing the mask.

Removing Masks
Removing your emotional mask allows others to understand and notice your needs. When you show you are sad or hurt, others can respond with help. If your mask is in place, others will not know that you are hurting

and will not be aware that you need reassurance and help. By removing your mask, others will be able to share in your joy as well!

To remove masks, it is usually necessary to go out of your comfort zone. Joining a support group and actively participating by sharing at meetings can help build a sense of confidence in sharing your thoughts, ideas, and feelings. Public speaking classes such as the Dale Carnegie course or Toastmasters can sharpen your sharing and presentation skills in a supportive learning environment. Learning to stretch yourself in terms of emotional expression can be accomplished by taking risks.

It is also helpful to imagine how far your own energy field extends from your body. The further we extend our own energy boundary, the more confident and visible we can feel. One of the most difficult challenges I faced was at the end of a stand-up comedy course when all the classmates were required to perform a six-minute comedy routine in a club. After completing this experience, I found myself being more dynamic in my presentations, and when around my friends – a valuable benefit of going out of my comfort zone!

Mark Linden O'Meara

5. How You Avoid Your Feelings

In addition to masks, there are several behavioral patterns you may use to keep your emotions (and the pain that comes with them) at bay. Unfortunately, these techniques eventually catch up with you and may block you from experiencing joy in your life. Emotional avoidance methods can be subtle, and you may not be consciously aware of how you run from your feelings. Below is a list of some of the techniques used to avoid emotions and the reality of your life. Which ones do you use to avoid issues and feelings?

Keeping Busy

By taking on extra responsibilities, whether at work, in our families, or as a volunteer, you end up keeping yourself so busy that you simply do not have the time to feel. There is no balance in your life. You end up rushing around and being unable to slow down. Eventually, you can burn out and then need to face the emotions you have been avoiding. Escaping from your emotions by keeping busy dampens the pain but does not allow you to heal.

Keeping the Focus on Others

By focusing on other peoples' problems, you distract yourself from your own problems and avoid them. You may derive a sense of self-worth in helping others, but you are unable to take a close look at yourself. You may become defensive when someone tries to talk to you about your own problems.

Taking Drugs

Drugs (even prescription drugs) are often used to avoid feelings. Unfortunately, many have resorted to the overuse of medication to block feelings of sadness. To gain a lift, some may take hallucinogenic drugs and alter their perceptions of reality. You may get a false lift – a false sense of joy, but what goes up must come down, so you try to get the feeling again and end up addicted to a drug with your emotions unresolved. Facing pain can be difficult. In his book, *Try Being Human*, Alec Forbes writes: "Addiction would not occur if people took responsibility for their emotional states." This is not necessarily easy, but the goal is to learn and experience the wonderful range of human emotions rather than the limited, painful range you might be currently experiencing!

Drinking Alcohol

Alcohol can work as a suppressant. Having even an occasional drink or two can end up suppressing or numbing your emotions. When you start to feel pain, you reach for a drink to soothe and numb that pain, but the emotions are never actually resolved, only masked. Often after a few drinks, you may think that you have achieved a greater sense of self and feel more centered. This is because alcohol affects your judgment, and, on a very subtle level, you may be letting some defenses down. Some of us may have wonderful sharing experiences under the influence, but the sharing ends once you sober up.

Sobriety is not just an absence of drinking. As Dottie Hollingsworth states: "Sobriety to me is about being present in all situations, about feeling our emotions and being aware of our actions. It's about staying when we want to run."

Taking Legalized Drugs or Prescription Medicine

While some states and countries have legalized marijuana, the true cause for concern is that many people smoke marijuana mainly to deal with anxiety. Would it not be better to learn to deal with anxiety through meditation and healing techniques rather than relying on drugs? The same holds true for long-term antidepressant use. Sometimes a boost or temporary reprieve is needed by taking antidepressants, but in the long run, perhaps people need to learn how to deal with emotions and life challenges. With very poor access to mental health services, sometimes the only tool the doctor has is a prescription pad. Some people do benefit from these drugs, and the legalized drugs may help calm the current situation. For myself, the side effects were intolerable. The medicines seemed to completely numb my emotions, leaving me incapable of experiencing the emotions I needed to feel to continue my personal growth.

Maintaining Denial

The simplest way to avoid feeling is to maintain a wall of denial, saying that "I'm not hurting" or "I'm not angry," even though all the evidence points to the fact that you have unresolved emotions. You may even be so good at denial that others actually believe that you are not hurting.

Maintaining Noise

To keep your mind occupied, you might often turn on a television or radio just to fill the silence. Even when you are out in nature, you may need some stimulus to keep your mind from feeling your emotions. If you are running from your emotions, it is difficult to sit still and enjoy the peace, so you create some artificial noise to overwhelm the quietness. When you begin your healing, you may find that enjoying the sounds of nature will be healing and peaceful.

Smoking and Other Compulsive Behaviors

Smoking can be linked with several behavior patterns. It is quite explicitly used as a way to "take a break" – often from stressful or otherwise difficult situations. Smoking has also been linked with depression. Not only have some studies observed directly the effects of cigarette smoking on the chemicals in the brain related to depression, the inability to quit smoking has been found to point to underlying depression. Treating the depression made it possible for individuals to give up their smoking habit.

Compulsive Shopping

A recent treatment program for compulsive shopping was successful when the patients were treated for their depression rather than for their shopping habits. As adults, we seem to be able to develop numerous methods for dealing with depression that do not get to the root of the problem. In many cases, if the depression is treated, the compulsive behavior simply disappears. It isn't helpful that marketers prey on you by associating a purchase with feelings of happiness. True happiness is self-generated.

Let Go and Heal

Self-Abuse and Self-Harm

In recent years the medical profession has become aware of various methods of self-abuse that go beyond well-known behaviors such as smoking, drinking, and taking drugs. These forms of self-abuse include sexual addictions, self-cutting, and other behaviors such as hair pulling and physically hitting oneself. Such behaviors are often used as a distraction: the physical pain inflicted allows one to focus on something other than the mixture of overwhelming, painful emotions. The experience of physical pain causes the release of endorphins, and the self-abuse becomes an addictive ritual. This method is usually rooted in low self-esteem and an inability to express emotions in more constructive and appropriate ways. For this type of difficulty, it is important to find counseling and an appropriate support group. Learning new behaviors, such as reaching out, self-reassurance, or stress-reducing techniques, will help in coping with distress and hopefully reduce the incidence of harmful coping mechanisms.

The Racing Mind and Obsessing

One way of avoiding emotions is to think obsessively about something or someone. Often you may find your mind racing, resulting in insomnia or an inability to focus on the task at hand. A racing mind is a protective device that your subconscious mind evokes to avoid feelings. If you are thinking all the time, you will be experiencing yourself only on an intellectual level and will be blocking out the feelings that are the root of the problem. Simply acknowledging this and slowing down the mind to discover the feelings can often resolve this problem.

Technology and the Internet

One of the greatest inventions in the last few decades has been the availability of information and entertainment via the Internet, cellphones, tablets, and games. All these things have become a valuable resource to many people, and I do not want to undermine its value as a communication tool. Unfortunately, many people spend far too much time focusing on the screen rather than themselves and their relationships.

There was a famous experiment by Pavlov in which he trained his dogs to salivate when a bell rang. At first, he rang the bell when food was placed out, but later, when no food was placed out, and he rang the bell, the dogs still salivated. Don't be one of "Pavlov's dogs" when it comes to notifications from your cellphone!

Comparing Yourself to Others

An emotionally hurting person may try to deny their pain by focusing on how others are worse off than themselves. You may take note of someone who, in your eyes, has had a more difficult time. You then remind yourself that things are better for you. This denial technique is a rational way of getting yourself to think that your pain is inappropriate or unjustified. But each of our circumstances is unique. To expect two people to experience an event and react exactly the same is not reasonable. Your troubles and your reaction to them belong to you alone, and you should not try to compare your troubles to others to try to make yourself feel better.

Sometimes you may feel guilty for feeling pain or hurt because your problems may seem insignificant compared to other people's problems. You may even feel guilty simply because you may not have been given permission, by yourself or by others, to feel bad. I've read many comments on the Internet telling people that they shouldn't feel so bad because others are worse off. Though factually true, this line of reasoning demonstrates a lack of empathy. On the other hand, I remember a time when I was dealing with significant health problems, a relationship that had ended badly, and the grief over the death of my father. I overheard a friend talking about how stressed she was because she could not decide what model of car to buy. A counselor I was seeing while doing my undergraduate degree took care of this problem by saying, "It does not matter how big the pile of poop is. The smaller pile smells just as bad!"

Dissociating

One way of avoiding emotions is to simply tune out what is going on around you. In cases of childhood trauma, dissociation is a common occurrence. Dissociation is now being recognized as a symptom of early sexual or emotional abuse often experienced in childhood rather than a pathological state. By dissociating from yourself, you become more of a distant and numb observer, less present, and less connected with yourself, thus avoiding the possibility of emotional pain or discomfort. The individual who is dissociated may be able to function at high levels in social and work situations but may be disconnected emotionally.

Living Too Much in "The Now"

While living in "The Now" has become very trendy, it actually can be used as a method of denial. Being here in the now does not mean denying the past or not having goals or aspirations for the future. It involves being aware of all the feelings you are having in the present moment regardless of when the event that triggered the emotions occurred. When working through my own pain, I observed many people who denied their own pain and mine by telling me, "That was in the past, just be here, now! There is no point going back into the past." In fact, I was not going into the past but was using the emotions in the present and in doing so, was able to release the present moment's repressed energy of those events, which in turn allowed me to be a more objective observer, gain a greater understanding, and heal. Being here in the now does not mean restricting the range of emotions that you are allowed to feel, nor does it mean refusing to acknowledge what happened in the past and what is currently affecting you. Being here in the now should not be used as a tool for restricting your experience or to push away any feelings that are not viewed as positive by yourself or other people. It should be the exact opposite, allowing you to fully feel and understand the totality of what you have experienced so far and the potential you have for growth.

Most of us have behaviors that help us avoid pain. We try to move towards happiness and move away from pain. Marketers know this and try to sell you things by using the avoidance of pain as a sales tactic.

Sometimes avoiding pain is necessary until we are ready to deal with it, but avoiding pain all the time, even when we are ready to deal with it, leads to being stuck in avoidance of our issues. Avoiding pain leads to stagnation, and an inability to move forward.

"I said to my heart today: I am sorry I didn't come and visit you until now."
– Shiyun Tang

6. Hurts of the Heart

> "History has demonstrated that the most notable winners usually encountered heartbreaking obstacles before they triumphed."
> – B.C. Forbes

One of the first crucial steps in healing is to admit you are hurting. You may feel a sense of aching or a longing for something better. You try to live in the present moment, but something keeps bringing you down.

The present discomfort you are trying to resolve may be the result of events that happened years ago. You may think you have completely forgotten about them, but notice that certain situations trigger uncomfortable feelings.

Many things can cause hurt and pain. Sometimes the hurt occurs because we misinterpret the actions of others, while sometimes others behave badly. In the workforce, managers are often called upon to make decisions that will be painful or troublesome for employees. Just like doctors need to cause pain through surgery to remedy an illness, so, too, must business managers make similar decisions. There are guiding principles to follow to ease the pain, but many managers are poorly trained to effectively minimize the discomfort of difficult decisions.

While this chapter lists many painful things that can happen, the purpose of this chapter is not to compare yourself to others and claim a right to more suffering. The purpose is to examine your life and see what difficulties you encountered and determine which still need healing. Take note of what you've been through and what is still impacting your life.

Dealing with Loss and Grief

Although losses are as much a part of life as gains, it is usually easier for most of us to deal with the gains. Alexander Graham Bell said: "For every door that closes behind us, another door opens." Bell went on to say that often, too much time is spent focusing on the closed door and not enough time on the open one. On the other hand, some of you may have never acknowledged the door that closed behind you as you began a new career, started a new relationship, or moved to another city, creating an ungrieved loss.

In *How to Survive the Loss of a Love*, authors Colgrove, Bloomfield, and McWilliams describe various types of losses. There are inevitable losses (situations in which death or separation is imminent), temporary losses (absences from work, a lover going away for some time, a child going away to camp), and some not-so-obvious losses. There can also be losses related to missed opportunities and minor losses that may accumulate during a day. Missed telephone calls, a missed connection, or not hearing about something you wanted to attend until it is too late are examples of missed opportunities and minor losses.

At some time or another, you may have experienced multiple losses. When this occurs, it is as though the stress of the events is not added but multiplied. You may require the use of avoidance techniques until you are ready and capable of dealing with the event or events. Several smaller or seemingly insignificant losses can bring about depression, especially if they occur around the same time. Even a string of bad luck can bring about depression or a sense of loss. Whatever the loss, you need to allow yourself to go through the natural process of grieving and healing.

Sometimes a loss may not become apparent until later in life. For example, many women unconsciously bond with the child in their womb and feel a great sense of loss after an abortion. Support groups are now offered for women who later in life, look back on abortion with grief. Healing work needs to be done. There can also be less obvious losses that emerge later in life. Realizing that you may have been deprived of a happy childhood can be considered a nonobvious loss. There may be no external event that triggers the recognition of loss, rather a creeping internal realization about the nature of your upbringing. This type of loss is just as real as other types of losses and needs to be felt, expressed, and grieved.

As discussed previously, any change in your lifestyle can bring about a sense of loss even if the change ends up being for the better in the long run: graduating, moving, changing relationships, and starting a different job are all stressful events. Again, the important principle you need to follow to keep yourself emotionally healthy is to feel and express the emotions regarding these events.

One of the most difficult and stressful losses to endure occurs when you are placed in an indeterminate state. Is the relationship going to end? Am I going to lose my job? Is my health OK? Continually wondering about these and other questions can be more stressful than the outcome itself. Often when and if the event occurs, a sense of relief is felt because the feeling of not knowing is finally removed. Once the state of limbo ends, you can begin the process of healing and move on.

In addition to feelings of physical and emotional pain, some symptoms of loss include:

Anger	Anxiety
Changes in energy	Changes in sexual drive
Despair	Emptiness
Feelings of helplessness	Guilt
Lack of concentration	Loneliness
Mood swings	Proneness to error
Reduced ambition	Sleep disturbances

The key thing to remember is that all or any of these symptoms are normal for anyone who has experienced a loss. Too often, these feelings are fought rather than expressed and experienced. If you have not had an obvious loss yet you relate to a number of the above reactions, you might wish to examine your past for a not-so-obvious loss or a series of such losses. Some of the nonobvious losses can be a loss of an ideal or goal, achieving success, moving, or similar changes. Learning new things about yourself can also be construed as a loss, especially when it involves a loss of innocence.

Keep in mind that your losses are personal and how you feel may be different from how others may feel in situations of apparently similar losses. In providing support to the bereaved, counselors are often advised to refrain from saying, "I know how you feel." The grieving person has no words to express the rainbow of feelings and thoughts that are occurring. It is not possible to match their feelings with our own.

In all losses, it is important to feel the loss, to admit that you have lost something, and to allow the natural healing process to take place. Often your body has begun the healing process without your knowing it. Often you try to block this healing process because you do not understand it or because you do not understand the process of letting go. Colgrove, Bloomfield, and McWilliams state that to feel pain after a loss is "normal, natural, proof that you are alive, and a sign that you can respond to life's experiences" and "to see pain not as hurting, but healing."

Day-to-Day Events

Day-to-day living is not without its minor inconveniences and troubles. A bad day occurs when you have several small mishaps. A missed connection or telephone call, poor timing, being splashed by a passing vehicle, or causing a minor dent in your car can all add up to emotional stress in your day. It is necessary to acknowledge the troubles but not dwell on them. Since daily life can be full of annoyances, you need some outlet to release the emotional tension and stress created by these incidents. If you do not find these outlets for yourself, you end up building a backlog of emotion that adds to your stress level. Eventually, you may find that, as in the phrase "the straw that broke the camel's back," at some point, a seemingly insignificant event triggers a flow of emotion. Unfortunately, this can be a rather unhealthy method of stress release because it can generate a habit of failing to deal with each issue individually as it arises. You can reduce the level of stress sufficiently to be able to cope, but you do not resolve the underlying issues.

Day-to-day stresses can be viewed as minor losses that individually might not even be noticed or remembered a few days later, but the stress of the events takes its toll on your emotional health. After a buildup of minor losses, you may find yourself crying unexpectedly or bursting in anger when you can "no longer take it." You may appear somewhat irrational in your behavior because another person viewing your reaction to an event does not know about the little events that have added up to create your discharge. If you maintain healthy emotional habits, you will find ways in which you can reduce your emotional tension before you reach your breaking point.

Holidays and Christmas

For some, the Christmas holiday season measures closeness, while for others, it measures distance. It is a time of gathering and for some, a time of aloneness. It is a time of joy; for others a time of despair. I've experienced both. From my studies in counseling, and from talking to my friends and co-workers, I have learned that I was not alone in my difficulties. Our holiday rituals have a profound effect on people. Counseling intakes are highest after the Christmas holiday. Sadly, suicide rates are highest at Christmas, and in the spring months, when the weather gets better, but people don't. Christmas is a very stressful time for many. With healing and self-control, you can bring back the joy of holiday gatherings, finding safety in your ability to cope and self-acceptance. It's always great to have an escape plan though. I recommend having a friend to go visit so that you can take a break from the family setting should you need one!

Chronic Conditions

Having experienced the painful effects of several whiplash injuries combined with stress, I can easily identify with the difficulties of putting up with chronic pain from injuries. It was not until I took a course on living healthily with a chronic condition that I fully comprehended the impact that the condition was having on my emotional and mental health. I soon learned that chronic pain could lead to frustration and depression. In learning to take better care of myself and to be more proactive in my health management, I was able to minimize the effects of my condition. Chronic fatigue or pain is a condition that many of us live with. We need to learn to differentiate between physical pain and mental pain. The physical pain often needs to be accepted, hopefully with some relief in sight. The mental anguish of wishing it were different or thoughts of anger, and "Why me?" only exacerbate the suffering. With the suffering of the mind, mild pain becomes severe pain.

Fortunately, there are support groups available that can help us deal with the mental health aspects of chronic pain. As you learn to acknowledge your difficulties and to reach out, you can find helpful support in your community. It helps to know that your problem is a common one. It ends isolation and also reminds you of your humanity.

Living, Loving, and Learning

Living and sharing with others can bring great joy to your life, but in doing so, you open yourself to the risk of losing someone you care about. With the divorce rate hovering at the 50 percent level depending on where you live, there are great numbers of people who have lost their ideal of having a marriage that will last forever. Many people experience anger and hurt over things that went wrong in marriage or a relationship. If these life challenges are not resolved, they will be carried into the next relationship or marriage, bringing a greater vulnerability to other issues.

Some people may unintentionally hurt you. They are not mean people, but they may not know or understand how their actions or words could be hurtful. Simply put, they may not know better. People may grow and as a result, outgrow a relationship. They may no longer feel the need to be fixed through a relationship. Everyone changes. Their new goals may result in focusing on new career opportunities that result in growth for them but a loss for you, possibly leaving you feeling frustrated and hurt.

All of us go through breakups and letdowns. You have your successes, but you have your failures, as well. The events occurring in your life will create emotions that need to be expressed and resolved. If you resolve the issues, you end up living, loving, and forgiving, which brings about learning.

Rejection, Betrayal, and Letdowns

Whether you are asking someone out on a date, for a job, or for a raise, you feel a certain amount of vulnerability. I have heard that a simple answer for dealing with rejection is to say, "Next!" Yet at times, rejection is not so simple to deal with, particularly when you have to reconcile the discrepancy between what you were promised or wanted and how things turned out. I don't know of any couple who did not mean what they said when they recited their wedding vows, yet many couples end up divorced.

Even if you have not married, the love that was once there must be reconciled with the fact that a partner is leaving.

Rejection and betrayal leave you feeling wounded, with feelings and thoughts that come faster than you can process. Initially, you may even feel shattered. MRI studies have shown that rejection and social pain are similar to physical pain. It is hard to accept that someone you love has chosen a different path that does not include you in their picture. Similarly, you may have to face the fact that someone has lied to you, or had an affair, and you must reconcile the truth of their actions with what you did not believe possible. You need to acknowledge your deep feelings of disappointment and the challenge to your sense of worthiness. In your healing process, you may come to understand that you don't have to take the issue personally, that it is more about the other person than it is about you.

Tony Robbins says in the documentary *Tony Robbins: I Am Not Your Guru*, "Rejection breeds obsession." That obsession can manifest in various ways. People who are experiencing the pain of rejection are more likely to commit fraud. Rejection is painful and felt as strongly as physical pain. Coupled with already low self-esteem, rejection can challenge our self-worth and lead to numerous obsessive behaviors. The antidote to rejection is healthy self-esteem, which can be restored through the process of developing resilience.

Jealousy

Relationships and friendships come and go, but many fail due to either your own or someone else's jealousy. When an ex-partner develops a new relationship, jealousy can destroy your current friendship. You may stop calling friends of the opposite sex because of your own jealous partner. Many of us have lost companionship due to the jealousy of other peoples' new partners. Insecurity and fear are the basis of jealousy. You must remind yourself that, like excessive pride, hatred, and anger, jealousy is one of the seven deadly sins. What a better world it would be if you could put aside your jealousy and, in true love for your partners and friends, support their growth, health, and wealth.

Parents Wanting "The Best"

I was recently attending a course on happiness in which the teacher described three types of love. A parent loves a child when born with awe, then loves the child as a nurturer; then as the child grows up, the parent loves the child, wishing for the best for the child. After my father passed away, we had to go through all his belongings to clean out his house. I came across a letter he and my mother had written to the Blessed Virgin, praying that the utmost suffering that we could bear be brought upon the family so that we could be redeemed and get into heaven. While they clearly wanted "the best" for us, their definition of "best" was clearly sick. Finding these letters helped explain some of the reasons why my mother and father behaved the way they did. When I was bullied, they would console me, but secretly, they saw this as a suffering opportunity to help me get into heaven. It explains why they would never do anything about the bullying. Sometimes the parents' idea of what is "best" is messed up!

Bullying, Teasing, and Humiliation

Bullying and teasing in school are now being recognized as a major contributor to problems later in life. Both leave a child or young adult with a low sense of worth as well as a lack of confidence in social skills and a low sense of acceptance. In my own personal work, I came across several men and women who had been teased and bullied. The scars lasted long into their adult lives. It seems that although children can demonstrate a beautiful understanding of how the world should be, they can also exhibit a level of cruelty rarely found in people once they reach adulthood. In my own healing from bullying and teasing, I learned that children need an outlet for their anger and frustration. I was an easy target because I was trained to not stand up for myself, I was physically weak, and I lacked self-esteem. I've learned not to take it personally, yet it has been quite a journey to get to this point. I realize that many children are unaware of the hurt they cause. One of the most successful programs to promote empathy and reduce bullying is *Roots of Empathy*, which was founded by Mary Gordon. This program involves having a class "adopt" a mother and her baby. Each week the mother brings the baby to the school, and the children interact with and watch the growth of the child. As the school children bonded with the little baby, the incidence of bullying and teasing dropped significantly: as the children developed their sense of compassion and love, bullying seemed out of the question.

Creative Soul Wounding

In your emotional development, there are many factors that either facilitate emotional expression or encourage you to avoid it. The causes of your own emotional abandonment are numerous. Some of you were never taught to value your emotions. You may have had poor emotional role models and may have never been taught how to effectively communicate your feelings.

Parenting not only involves putting food on the table but also includes nurturing and paying attention to the emotional needs and concerns of children. Children need encouragement to help them in their development, growth, and decision-making. In some families, emotional expression, decision-making, and expression of thought may be devalued and ridiculed, or you may even have been shamed for having emotions. In some cases, you may have been hurt so deeply by the actions of others that you choose to avoid your emotions as a way of coping with your pain. Often you may refrain from expressing yourself when there is a lack of trust and safety.

In all of the above cases, the neglect, suppression, and shaming of your emotional side is an injury to your soul or heart. These injuries can run deep into your consciousness and affect your emotional state and comfort in expressing yourself until the issue is re-evaluated. Although you may not be able to recall a specific incident or trauma, an environment of constant shame, scolding, or subtle put-downs can lead to a demoralized spirit that will likely result in unresolved emotional trauma. This trauma will come to the forefront when later, you discover that your treatment was unhealthy, unfair, and undeserved, or possibly when you become involved in a relationship.

Another type of emotional abuse or scarring occurs when a child is overly criticized for creatively expressing themselves. Children will creatively express themselves through inquiring and wondering, dancing, singing, or playfulness. Often children are robbed of their freedom of self-expression when they are shamed or ridiculed for their spontaneity.

Excessive controlling will lead to a loss of connection with their creative side.

Actions that ridicule or shame your creative center or that shut down your expression of self are a crime against your creative soul. You may have been taught to suppress the expression of creativity – one of the greatest sources of human joy and expression. Fortunately, though, you can still find your creative center within. You can learn to be comfortable in letting your creative aspects and talents shine again, perhaps even for the first time. Through emotional release and resolution, you can reconnect and rejuvenate your creative personality.

Reality Can Hurt!

Reality can be hard to take when situations turn out differently than you expected. Most people who are divorced, separated, or widowed never thought this could happen to them. The shock of separation, starting over, or even just losing the innocence of childhood, can be challenging. For many of us, it is a difficult lesson to learn that the only thing in life that seems constant is that it is changing.

I have often been troubled by the claims of some people that we create our own reality and that everything that happens to us is a result of our ability to attract things into our lives. The problem with this concept is that it feels great to have this belief system when things are going well. But when the tables turn, as they often do at various points in life, this belief system becomes a punishing frame of mind to live under. In his book *Leading from Within*, Parker Palmer defines "functional atheism" as "the belief that ultimate responsibility for everything rests with me." He states that this is "a belief held by people whose theology affirms a higher power." Simply put, people who act out of functional atheism go around saying, "I guess it wasn't meant to be" when things don't go their way, but say, "I create my own reality and universe" when things work out. They take credit for the good things but don't accept responsibility for failures.

The problem with functional atheism is that it appears to be a belief that has been extrapolated to include more than was originally meant. You can indeed learn to control your reactions, but sometimes things happen that are beyond your control. There are other people in the world, and I cannot control their choices or actions, any more than can I control the weather. Things often happen for a reason, but sometimes that reason is not about you or me.

Internal conflict arises when you believe that you are 100 percent responsible for your destiny, and things don't work out. You can experience periods of deep guilt, shame, and low self-esteem. Natural disasters, accidents, crimes, and even decisions made by other people are outside your realm of control. Some ancient wisdom books that I have come across state that we control our actions, thoughts, and feelings, but not the results of our actions. There is great wisdom in the statement "grant me the serenity to accept the things I cannot change, the courage to change the things I can, and the wisdom to know the difference." The wisdom to know the difference is the key to living in a world of billions of people with different viewpoints, agendas, and outlooks on what is best.

On the other hand, it is important to have a belief that things happen for a reason and that the universe will somehow help us to handle our problems. While I am skeptical of *"Law of Attraction"* seminars, the universe has often offered up a sense of humor to me around this topic. At a music festival, I was ordering some food at one of the food trucks. As I got nearer to the front of the ordering line, the staff announced that they were out of fish and chips, which was what I had planned to order. When I was asked what I wanted, I replied: "I'd like fish and chips, please!" The order taker looked at me quizzically and replied: "Umm, sir, we just announced that we are out of fish and chips…" I replied coyly: "Well, I believe in manifesting, and I just paid three thousand dollars for a seminar on attracting what you want, so I'm trying to manifest fish and chips!" I waited a second or two for effect and then burst into a smile and said, "Wow, I guess I wasted that money, and now I have to tell my teacher it doesn't work. I'll have pizza then…" We both had a good laugh, I paid for my order and then got into the line to get my food. As I neared the front of that line, the staff announced that they actually did have three more orders of fish and chips! As I picked up my fish and chips, I chuckled to myself that the universe not only provides for us but has a sense of humor too!

Shame and Guilt

Being given or taking on inappropriate responsibility is another crime against the soul. Children are sometimes inappropriately given and accept responsibility for what has happened to them. Many adult children of alcoholics learn through recovery programs that they were not responsible for the treatment they received as children. Without any other models, many of these children assumed that their environment and the treatment they were receiving were normal.

Realizing the falseness of the image of their family, and that their environment was not normal, leads the adult child to try to reconcile their past. This usually involves revisiting the past and resolving the fear and pain associated with their upbringing, and then allowing the development of healthier patterns of behavior in their current and future relationships.

Infidelity and Divorce

No one ever walks down the aisle in a marriage ceremony, thinking that they will be one of the many couples that divorce. People change over time, and a couple may end up discovering that they are not meant for each other after all, or there may be strains in the roles that each expects the other to play. On a trip to Beijing, I struck up a conversation with a friendly older gentleman in a coffee shop. We ended up talking about several things, but the one that has always stuck in my mind is his description of marriage. He said: "Marriage is like two people jumping into a swimming pool. One person needs to be aware that someone must be holding on to the side of the pool at all times. Otherwise, both will drown. They may take turns holding on to the side of the pool, and sometimes it's necessary to hold on to the side even when you are tired and don't want to because the other person doesn't have the energy to hold on." This metaphor explains why some couples fight and end up divorcing. No one was holding on to the side of the pool!

Why we are attracted to someone is complex, and after years of being with someone, you often discover things about yourself and how you subconsciously chose your partner. One of the dangers of romantic love is that some people hope to find a partner who will heal what we didn't get from our parents, teachers, or family. When they don't or can't give it to you, you get angry and relive the old drama. You can recognize that your partner has more skills than your mother or father did, and your partner is not your mother or father, but you are projecting your needs onto them. Unless this internal conflict of seeing your partner as the enemy can be resolved, and you realize they are not an enemy, the likelihood of the marriage succeeding is not high and it will lead to separation and divorce.

Going through a divorce can require you to face up to a loss of ideals, questioning your choice of a partner, and a re-evaluation of life plans. Financial considerations can also play a large part in negotiating your way out of a relationship and re-establishing yourself. The social construct is that divorce is a painful, messy, long, drawn-out event, rather than a clear break from a relationship. On the other hand, I have met couples who have amicably divorced, reached an agreement, and remain friends. In one case, I heard of a couple who both fired their lawyers because the lawyers were bent on being vindictive, which was not in the couple's nature.

Another painful relationship issue is learning that a partner has had an affair. The experience of learning about the infidelity of a partner can bring about physical reactions such as nausea, diarrhea, gastrointestinal disturbances, heart palpitations, shortness of breath, headaches, loss of appetite, and insomnia. It is now understood that infidelity can lead to "Post Infidelity Stress Disorder."

Whether dealing with infidelity or going through an actual divorce, such disruptions bring up a wide spectrum of emotions and challenges. Keep in mind that divorce can be an opportunity for a new beginning, new hobbies and interests, and new relationships. But as the saying goes, "As one door closes, another opens, but it's the hallway in between that is the difficult part!"

Betrayal and Loss

You often have expectations that certain friends will stick by you and that you can count on their loyalty, yet it is a fact of life that each of your friends will sometimes let you down. But, worse, sometimes a friend will make statements behind your back to take care of their own self-interest and protect themselves, which leaves you with a feeling that is deeper than disappointment. It leaves you with a sense of shock and thoughts of "How could you?" mixed with anger and disappointment.

When you change and grow, you may find that you find new, healthier friends or your friendship with some people will deepen. Unfortunately, some people who are going through difficult times isolate themselves. In doing so they "ghost" their friends. In Korean culture, the term "submarining" refers to a friend suddenly disappearing, but like a submarine, they will likely resurface at some time, but unaware of the emotional consequences of their behavior. Ghosting and submarining, or the outright ending of friendship, will bring forth a mixture of emotions and challenge our self-worth. I call this a "deathless loss." We experience grief and rejection and are left wondering why. Some people run away from friendships if they have overshared, others withdraw for reasons that may have little to do with you.

Keeping a Secret

Keeping a secret is difficult for anyone, but when the secret is something you fear will cause others to reject you, the emotional stress is much higher. Keeping a secret about yourself from others can substantially compromise your immune system, according to a study at the University of California. We all have things we wish we had done differently, but the secrets that are the most troublesome are the ones that are ever-present in your mind, even if you have fabricated a story to cover them. The religious practice of confession has been a powerful healing tool for dealing with these kinds of secrets. The power comes from sharing your deep fears and pain with a trusted witness. I remember the fear I experienced in Grade 8 as I changed schools due to being relentlessly teased. I was told to make sure no one knew what school I had come from. I was in a state of fear most of the time that someone would find out about me. Taking this personally, I developed a shadow side to myself that needed to be resolved in my later years.

Sexuality and Orientation

While there are now laws that protect against discrimination based on sexual orientation, there are still many incidents of negative treatment towards people who are gay, lesbian, or transgender. I remember the teasing I went through in my grade school class as some students thought it was fun to suggest I was gay, though I was and am straight. This experience taught me to have empathy for the difficulties others go through. I have heard people talk of parents disowning their gay kids and selfishly thinking, "Where did we go wrong?" but also of wonderful stories of acceptance. It seems the difficulties with parents usually occur when the parents expect their children to fulfill their dreams of grandparenthood and their idealized notions of family life as depicted in TV shows from the 1960s. Kahlil Gibran says: "Your children are not your children. They are the sons and daughters of Life's longing for itself... You may give them your love but not your thoughts, for they have their own thoughts. You may house their bodies but not their souls." The wisdom in these words means that parents need to raise their children without any expectations of their own, only with the best intentions for their child.

I have read many articles and books on precontact Hawaiian culture, which was much less restrictive and less prudish than some other cultures when it comes to sexuality. Many of us were taught to hide our sexual organs out of shame and guilt. In the Hawaiian tradition, however, young girls and boys were required to cover their private parts out of the recognition that these parts of the body are sacred. How many of us were ever taught that?

Becoming More Aware

Each of us builds constructs about how the world works, how people really are, and how we fit into the world. Sometimes we grow into a new belief system gradually, but sometimes life hits us harder than we expected when we realize how people have really been behaving towards us. An overheard conversation or a realization of the lack of genuineness of some people becomes painful when you have to face up to the way people are really thinking about you. I remember a time when I had faced a lot of emotional pain. I had truly been dissociated and had been putting up a fake smile. When I worked through the pain and became present, I dropped the mask, but there was a great deal of pain as I realized that some acquaintances were sarcastically reflecting my mask back to me. There were many moments of awkwardness and embarrassment as these people realized that I was now aware of what they were doing. It was painful, but I reminded myself of my growth and practiced self-compassion.

Moral Trauma and Demoralizing Inaction

According to the Canadian Mental Health Association, "A moral injury is a loss injury; a disruption in our trust that occurs within our moral values and beliefs. Any events, actions, or inactions transgressing our moral/ethical beliefs, expectations, and standards can set the stage for moral injury. When moral injury hits, it hits hard and can have a long-lasting emotional and psychological impact."

A former friend of mine was traumatized after working tirelessly to survey a homeless situation and provide recommendations. The report was completed after many hours of work but resulted in no action by the organization. Similarly, many journalists silently suffer in depression after reporting on a human tragedy when they realize that nothing is being done to help the people in the story.

Symptoms of moral injury include:
- Feeling anxious and afraid, demoralized, guilty, and ashamed
- Feeling "haunted" by decisions, actions, or inaction
- Anger in particular following betrayal
- Feelings of worthlessness, helplessness, powerlessness, and anger
- A sense of loss of identity and role
- Persistent self-blame or blaming others
- Impairment in social, personal, and occupational functioning
- An increase in substance use
- Suicidal ideation

Crimes of Personal Invasion

Many people's homes are broken into each and every day. It is sad to realize the impact that this has on the victim's mental health. Knowing that someone has been in your personal space without your permission can leave you feeling angry and vulnerable. It is common to have disturbed sleep patterns and increased sensitivity to unfamiliar noises for a long period after a burglary. I can remember clearly the day my van was broken into during my university years. Like many others, I am now awakened easily by noises on the street. There is a spectrum of emotions that you may experience when your personal property is taken, ranging from anger to disgust, but hopefully settling on eventual forgiveness.

Instances of Injustice

It is a sad reflection of society, but sometimes people do mean things to you and justice does not prevail. You may have been told as a child that what goes around comes around, but it may not appear to be true. You may even find yourself being the victim of gossip, lies, and even false accusations. The consequences can be severe, such as a job loss, loss of housing, or financial problems. Finding help may be difficult and others may not want to get involved, leaving you feeling betrayed. Situations like this can leave you with symptoms of traumatization. All attempts to change your thinking do not relieve the cycle of ruminating thoughts. The key to resolving the trauma is to focus on the emotions in the body, feeling them, expressing them, and forgiving others so that you can return to a sense of serenity.

Long Periods of Unpredictability

While low levels of stress can be a positive motivator, high levels of stress can do harm to the mind and body, especially if it continues for a long time. One of the most difficult situations to deal with is unpredictability and a lack of control over things in your life. When the stress of trying to solve one problem after another continues and continues, the body remains in a heightened state and seems to adapt, albeit unhealthily, to remaining at high-stress levels. The hormones produced by stress remain at elevated levels resulting in a sense of burnout and fatigue even after the original stressful period has ended.

Perfectionism

While doing something well is a goal we all strive for, trying to do something perfectly often gets in the way of doing anything at all. Gifted performers express their talents in what appears to be a perfect performance, yet the artists themselves often notice mistakes that are completely missed by the audience. When I played in a rock group, we would comment after

Let Go and Heal

a show about the mistakes made. As professionals, we would take pride in improving our craft, while most audience members did not have the knowledge, skill, or perceptual capacity to notice that any mistakes were made at all! Artists, writers, teachers, or hobbyists often limit their ability to enjoy their efforts. At some point, someone told you, or perhaps you developed the belief that if something is not perfect, it is of no value. This is not the real-world truth of expression and creativity.

Perfectionism can range from thinking that what you've accomplished is never quite enough to procrastinating so that you never actually have to measure your accomplishments. It can be rooted in fear of disapproval, failure, embarrassment from making mistakes, or from not living up to what you think you should be doing. Ironically, the ideal of always trying to attain perfection can be quite harmful, even though it may be considered a desirable trait. For gifted people, perfectionism is usually necessary to attain an extremely high level of performance and success. However, it is far better to have a sense of healthy striving than an all-or-nothing, compulsive, and obsessive attitude of perfectionism. When you are unable to attain the high standards you set for yourself, anxiety and depression can set in. John Henshaw states: "Don't let perfect get in the way of the good."

Other People's Rules and Decisions

Sometimes you are faced with the reality that there are other people in the world with different viewpoints, different ways of going about things, and different styles of communicating. When you combine this with organizational rules and a legal framework that is slow to change or recognize mistakes, it is easy to get caught up in a challenging scenario. Rules that at one time made sense simply don't in our situation, leaving us with frustration and sometimes disastrous financial repercussions. It is easy to spiral down into a sense of hopelessness since challenging the rules can take a lot of time and energy. In the justice system, many people have been wrongfully accused and convicted, stealing months or years of their lives while trying to fight to uphold their innocence. In the administration of government programs and tax laws, sometimes you find yourself in a unique situation where rules become unfair. It is sometimes necessary to accept that the rules won't be changed immediately and to try to move on and rebuild.

Experiencing Poverty

Sometimes things don't go as planned, or you may experience situations that you can't control that greatly affect your finances. It has been shown that poverty can have a very negative effect on your morale and self-esteem. While some people come out stronger from experiencing childhood poverty, others experience lingering issues. What seems to differentiate the two groups is the level of cognitive stimulation available in the home, and to a lesser degree, parenting style.

The idea that hard work will get you ahead can come crashing down in a recession or even with a change in governmental rules and regulations. You can find yourself in a situation of joblessness and unable to meet your financial obligations. Poverty can happen to anyone.

Ostracism, Isolation, and Humiliation

Recent studies have shown that ostracism, isolation, and humiliation are far more painful than previously thought. My travels to China and learning about the concept of "face-saving" have taught me that, in some cultures, humiliation (even if unintended) has profound effects on individuals. Humiliation is a highly emotive negative state in which your status is lowered in front of others. It is more powerful and destructive than anger and more intensely felt than the feeling of happiness. Bullies thrive on humiliating people.

Ostracism and isolation involve being ignored, excluded, or overlooked. They can occur in the home, at work, or in social groups and have profound effects on your physical and mental health. Ostracism, while being more common than harassment, has actually been shown to have harsher effects on well-being, result in health problems, and contribute to a greater likelihood of quitting your job.

Dealing with a Sociopath

As I look back on my life with new knowledge, I realize that, at times, I was dealing with a sociopath. The sociopath often comes across as charming to win your trust but then works against you behind the scenes.

Because of their charm, it is difficult to convince other people of their two-sided nature. Others have only seen the warmth and friendliness that the sociopath exhibits. Unfortunately, the warmth and friendliness are only superficial. The sociopath will lie frequently, often believing what they say. They rarely apologize and always deflect blame to other people and other factors. They appear to want friendship, but in fact, only want loyal followers. If they cannot control you, they will try to control how others see you. They twist any information you give them to make you look bad or harm your reputation. Other people may not complain due to fear of being picked on by the sociopath. Sociopaths live in a different world. They lack the capacity to feel compassion and remorse.

Sociopaths are often more likely to see empathic people as targets. Studies show that people can easily spot someone's genetic disposition for empathy. Therefore, one should not feel any shame for being targeted. Your kindness and thoughtfulness are positive qualities that the sociopath tries to exploit. In dealing with a sociopath, you get worn down by being constantly on guard and fighting a battle to preserve your reputation. In the BBC version of *Sherlock Holmes*, Sherlock stated that it is very hard to kill an idea once it has been given a home. The sociopath counts on this – planting ideas and then forcing you to defend yourself.

Most of the literature I have read on dealing with a sociopath suggests that the solution to the sociopath problem is to look for another job or place to live. I don't believe this advice is fair, as many people are not in a situation that allows them to easily leave or move. The best defense is to be informed and knowledgeable about the traits of a sociopath and to defend yourself without trying to outwit the sociopath.

If you stick it out and the sociopath leaves, it may take some time to heal. In my own experience of dealing with a sociopath, I found that the strongest emotions were felt after the sociopath left. As my counselor stated: "The bleeding has stopped, but you still need to heal."

You may look back at past events and, now knowing what sociopathic behavior looks like, attribute past difficulties in relationships to sociopathic behavior. I now have a greater understanding of some of the people I worked with and the workplace politics and sabotaging behavior of some co-workers. One thing that has helped me is to give attention to the positive working relationships I have had and to remember that other workers may remain quiet out of fear of becoming the sociopath's next target. Also, since they aren't currently a target, it could be that they don't see the dark side of the sociopath that you have experienced.

While dealing with a sociopath can be a draining experience, there is a silver lining to the cloud of troubles. Dealing with a sociopath leaves you more aware of the complexities of human interaction, and you can spot sociopathic behavior from a safe distance much earlier in your interactions.

A Broken Heart and Unrequited Love

How many of you have at some time fallen in love, only to find that the person you have fallen for does not share the same feelings for you? Unrequited love can be disheartening as it challenges your notions of fate and feelings of self-worth. You find it painful to accept that someone you have fallen in love with has chosen someone else, even though you feel a strong bond with this person. You wonder whether to give up and move on or hope for a change in the other person's feelings. True heartache can occur when you tie all your hopes to one person, yet a beautiful romance can blossom when the attraction and love are reciprocated. Recent research has shown that the part of the brain associated with physical pain is activated when we experience heartbreak. What inspiration this topic has been for the poets, writers, dreamers, songwriters, and romantics throughout the ages!

Revictimization

Sometimes our court system is not perfect. There have been concerns that the justice system focuses more on the offender than on the victim. Although this has changed recently with the introduction of victim impact statements, going through the process of the court system to obtain justice requires telling your story numerous times. Well-intentioned officials may question why you did things and repeatedly question facts and figures, leaving you exhausted, feeling judged, and with your integrity questioned. Justice takes a lot of energy. This may even happen outside the court system when pressing for fairness in other matters.

Vicarious Traumatization

It is commonly known in the health professions that observing or treating people who have experienced trauma can, over time, result in traumatizing the caregivers themselves. This form of trauma can also happen to the average person as they watch the horrific images of terrorism, war, and crime on the daily news and the Internet. It is only in recent history that so many troubling images are presented in our daily lives as we go about our family activities and business. It is easy to become numb to these images, but on a subconscious level, the images trigger thoughts and feelings that compromise your mental health and cause you to question your values, the moral standards of society, and your sense of safety.

Creative Constipation

One of the most frustrating experiences I ever encountered was during a time when I was quite ill with Lyme disease and could not write, nor could I focus on my other projects. Other events and conditions also interfered with my ability to write, sing, socialize, and do the things that I truly enjoy doing, and that give me energy. In the classic psychology book *Conditioned Reflex Therapy*, author Andrew Salter theorizes that many anxiety issues and social phobias arise from conditioned inhibited expression. A conditioned reflex is a habit that has formed based on a cue, reaction, and response. In his book, Salter describes numerous cases where expression became uninhibited after understanding the cue, changing the reaction, and instituting a new response. In many of his cases, uninhibited expression led to a reduction of anxiety and an increase in happiness. Expressing yourself through creativity, whether it be organizing, planning, or just doing the things you enjoy, brings satisfaction on a deep level. If you are not expressing your creativity, try to figure out what roadblocks are in your way and then go around, above, or below them rather than inviting frustration by persisting in attempts to plow through them!

If you have talents that you are not expressing, then you may be experiencing an inner turmoil of blocked creativity. Begin to explore your talents that you put away and learn to discover new talents that lay hidden beneath the surface of your fear of expressing yourself.

Mark Linden O'Meara

Classifying Human Suffering

While several possible causes of suffering are listed above, it is impossible to describe all of the things in life that cause suffering. According to Buddhist texts, there are several categories into which human suffering can be classified. The first category is something we have all experienced. It would seem that even the act of being born entails an experience of pain. I have not heard of any babies who were born laughing or singing; all are born crying as they leave the safety of the mother's womb to begin the journey called life. Other categories are aging, sickness, death, separation from loved ones, undesirable confrontation with another person or thing, denial of desires, and suffering due to the characteristics of the human body and mind. This last category is one that you often need to work on the most. By understanding the nature of the mind, you can learn to reduce your suffering and practice acceptance, forgiveness, compassion, and kindness towards yourself and others. This is what ends suffering!

I have often witnessed how telling someone in a warm, focused, and sincere manner that they are special, good, and loved can reduce a person to tears. I believe such statements call forth the incongruence between the thoughts and beliefs of your subconscious mind and what you are being told. Many people have a fragile sense of self-esteem. I notice that those who have healed their suffering and past pain can more readily accept words of love and encouragement.

The purpose of this collection of possible hurts in this chapter is not to collect suffering points to prove how difficult your life has been. It is, however, an opportunity to acknowledge the past and not push away any unresolved emotion and painful images of those times. It can be a starting point for looking within to examine what we have not yet healed from and examine things that happened that we need to work on.

In traumatic events, there are many components. The first is the event itself, a second component is the reaction you had given your knowledge and awareness at the time. A third component is how people around us reacted or did not react, perhaps shaming you for something that was not your fault. Perhaps with your limited understanding, you incorrectly arrive at the conclusion that something was your fault and developed shame. As a child, teenager, young adult, adult, or even as a senior you would not have the tools to deal with what has or is happening. There should be no guilt about how you reacted or the attributions and beliefs you formed at the time, but there should now be a commitment to healing.

I have met many others who, in their quest to end suffering and help others, have expressed a desire to set up a healing retreat or healing center. Keep in mind that a healing center is not located in a remote place in the mountains, nor is it a place to retreat from the world, even though that may be beneficial at times. Your healing center is in your place of work, your home, your friends and family, the places you visit daily, and, most importantly, in your heart and mind. It is here that you will end suffering.

7. Abuse, Trauma, and the Wounded Soul

Defining Abuse and Trauma

> "If we could somehow end child abuse and neglect, the eight hundred pages of the DSM-IV would be shrunk to a pamphlet in two generations."
> – John Briere

I doubt that my parents had ever intended to be abusive, but their own issues and lack of personal growth had resulted in numerous incidences of neglect, emotional abuse, and in one situation, physical harm to another family member. I also realize that although I had never used the term before my healing began, my mother was an active alcoholic until the last year of her life, and my father exhibited numerous dysfunctional traits that resembled an alcoholic who had given up the drinking but hadn't healed. Did my parents love us? Absolutely! Were they emotionally healthy people? Clearly not! I have come to understand how they got to be who they were, forgiven them, and healed. That process began by acknowledging the abuse that I experienced.

According to United States federal law, childhood abuse is defined as "Any recent act or failure to act on the part of a parent or caretaker which results in death, serious physical or emotional harm, sexual abuse or exploitation"; or "An act or failure to act which presents an imminent risk of serious harm." While federal law does not define neglect, many states have legislation that defines it. In some states, the term abuse has been replaced with "maltreatment." Childhood abuse, neglect, and maltreatment overwhelm the resources of the child. They result in a loss of physical safety and trust. The effects can last into adulthood with a sense of lost opportunities, repeated failed relationships, incidents of domestic violence, and revictimization.

There is a strong link between some mental health disorders and childhood trauma, but there are also fascinating stories of people healing and accomplishing great things in life.

Let Go and Heal

Without intervention or a calling to heal, adults who were abused emotionally or psychologically, or who witnessed abuse, are more likely to develop mental health issues than those who have not. It is interesting to note that repeated abuse results in individuals exhibiting a higher total trauma score than those whose past included singular abusive experiences of perhaps greater intensity. This seems to support the idea that prolonged emotional abuse can be as damaging as other seemingly more violent forms of childhood traumas.

The combined effect of numerous incidences of emotional abuse may lead to similar symptoms of repressed emotions, numbness, and the irrational thinking that comes with unresolved issues and loss of your inherent nature. As a child, I had a sense that I was in pain, but I did not have the words or understanding to deal with the emotional injury until I became an adult and made a conscious decision to heal.

The fact that your needs as a child were rarely met may bring about emotional pain and habitual patterns in your adult life. Through healing work, you can free yourself of these patterns and resolve the pain that has lingered below the surface of consciousness for so long.

One fellow author posted the following in a newsgroup topic about families: "Families are prime breeding grounds for astonishing acts of love but also for disastrous emotional tangles that would stun anyone from the outside… and the difference between the parents' version and the children's can be like night and day." Furthermore, as I heard in the Netflix series Mad Men, families can be a wellspring of confidence. Unfortunately for some, they are a deep, dark well that is filled with denigration and shame. As I watch my grandkids grow, I see them freely expressing themselves with dancing, singing, joking, and being raised with a sense of safety. It wasn't the situation in my upbringing, but I acknowledge it, understand it, forgive those who did not know what they were really doing, and have learned to be my own parent, giving myself safety. Self-expression no longer takes the courage that it once took.

Perhaps it could be argued that it is not only pain that causes insanity, but the lies you tell yourself about the pain. These lies are often the only way you know of coping through the pain. Fortunately, as I did, you can heal by beginning to tell yourself the truth about your pain, accept your emotions, and give them up to the universe. By learning that you are in charge as an adult, you can parent yourself and give yourself the love that you know now that you always deserved. You can let go of your pain.

Recognizing Abuse

Often it is not until later in life that you may realize the impact your upbringing had on you, and that your family situation may have been abusive. As a child, you came to accept your environment simply because you knew of no other. You did not know that in other families, parents were and are supportive and nurturing. Instead, you may have experienced parents who could be classified as inadequate, controllers, hinderers, alcoholics, verbal abusers, physical abusers, or sexual abusers. They even may have fallen into more than one category. With all these types of abuse, crimes are perpetrated on an innocent victim who often feels shame, blame, and low self-esteem. In your case, that is you.

Though presented here as abusive parenting types, these characteristics are not limited to parents but may also be applied to spouses, employers, friends, and other members of the community:

Inadequate: Inadequate parents are so focused on their own world that they pay little attention to their children. They are often overly sensitive and cannot deal with any criticism. These parents often make excuses for themselves and hide their problems with statements such as: "We're doing the best we can." Inadequate parents often lack listening skills and have not experienced their own emotional development.

Controllers: Controllers often experience a fear of letting go. They frequently believe that their children were created to serve them and that their children are possessions. The children are not allowed to develop their own set of standards or values and have difficulty exercising decision-making skills due to guilt and manipulation by the parents.

Addicts and Alcoholics: Addicts and alcoholics often make promises that are not kept. Denial of problems, mood swings, inconsistency, and blaming are all characteristics of an alcoholic home. Keep in mind that drinking is only one of many symptoms of an alcoholic. Many parents could be considered "dry alcoholics" who have given up the drinking but do not have the skills to nurture and assist in problem-solving. Addictions tend to follow family patterns. Children of alcoholics tend to develop certain characteristics, often referred to as para-alcoholism. Para-alcoholics show the same style of distorted views and thinking, although they may not actually drink. A familiar saying in support groups is: "If you shake your family tree hard enough, you are bound to find some alcoholics."

Verbal Abusers: Verbally abusive parents often try to motivate children with disrespectful comments. They can be verbally direct, or their comments may be subtly abusive. Abusive statements may be in the form of comparisons to others or subtle put-downs regarding choices of clothing, friends, or interests. The parents exhibit a great degree of insensitivity and rob the children of autonomy and self-confidence. Challenging the parent often leads to denial and attempts by the parent to make the child feel guilty.

Hinderers: The hinderer is someone who says or does things that hinder our development and maturity process. Hinderers do not provide the guidance children require to develop a sense of worth and autonomy. They also go further by saying things that erode confidence and trust in decision-making abilities. Hinderers instill self-doubt and discourage the development of interests and, thus, opportunities to socialize.

Physical Abusers: Physical abusers are those who use physical force to control or harm their children. The parent may often apologize for the striking, placing the child in the awkward and difficult situation of being expected to love and forgive an abuser. Physical abuse may also occur as threats in which a domineering parent may behave in a manner that threatens the safety of the child. Although they might express remorse for striking or acting out, physical abusers often have not learned the skills necessary to cope with their anger. This makes it unlikely that they will be able to restrain their anger any better in the future.

Sexual Abusers: Sexual abuse has always been more prevalent than society would care to admit. Even in the Victorian era, the number of clients who reported sexual abuse astounded Sigmund Freud. Sexual abuse is not limited to unwanted touching or intercourse. Sexual abuse involves power and a lack of respect for a child's innocence. Abuse can be in the form of inappropriate comments, exposure, or teasing. Abused children often experience numerous problems later in life that they may not attribute to the earlier abuse.

The Sexualized Environment: As noted in many online blog posts, many fathers grow uncomfortable with physical contact with their daughters as the daughter begins puberty. Some fathers talk openly with their daughters and involve the mother in the discussion, but in unhealthy environments, the father and mother do not respect boundaries, make sexualized comments, or make fun of their daughter's developing body. In some situations, fathers, uncles, and their friends openly joke about and make unwanted comments about women's bodies and are a poor role model for the girls and the boys in the family. I have even heard of extreme cases where the parents openly watched pornography in front of their teenage children. In another situation I knew about, a friend's menopausal mother tried to seduce his best male teenage friend. This led to the end of the friendship and severe embarrassment and humiliation within his circle of friends. Teenagers should not be afraid of awakening a predator in their family because of their changing bodies.

Let Go and Heal

Helicopter Parents: This parenting style is characterized by the parents spying on their children and doing everything for the child out of fear of the child getting hurt or failing. Unfortunately, this parenting style leaves the child with low confidence, an inability to make decisions for themselves, and high stress levels. In some cases, the overinvolved helicopter parents intervene in situations causing humiliation to the child or young adult in front of their peers.

Uninvolved Providers: While children may be given a roof over their heads, clothes to wear, and food at the dinner table, parenting involves much more. Many parents are unaware of the needs of children concerning the development of a healthy sense of self-esteem. Children of uninvolved providers are raised without the encouragement, affection, sense of belonging, and respect that all children need to develop a positive view of themselves as well as a positive outlook on others and life. The parents may be completely unaware of the problems their children are having. This leaves the children with no primary relationship in their lives unless they find a teacher or other mentor.

Discouragers: Fear-based parents tend to say no to everything. A fear of failure or of harm coming to the children results in an overprotective manner in which the children are discouraged from making decisions and taking risks. Part of growing up and assuming the role of adulthood involves learning to evaluate information and act appropriately. The timing of a decision is also important. If you do not pick the apple off the tree at the right time, it will either taste bitter because it is too early to pick or will rot and eventually fall off the tree if too late. Discouragement teaches children that their goals cannot be attained, or that they are not good enough, when, in fact, they may be able to form great friendships and community in pursuing their talents.

Invalidators: Invalidators make sure that you don't feel good about yourself or your accomplishments. They constantly point out that someone is better than you, or they diminish your accomplishments. In this kind of environment, it is difficult to develop self-confidence. You also become fearful of expressing yourself as any accomplishment makes you a target for a put-down.

Destructive Communication Styles

Sometimes it is the communication style of the person you are involved with that puts a damper on your goals, efforts, and enthusiasm. Some people have a natural habit of being encouraging, while some practice subtly dismissing your goals and negating your positive achievements. A person can say nothing, but the look on their face can convey discouragement. A subtle change in the tone of voice can alter their message. They may ignore your statement about your achievement or offer a reason why your goal is risky. Once you recognize these patterns, you begin to notice the impact this form of discouragement has on you, and you can choose to not let this type of behavior impact your goals. You may also choose to find more supportive relationships.

While reading about a study on communication styles, I recognized the behavior pattern of a few people who had not been supportive. I remember announcing to my parents at the age of twenty-three that I was going to go to university. My parents responded with "How will you support yourself? What will you do if you don't get a job when you finish?" These are examples of "active, destructive communication." Passive destructive communication can occur when you are simply ignored, or someone responds, "That's great!" but with a snide tone of voice and no follow-up engagement in discussing what you have shared. Active constructive communication would have sounded something like, "That's good news. We were always hoping you would do that." In the end, my father was proud of me when I graduated five years later, and impressed when I got a much better job having sent out only one résumé! Active constructive communication is now considered one of the cornerstones of healthy parenting and relationship communication styles.

Other types of abuse include verbal abuse disguised as jokes, withholding approval or attention to gain power, putting down for having a different point of view, discounting achievements or feelings, accusing and blaming, and denial of the fact that the actions of the abuser hurt.

Often an abuser will use various blocking techniques to avoid accountability for their actions. Examples of blocking are statements such as "It was only meant in fun," "I was only joking," or "You're too sensitive." These are statements that deny that abuse is occurring and puts the onus on the victim to change.

Defining and Identifying Dysfunction

While abuse may have not occurred in your family, you can still be greatly influenced by dysfunction. While "dysfunction" is a broad term, there are a few characteristics and behaviors that can be described as dysfunction in a family.

In *The Politics of the Family*, R. D. Laing describes a number of these classifications as well as a great observation about the dynamics of a dysfunctional family:

> "Maybe no one knows what is happening. However, one thing is often clear to an outsider: there is concerted family resistance to discovering what is going on, and there are complicated stratagems to keep everyone in the dark, and in the dark that they are in the dark. ... When one is a child, one is usually taught to believe by one's teachers that what one is taught by them is true. We are taught to think we are wrong if we can't see they are right. If one does not believe what they say, there is something wrong with oneself, morally or medically. ... Lying is against the rules: children are not supposed to lie to their parents, and they are supposed to believe their parents if or when their parents lie to them. Yet parents may feel guilty to tell the truth, are often embarrassed by it, and may even come to believe their own lies. This can become diabolical."

Laing also describes some important distinctions we learn as children, or at least are supposed to learn: inside and outside, pleasure and pain, pleasant and unpleasant, real and not-real, good and bad, me and not-me, here and there, then and now. Unfortunately, some of these distinctions did not become clear, especially "me and not me." You likely took on the responsibility or were blamed for things that were not your fault.

Many of the following defense mechanisms are utilized to keep the family image and reputation in place, or they simply become unhealthy patterns of behavior passed on through the generations:

Denial: A flat-out statement that what is true is not true. This is done with a statement such as "We are a happy family," which one knows deep down is not true.

Splitting: Two groups of ideas or even people will be separated into two groups with no overlapping communication or discussion about or between the two groups. This is also referred to as "all-or-nothing thinking." People are good or bad, right or wrong – thinking tends to be in an "either/or" mode with no room for anything in between.

Displacement: This is the classic tale of taking one's anger at one person out on another. As a newspaper carrier, I witnessed this a few times. A customer had a difficult day, then takes it out on the paperboy for being a few minutes late with the paper delivery. Call center representatives deal with this daily.

Blindfulness: This is a play on the term mindfulness, but instead of being open and aware, people choose not to see what they don't want to see. This can move into the realm of replacement, where people see something else.

Projection and Introjection: Projection is when you think other people are feeling or thinking about what you are feeling. Introjection is when you begin to take on the feelings and beliefs of others. Both of these are the result of lacking the development of "me and not-me" and "outside vs. inside" boundaries.

Rationalization: People come up with all kinds of reasons to explain why they do things. It temporarily calms their conscience.

Repression: Repression is forgetting and forgetting that something has been forgotten, and then forgetting that we have repressed.

Regression: Regression is going back into previous patterns or living in the past and repeatedly reliving memories.

Identification: Identification is really an issue of misidentification. In this style of dysfunction, two situations are taken to be the same problem when, in fact, there are two separately identifiable problems.

Mystification: In this form of dysfunction, the problem is not identified correctly.

Reversal and Inversion: When someone speaks up, the other person is labeled as the troublemaker. With inversion, the workers are blamed for the management problems, and the children are blamed for the parent's problems.

Reaction Formation: This is another dysfunction in which feelings are dealt with by a subsequent action. A better name for this would be "Event – Reaction – Action" in which sometimes the action is the exact opposite of what one would desire. The action is usually done to protect oneself from harm. Due to the bullying and harmful things that people would say to me, I developed a common reaction formation. When people would look at me, I would instantly look away. It took years of awareness and practice to try to reverse this pattern.

Social Isolation: Many dysfunctional families do not allow their children to socialize, or their friends are chosen very carefully, but a reason is quickly found to reject those friends and again isolate the children. There may be behaviors that isolate the children by not having a TV or Internet or accusing other kids of taking advantage of these things when, in fact, it is just normal socialization and sharing. This protects the family from outsiders looking in and seeing what is going on.

Thought and Feeling Isolation: In this situation, the feelings and thoughts arising from a particular situation are isolated and separated from the real cause and attributed to something else, if attributed to anything at all.

Turning Against the Self: If one cannot express anger or even love, then a person may turn against themselves, self-blaming, being their own inner critic, and doing the harm to themselves that their families have been doing to them.

Displacement: This involves denial and then placing blame on others.

Bulldozing: Bulldozers impose their beliefs and standards on others without any discussion. They push very hard, and the people feeling bulldozed feel powerless to stop the bulldozer. They don't take in new information, and they yell with the purpose of overpowering. Trying to be rational with the bulldozer is futile. They have no intention of listening and reaching a compromise and will never apologize.

The Rule of the Unspoken – Expected Collusion

Trying to navigate through childhood and into adulthood in a dysfunctional family is challenging. Part of this dysfunction is that there is a family rule that the dysfunction is not to be acknowledged or talked about. The family rules state that the rules must not be spoken, but to the child or young adult, this is felt as an internal emotional conflict. The result of this unspoken environmental rule is the loss of self, as described by Dr. Laing.

The thought process Dr. Laing describes is similar to this:

> "We are a happy family, but I am not happy, but I can't tell anyone about it, because that would expose our family lie. I have to keep it a secret, and I am unhappy that I have to keep it a secret, and keeping a secret is hard. It wears down my mental health and self-esteem, because deep down, I know that we are a happy family, and I should be happy, right?"

Laing suggests that it is very difficult for a child to admit that their parents are flawed. If they did, they would lose all sense of stability because the child relies on the parents. Therefore, the child, applying logic, says that his or her parents must be wise and loving, so if they are not, it must be me.

The Explosive or Low Resiliency Personality Types

In addition to the dysfunctional patterns, there are unhealthy patterns of dealing with stress within the family. Some people let stress build and build and then explode. Their bubble bursts for some trivial reason, and they attack, yell, and berate to let off their steam. After their outbursts, they feel calm and relaxed, but the recipient feels as though they have been tasered. The process is then repeated over and over again, leaving the victim feeling helpless. Reasoning does not help when they are venting and only feeds the explosive person since they turn everything you say against you. Explosive people often fail to learn that this type of release is destroying their relationship.

Another type of unhealthy pattern is the low resilience parent or caregiver, who is always fragile emotionally and mentally. The slightest out-of-place comment or even a compliment can trigger them to fall apart. In this situation, the child is being expected to parent the parent. The child end ups "walking around on eggshells" in fear of upsetting the parent. This leads to a pattern of fear that, in turn, leads to withholding communication and not being open with other people.

The Rule Book

Each family, whether conscious of it or not, has a set of rules that governs how things are done, and how the family and members relate to each other and to the outside world. Some of these rules, behaviors, and ways of thinking have been passed down unchanged from generation to generation while others have been shaped through the influence of religion, careers, culture, and worldview of each generation. Some of the rules were shaped by a parent's drastic attempts to not become their own parents, yet by having the pendulum swing fully from one side to another, have created new problems.

These rules are often not conveyed as commandments, but by responses you receive to your behavior, statements of belief, career choices, and so on. There is an unlimited number of dos and don'ts in each family. Some of them are listed below:

- You must carry on the family business.
- You must go to university or college.
- You must choose a respectable profession.
- You should be introverted.
- You should be extroverted.
- So and so is the musician/artist/doctor in the family.
- Don't get angry with your parents.
- Don't get involved.
- Don't invite people over.
- Other families or people are bad.
- Do as you are told.
- As parents, we will choose your friends.
- You answer when asked a question.
- Don't draw attention to the family.
- Keep up the image.
- Don't ask others for help.

Try to think of any rules that might have existed in your home. How are your beliefs different? Not only does your healing process involve examining your emotions and thinking, but you also need to understand the people around you. Problems do not exist only in you! They exist in your family, friends, workplace, and social network. A lesson to learn is that you can truly only change yourself. Others may follow, but it is ultimately up to you to examine your relationships, be more objective, and determine how you relate to the world in which you live!

An Adverse Environment

This section came about through some synchronicity. I came home from a vacation and noticed a piece of paper on the ground neatly folded, near the entrance to our building. Thinking someone might have lost it, and with a sense of intuitive calling, I picked it up. When I opened up the paper, I found it was a copy of the Childhood Adversity Scale. Although I've identified some flaws in the questionnaire, it does ask some meaningful questions about your family dynamics and upbringing. To correct a flaw, I have changed "mother or stepmother" to "parent or stepparent" so that male spousal abuse is also included in the survey. Read through the questionnaire and answer the questions honestly. Note that answering yes to even one of these questions is cause for concern.

Adverse Childhood Experience (ACE) Questionnaire

While you were growing up, during your first 18 years of life:

1. Did a parent or other adult in the household often… Swear at you, insult you, put you down, or humiliate you? **or** Act in a way that made you afraid that you might be physically hurt?

   Yes No If yes enter 1 _____
2. Did a parent or other adult in the household often… Push, grab, slap, or throw something at you? **or** Ever hit you so hard that you had marks or were injured?

   Yes No If yes enter 1 _____

3. Did an adult or person at least 5 years older than you ever... Touch or fondle you, or have you touch their body in a sexual way? **or** Try to or actually have oral, anal, or vaginal sex with you?
   Yes No If yes enter 1 _____
4. Did you often feel that... No one in your family loved you or thought you were important or special? **or** Your family didn't look out for each other, feel close to each other, or support each other?
   Yes No If yes enter 1 _____
5. Did you often feel that... You didn't have enough to eat, had to wear dirty clothes, and had no one to protect you? **or** Your parents were too drunk or high to take care of you or take you to the doctor if you needed it?
   Yes No If yes enter 1 _____
6. Were your parents ever separated or divorced?
   Yes No If yes enter 1 _____
7. Was your parent or stepparent: Often pushed, grabbed, slapped, or had something thrown at him or her? **or** Sometimes or often kicked, bitten, hit with a fist, or hit with something hard? **or** Ever repeatedly hit over at least a few minutes or threatened with a gun or knife?
   Yes No If yes enter 1 _____
8. Did you live with anyone who was a problem drinker or alcoholic or who used street drugs?
   Yes No If yes enter 1 _____
9. Was a household member depressed or mentally ill or did a household member attempt suicide?
   Yes No If yes enter 1 _____
10. Did a household member go to prison?
    Yes No If yes enter 1 _____

Now add up your "Yes" answers: _____

While my family was considered a "wonderful happy family" by our community, my score adds up to 5, perhaps higher depending on the definition of "often" and extending the behaviors outside of my family to my school and church environments. Completing the survey helped me realize that my family, school, and church upbringing was not healthy. It also helped me realize that despite my upbringing, through my resilience and perseverance, I have turned out fairly well!

While the questionnaire above helps identify an adverse environment, it has its limitations. Perhaps you felt unsafe at school, or experienced bullying, or experienced a traumatic event. These items are not accounted for in the questionnaire. It is important to evaluate your childhood for events that deeply affected you. You may not even actively remember these events or understand the impact they had on you. I remember walking home from school one day and coming across an automobile accident in which a woman was lying dead on the ground after being ejected from the car. This was clearly upsetting to me, but I had no one to talk to about it either at school or at home.

Commonalities of Dysfunctional Families

I've come to learn that there are some commonalities of dysfunctional families. These are a lack of empathy, poor communication skills, an unpredictable environment, and unpredictable responses from parents. There is usually a disrespect of boundaries, excessively controlling behaviors, and excessive criticism. As an adult, you may strive to set boundaries with dysfunctional people, but trying to do so is more of a negotiation process than setting hard boundaries. It is important to keep in mind that some dysfunctional people are serial boundary violators. No matter how hard you try to set boundaries, they will always continue to violate them.

One of the impacts of dysfunction is that the child ends up trying to win a battle of trying to prove their worthiness by challenging the parent's criticism. Unless the parent has a moral and conscious awakening, the battle can never be won. You can learn to understand yourself and end the internal battle.

Many of these dysfunctions get combined into harmful messages. When the parent doesn't like others, and they project and misidentify, they tell the child harmful messages such as "Nobody likes you" or "You're no good" when the real problem is the parents are angry and helpless, and are unable to nurture, and blame the child for their problems.

Growing up in an adverse situation can leave you with a feeling that you are fundamentally flawed, not wanted, or different from others. You may have been neglected and don't expect love or warmth from others. With these feelings developed at an early age in your family, you likely extrapolate them into the larger world.

You Are Not Your Abuse

Many of us are left with low self-esteem, an inability to make decisions, a lack of clear self-identity with regards to our talents and traits, and a fear of intimacy. You may also have low feelings of worthiness due to the view of yourself that was imposed on you by other people.

In working through issues, you discover that your human experience can be far greater than what you currently believe it is. Once you commit to healing, your subconscious mind will attract key answers through synchronistic events, dreams, and people you meet. Within you is a force that helps you, in its own mysterious ways, to solve your problems. While trauma and pain do harm you, you have a fundamental ability to direct your mind and body towards healing. With a commitment to healing, you begin a process that can result in dramatic and seemingly impossible changes in your life. This holistic healing acknowledges all aspects of your humanity and becomes your new guide.

8. Memories – Fact or Fiction?

"Memory said, 'It was like that,'
and Pride said, 'It couldn't have been!'
And Memory gave in..."
– Friedrich Nietzsche

"Those who cannot remember the past are condemned to repeat it."
– George Santayana

A Forgotten Past

In my own case, I had forgotten numerous aspects of my own childhood. My own repression of painful memories was due to the simple logic of "out of sight, out of mind, out of memory, no more pain." But had I really forgotten, or simply repressed them? There is a distinction between the two. Due to the emotionally painful nature of the events, I was unable to bring those events and the associated affect into my present existence, for to do so would have taxed my coping resources beyond my capabilities. To protect myself, my mind kept them in my subconscious. The price of doing so was living in a heightened state of anxiety and emotional numbness.

The statement by Nietzsche reflects the tug-of-war that your mind and your consciousness can play about the recall of traumatic or distressing events or times in your life. I find Nietzsche's words also provide insight into the denial of those who are accused of abuse, or of those who were present during situations in which unpleasantness occurred. With these people, it is pride that keeps them from admitting the true nature of their own experience. It is difficult for them to admit that things were a certain way, for to do so would bring a plethora of painful emotions and shame.

Voluntary attempts at recalling my childhood did not bring about any memories. It was the development of appropriate support and community, and the acceptance of my emotions in a safe place, that eventually brought about the recall of my memory. This recall occurred little by little, like flashbulb experiences, one at a time. As the memories returned, my self-understanding grew exponentially.

I have learned that my experience is not unique. Many adult children report that once they start on their path of emotional healing, they begin to remember events they had previously seemingly forgotten. You may even entirely forget severely traumatizing events. In my own experience of healing, I have met numerous people who have retrieved memories that were put away long ago. Many situations bring forth a mix of conflicting emotions. Research has shown that when a situation involves mixed emotions, there is often difficulty in recalling the individual emotions that were experienced. In my case, these emotions felt like a foggy cloud of energy that was difficult to understand.

It is also possible to forget the nuances of a situation. You may repress memories of how things were in a household or relationship. The tone of the environment may be repressed to avoid dealing with your emotional state at the time. For a long time, I had forgotten how depressed my mother was when I was a teenager. One of the memories I began to access was the time I went away to summer camp for three weeks as a teenager to work as a camp counselor trainee. It was when I returned to my family that I could see how my family environment was severely depressing. Both my parents refused to admit they had problems. I had forgotten how my teenage environment had been contaminated with my parents' depression, helplessness, and inability to cope, and a sense of extreme emotional sensitivity.

Emotional Memory Triggers

While writing this book, I came across a study about memories of people who had experienced abuse and what triggered the recall. Over two hundred female survivors of childhood sexual abuse were interviewed, focusing on their experiences, memory, and recovery process. The findings were consistent with other studies in that approximately half of survivors report some memory loss or disruption (other studies have put this number between 59 and 64 percent). Of the fifty-one women who reported recovered memories, over 62 percent reported that their memory returned during therapy.

The Carleton University study questioned the participants regarding which of twelve events had triggered the return of their memories. The following were reported as the most prevalent triggers:

Prior to any therapy:
An event similar to the original trauma	31.3%
Beginning an important relationship	30.1%
Watching a film or reading about sexual abuse	20.7%
Parenting	20.5%
A creative process	15.7%

While participants were in therapy:
A support group	47.6%
A creative process	41.7%
Watching/reading about abuse	36.6%
Beginning an important relationship	27.7%
An event similar to the trauma	22.9%
Stopping alcohol or drugs	15.9%
Ending a significant relationship	13.4%

According to the authors, "Trauma causes alterations in the production and release of stress-responsive neurochemicals such as norepinephrine and the endogenous opioids, and extreme levels of these neurochemicals disrupt everyday explicit information processing."

The Recovered Memory Debate

There has been considerable controversy regarding the concept of recovered memories and "Recovered Memory Therapy." It is very important to note the fundamental distinctions between the two. Recovered Memory Therapy is the name of a counseling technique developed by a group of people who believed that repressed memories were the cause of most psychological problems. In their approach to therapy, there was considerable pressure for the client to discover hidden memories. In some of these cases, the accusations that arose led to confessions, thus confirming the memories. In other cases, the abuse was denied, yet some convictions were obtained. Some of the memories were proven to be incorrect or simply challenged and labeled by lawyers as arising from "False Memory Syndrome." This method of therapy has come under the close scrutiny of licensing boards and, as a result, strict guidelines and ethical considerations have been put in place by several professional associations. In discussing the concept and existence of suppressed and recovered memories, it is very important to distinguish between 1) a type of controversial therapy and 2) the established knowledge that, as you begin to release your emotions, memories do often come to the surface.

When you start to remember incidents from your past, why do you recall some memories but forget others? What are the processes and conditions that cause you to forget or put away memories, and what brings them back? In *Unlocking the Secrets of Your Childhood Memories*, authors Dr. Kevin Leman and Randy Carlson suggest the answer is simply that "people remember only those events from early childhood that are consistent with their present view of themselves and the world around them." The authors call this the "Law of Creative Consistency." "Without Creative Consistency," they write, "you'd be in deep trouble. It is your God-given ability to keep the present and past in balance so that you don't fall over the edge into frustration, depression, or insanity."

What seemed to trigger my own memory recall was a change in my worldview. I now viewed my upbringing and difficulties differently. I saw them for what they were, and as a result, it was now safe to reveal those memories to myself. As I became more comfortable with feeling my own emotions and being more present in mind and body, I felt more comfortable with my past. This then triggered the release of individual memories. I had forgotten about numerous traumatic incidences: the death of a classmate in Grade 5 from a glue-sniffing overdose, witnessing a dead body on the side of the road after a car accident in Grade 2, and numerous details about my grade school environment. I had also forgotten numerous other incidents and aspects of my childhood and early adult years. I had experienced ostracization, emotional abuse, and sadistic behavior from the priest at the summer camp I worked at. He sadistically put kids in a boxing ring and enjoyed watching kids get beaten up. All these memories had been buried.

Clearly, in my case, the concealing and denial of my emotions hampered my memory of distressing situations. Suppression greatly drew on my mental and physical resources. The psychological cost was quite high. No one could get close to me, and a simple statement of empathy from a friend could bring about an overwhelming wave of emotion.

Facilitating Memory Recall

Trying to force the recall of events never actually worked for me, but some things were helpful. The first and foremost factor I needed to bring about a recall was a sense of safety and support. If I had a memory recall, I knew I had a support group, friend, or counselor with whom I could discuss the memory and the emotions.

Second, memory recall always occurred after the acknowledgment and recall of the emotion. The notion that memory reappearance will precede the emotion appears to be the reverse of what happens. Usually, a cue of some sort will trigger the emotion and, once the emotional expression is facilitated, the memory surfaces and reveals itself.

In *Unchained Memories: True Stories of Traumatic Memories, Lost and Foun*d, author Lenore Terr, M.D. writes that "in order for a repressed memory to return, there usually is a ground – that is a general emotional state and a cue." Often this cue may be only a smell, a taste, a simple reminder by way of a similar experience, or a cue from any of our senses. Terr suggests that vision is one of the strongest cues. Additionally, I believe that a visual cue, as seen through the "mind's eye," can also act as a strong stimulus.

The nature of traumatic memories has been controversial, as well as difficult to study. The recall of abuse often leads to confronting the abuser or realizing the true nature of individuals who have been close to us. Claims of abuse are often denied, but in some cases, full confessions have been obtained, and the guilty abusers have given apologies.

In times of recall, at first, I experienced some doubt and perhaps an echo of denial, but the recall was actually a relief. There was usually some additional emotion to work through, but there was a sense of relief as I now understood what the emotion was about. When recalling things, I had to be careful not to invoke a voice of victimization but to feel empowered that I was now safe and could act differently to take myself out of such a situation or ask for help. Individuals, like you, may experience self-doubt about the memories. It is often important to remind yourself that although you may be experiencing self-doubt, you are also experiencing a great deal of emotion, which likely has a basis in some event. If the emotion is processed, the nature of the event will be revealed to you when you are ready.

When memories come back, there may be a desire to confront the abuser. I believe it is better to wait until the emotions are processed. The abuser is likely to deny the abuse and accuse you of making it up. They do so not to harm you, but to protect their own worldview and the overwhelming shame they would experience if they admitted to themselves the harm they had done.

Even other family members may get involved in the denial as a fight, flight, or flock response. I remember having an uncle stay with us when I was very young. I remember telling my mom something about him that I knew but can no longer recall. The next day, he was booted out of our home. While packing, he walked by me and said, "This is all your fault!" which left me feeling traumatized and shamed. It could be that the events were not even related. Years later, at my aunt's funeral, I overhead two family members talking about him and how he had done something really bad. I ended up asking them later about it, and their response was a very direct "Don't have any clue what you are talking about!" While I was unable to uncover the details of my uncle, I remain satisfied with the knowledge that something had happened, and I was able to observe firsthand the strength of the denial pattern in my own family.

While recovering memories, I was constantly reminded by support group members that my mind would protect me until I was ready to remember. A flood of memories can be overwhelming. Your mind is truly your ally in times of memory retrieval. It seems that the emotion and memory will bubble to the surface as you are ready to face and process them. Although they may feel overwhelming, your subconscious mind seems to instinctively know that you have developed sufficient resources and support to work through the trauma. The key to retrieving these memories is the awareness and acceptance of what you are feeling.

Part 2 – Developing Insight and Growing

9. The Keys to Developing Insight

Breaking Free of a Closed System

One of the biggest problems I faced in my self-development was living in a closed system. I had no other families to compare my situation with, and few friends, let alone friends who would understand what I was dealing with in terms of the isolation, bullying, and pain I experienced as a child. I was afraid to reach out, and as a result, had no other sources from which to gather information.

I remember a time during my undergraduate degree when I decided to go for counseling. I recall how resistant I was to the questions of the counselor, due to my fear of bringing forth the pain in my subconscious. I also didn't know how to trust or how to ask for help.

A key turning point occurred when I had a serious emotional breakdown after a joke I tried to pull on a couple I knew backfired and I was horrendously embarrassed. Thinking back, it wasn't really all that bad, but it triggered deep feelings of repressed shame and pain. I was also grieving the loss of my mother. A friend took me aside and spent some time with me and assured me that it would be in my own best interests to seek some counseling, which I did.

This time I requested a male counselor because I knew it was harder for me to confide to another male. I deliberately challenged myself and began a process of learning about myself. He guided me on discovering my interests and where I would find similar people to hang out with. I learned more about myself and developed a stronger sense of identity by trying things out and getting involved in some volunteer work. The volunteer work put me in contact with some very supportive people who were excellent role models for accepting people and showing compassion and kindness, especially after my father died, and I was thrust into a period of betrayal by former friends. Fortunately, through volunteer work, I found new supportive friends, one of whom guided me into finding an appropriate support group.

The key to beginning a healing journey is to step outside the closed system of our families and our current circle of friends. To grow, I needed new information from new and old wise sources. My current sources of information could not provide information on how to live a healthier emotional life because they did not have that information to give to me. A decision to seek new information is often a crucial pivot point in breaking free of depression, crisis, or problems we are stuck in.

In his MasterClass on writing, Malcolm Gladwell talks about "an unwillingness to settle for the world you were given" and asking yourself, "Is there an analogous world [or similar group of people] that has dealt with this situation?" Developing insight and healing involves finding people who have dealt with similar situations, opening up to that new information, learning from it, and applying it to the new "you" you are creating.

Learning to Meditate

One of the best ways to regenerate your healing energy is to begin to meditate. The purpose of meditation is to develop a calm mind so that the mind can restore itself. Meditation can be done in just a few minutes, needs no special equipment, and is very easy to learn. Meditation is about learning to be an observer of your mind and to be aware of your thoughts and emotions. A practice can be started with just a few minutes of meditation each day. Some people claim they feel more anxious when they start meditation. It may be that they are not more anxious but are more aware of how anxious or stressed they really are.

Meditators use a metaphor of the mind being like twelve monkeys tethered to a pole with long leashes. The untrained monkeys all run about and create chaos with twisted and tangled leashes. Meditation trains the monkeys to sit calmly in a circle with their leashes untangled. The metaphor of the twelve monkeys is illustrated in a study that showed that a wandering mind is generally an unhappy mind. The untrained human brain spends a lot of time pondering what hasn't or isn't going to happen. People are less happy when their minds are wandering. Meditation can reduce wandering and increase focus.

While the term "mindfulness" is often used, I find the term "awareness" is better suited for our discussion. Mindfulness or awareness training helps you to be aware of and observe emotions without judging them as positive or negative. It also involves being open to new information, seeing new perspectives, and being able to create new possibilities. The outcome of meditation is that you can learn to regulate your body and mind.

Keep in mind that you don't have to meditate for hours to gain the benefits of meditation. Even a beginning practice of meditation for just a few minutes will bring benefits. Get a small kitchen timer from a dollar store and set it for two minutes to start. Try meditating for that time. Sit still, and just focus on your breathing. You will find that your mind has wandered off, but you observe and notice this. With practice, you will discover that your mind becomes more focused. I find that after just two minutes of meditating, my breathing changes to a deeper pattern.

At first, I found meditating to be challenging. With a writer's mind, I often find my mind is going over ideas, and sometimes inspiration comes in a flash. For myself, this constant review of ideas was tiring. I realize that the many monkeys in my mind were not running wild, but were sitting close to me having a lively philosophical discussion. I asked them to stop, and they did, and then I experienced the calmness of inner space.

Developing Inner Psychological Space

I believe the key to insight is expanding your ability to create inner psychological space. This space is developed over time. It is developed by practicing your own form of meditation, being open and honest with yourself, building your skills around the issue of asking for help, and developing your interests and thinking habits such as gratitude and empathy. When these are in place, if a difficult life event comes along, you are much better prepared to deal with it.

What is inner space? Try to imagine a beautiful beach that you have never been to before. Imagine the sand beneath your feet, the sun on your shoulders, and the beautiful blue sky above. Picture palm trees and the sound of exotic birds chirping. How is it that your mind can call forth images of a place you have never been to? This is your inner space. It is also your source of inner peace or inner turmoil.

Being aware of your inner space allows you to recognize that you, like others, can imagine any place at any time. Your inner space also holds aspects of your personality in the form of your inner voice. Your inner voice plays many roles in your life: the skeptic, protector, the victim, the inner critic, a martyr, lover, and childlike curiosity. I believe these different aspects of the inner voice are some of the twelve untrained monkeys that the Buddhists believe need to be trained to sit quietly. By learning to set aside these executive roles, you will find the undamaged self that is free of any pain and the effects of any abuse, hurt, or emotional pain. You will find that, like myself, some of these aspects of inner voice are overactive while some are underactive. Some may need to be tamed, while others may need to be developed further.

Developing the Inner Observer

In many instances of insight, it was my ability to invoke my inner observer that allowed me to re-evaluate incidents and attributions and gain perspective. To invoke your inner observer, you must step back from the event and the people involved in it and get some perspective. The inner observer allows you to realize that the strong emotions you may be feeling are not necessarily the only aspect of the event, and you may be able to gain more insight by asking the questions of who, what, when, where, and why.

In developing your ability to be an objective observer, you imagine that there is a camera filming the event from above. All characters can be seen in the film, and you try to see the event unfolding, free of judgment, and feel safe to see the truth. Try to have a calm mind and set aside your fears of what you might find. By becoming an independent observer, you invoke honesty and clarity. It is important to observe any beliefs that have an edge of discomfort. This can often indicate a bias in the interpretation of the event or an opinion that you should probably question.

Learning to become an observer through mindfulness training involves continuous nonjudgmental monitoring of experience. Your focus should be on your present experience rather than being preoccupied with past or future events. It is also helpful at first to make no attempt to interpret what you are feeling, and to make no attempt to change, inhibit, or escape what you are feeling. The interpretation and self-understanding come after you accept what you are feeling.

Let Go and Heal

You don't have to be sitting and meditating to accomplish the observation of your emotions and thoughts. A friend of mine confided in me that she was having feelings of resentment and anger when seeing postings and pictures on Facebook of her friends having fun. She asked me whether she should unfriend these people because of these feelings. I advised her to continue to view the pictures and observe the feelings. Through the observing of the pictures, she gained a deeper sense of her feelings and realized that she was actually resentful of her friends and others having fun because she had not had that kind of fun in her twenties.

Furthermore, she realized the true nature of these feelings and thoughts. She realized that grief was being triggered. The grief was being acted out as anger and resentment. With further observation, she recognized that the happy activities they appeared to be enjoying were not as valuable as she had once imagined. The desire for something was stronger than the value of actually having it. As Spock said in the episode "Amok Time," "After a time, you may find that having is not so pleasing a thing after all as wanting. It is not logical, but it is often true." In discussion with my friend, I realized that I also had this form of resentment towards one group of people as they appeared to be having the fun, friendships, and financial success that I lacked at the time. With this understanding, I, too, had my anger almost instantly dissolve when I realized where the resentment was coming from.

By becoming the observer, you can pull away layers of cloudiness and see the whole picture. The area I live in is often blanketed by fog in the morning. Yet I do know that above the fog is a beautiful blue sky. Just as the fog burns off, by examining the events that trouble us with a better perspective, we can clear away clouds of confusion and incorrectly assumed beliefs. Sometimes just imagining that the problem is moving further and further away from you will give you greater clarity.

Stop, Look, Listen

In the rural areas near where I grew up, there were train crossings that lacked the barriers that would stop traffic when a train approaches. Drivers were expected to stop before the tracks and use their own judgment as to whether it was safe to cross. These tracks were usually marked with a sign that said: "Stop, Look, Listen!" This same process can be used to identify your own feelings.

The first instruction is to stop. This may mean taking some time to put aside what you are doing and remove your distractions. To stop what you are doing means to suspend your thoughts and focus on yourself for a moment. It only takes a few seconds to do this anytime or anywhere. You can do it in the silent interval of a conversation or between responses. Quite often, the focus of counseling is to assist the client in looking inside.

The next step is to observe what is going on inside you. This may mean focusing on a vaguely felt sense of tension or anxiety in your body, a sense of lightness in the case of joy, or heaviness in the case of sadness or grief. While you may not be able to identify the emotion at first, you can identify that you are feeling something. At this time, simply listen to your body nonjudgmentally and accept that clarity may come later. In the case of repressed memories, there may not be an understanding of why emotions are occurring. Perhaps there will be no words attached to the feelings.

The third keyword of the sign is to listen. Slow down, look inside, notice tension, and listen to what sensations you are experiencing. You may be experiencing a combination of feelings. That is OK. Be willing to accept some discomfort and feel what is present. Give the emotions, space, and room to be present. This will help in the processing of the emotions and subsequent memory recall or increased awareness. Just as a doctor becomes quiet and uses a stethoscope to listen to a patient's heart, so, too, must you quiet the things around you, focus, and listen to what is going on inside. Doing this allows you to obtain the information you need to gain the awareness required to create a shift in your feelings, behaviors, and thoughts.

For many of us, facing feelings is frightening even though we may realize that it is necessary for healing. In your goal of expression and resolution, you can learn to face the feelings with a new sense of discovering new perspectives and new options. You can also discover that although the pain is being felt in the present, the incident that caused the pain is in the past and that you are removed from it and can experience it in safety. This sense of safety was not available to you at the time of the emotional injury.

Body Awareness through Chakras

A key problem for people who have experienced abuse is dissociation. It is a feeling of numbness and not being present in one's own body. In my quest to be more present in my own body, I learned how to scan my body for tension and by doing so, be more physically present. Learning to do so came from the ancient wisdom and practice of scanning and being aware of chakras – the energy centers of the body, mind, and spirit. Additionally, the ability to sense more than one chakra at a time brought a greater sense of being present. To fully heal requires you to be able to sense what is blocked and unblock it. For my particular energy, my chest area and throat were badly blocked, as confirmed by a speech and throat specialist who examined my vocal cords with the aid of a small camera. The vocal cords were fine, but the muscles in my neck were tight and constricted. My area of healing need was in the throat and chest, areas that correspond with communication and heartfelt love, both giving and receiving.

Most energy models identify seven basic chakras. The first chakra is the seat of the soul, located at the base of the spine. This chakra helps you feel grounded and connected to the earth. The next chakra is in the genital area and deals with your pleasure, ecstasy, and reproduction. Just above the belly button is the third chakra, or solar plexus chakra, which has to do with your center of power. The next higher chakra is the heart chakra, which is in the center of your chest. This area deals with love, openness, self-esteem, and compassion. The throat chakra is close to the thyroid gland and vocal cords; the openness of this chakra reflects your ability to communicate. The second to last chakra is slightly above the midpoint between the eyebrows and is also referred to as the third eye. It represents your wisdom and insight. The crown chakra is considered the highest-level chakra, and it connects you divinely.

An important area of the body to be aware of is the solar plexus or third chakra. In some faiths, the solar plexus is thought to be the "spiritual" mind of the body. It is considered to be the core of your personality, your identity, and your ego. This chakra also is the center of your willpower and self-discipline. From this chakra emanates the warmth of your personality. According to Yogic philosophies and studies, this is an area of the body that psychically, if not physically, is a powerful nerve and awareness center. It is located just back of the pit of the stomach, extending on either side of the spinal column.

While the medical community focuses on scanning the brain, recent insights have discovered that information flows from the gut and solar plexus to the brain, not the reverse, as previously thought. It is the solar plexus that gives you the feeling of butterflies in your stomach. In the early 1900s, the solar plexus was thought to be a powerful reservoir of life force, and both older and recent articles refer to the solar plexus as a "second brain." Boxers know that a powerful hit to the solar plexus can cause death. As Theron Dumont states in *The Solar Plexus or Abdominal Brain*: "The solar plexus is named so because of its central position and the fact that its filaments extend in all directions to the important abdominal organs, like the rays of the sun." This mirrors the Yogic philosophy, which understood the solar plexus to radiate energy to all parts of the body. Whether or not you believe in chakras or energy, I can attest to the sense of emotional awareness that is often centered in these areas. It seems the more aware you are of this energy area, the more likely you will be present in your body. When people say "think with the heart, and feel with the mind," perhaps they really mean "think with the solar plexus, and feel with the mind" with the solar plexus being the sense of feeling in the body.

While there are numerous books on chakras and the colors that they should be generating, I believe that developing your own sense of associated energy colors is critical to your healing and supporting your energy levels. I have personally found that remembering these chakras can be deep inside the body rather than on the surface helps to keep me centered and present. Putting my consciousness in these areas helps me focus on and release tension and helps me be a better singer. Try to be aware of these various points within your body and the sense of energy around them. Try breathing into and exhaling from each chakra and open up to giving and receiving healing energy.

Breathing in and focusing on the chakras one at a time will allow you to gauge how connected you are to your body. By practicing deep breathing, you can replenish your own personal energy with energy from

Let Go and Heal

the outside world. As you become more aware, you will become wise to the subtleness of your body. A deep sense of centeredness, self-worth, and compassion arises when you are aware of all of your chakras at once. To do so requires being fully present and in your body. It takes practice!

Invoking Your Insightful Higher Self

Some people call it "the mind separate from ego," while others call it the "Deep Mind." Eckhart Tolle calls it the "Deep I." I believe they are all referring to the sense we have of a higher self, which is the most intangible part of being. The higher self requires that we have faith for us to believe that it exists.

The higher self represents a knowledge greater than yourself that includes the healing and symbolic messages in dreams, your intuition, and the synchronicity of life events that brings you to the place where you need to be at a given time. It also includes your desire and motivation to do better and create a kinder world. When I started writing this portion of the book, I had difficulty figuring out how to incorporate the concept of the subconscious mind, yet this answer came easily when I learned that our subconscious is impressionable and responds to our creative thoughts and ideas through meditation and thinking. Since it seems to be a force that is more powerful than your personal nature or nurturing history, I found myself compelled to include it as a higher function that connects all of us to a consciousness that is greater than ourselves. According to Paramahansa Yogananda, it is the pure, intuitive, all-seeing, ever blissful consciousness of the soul. It is written in the Upanishads that "Ordinarily we know three states of consciousness only – waking dreaming and sleeping. There is, however, a fourth state, the superconscious, which transcends these. In the first three states, the mind is not clear enough to save us from error; but in the fourth state, it gains such purity of vision that it can perceive the Divine..."

Yogi Ramacharaka, in his book *Yogi Philosophies*, describes varying aspects of mind:

"Human beings possess mind powers that are greater than the animal world. We also possess an intellectual mind that is aware of itself as a person and aware of other people. This mind holds your belief system." The Yogis refer to even higher levels of mind, such as the spiritual mind. Ramacharaka describes the spiritual mind as "becoming conscious of a higher 'Something Within,' which leads them up to higher and nobler thoughts, desires, aspirations, and deeds..." Finally, Ramacharaka describes the highest level of mind as "...the Real Self. Words cannot express it. Our minds fail to grasp it. It is the soul of the Soul. To understand it, we must understand God, for Spirit is a drop from the Spirit Ocean."

The Higher Self or Higher Consciousness compels you to try to do better, to improve yourself, and to make things right. It is the part of your spirit that recognizes when an improper compromise has been made, or when a relationship doesn't feel right, or when an event helps you recognize injustice. The Higher Self brings to you the lessons you need to learn over and over again until they are learned, tested, and become part of your way of being. The Higher Self is involved in synchronicity as well as helping you to remember important dreams, both the sleeping and waking daydreaming kind. Your healing journey will take you through all the levels of the mind!

Follow Your Intuition and Hunches

In my journey, I have read many books, some of which I came across quite coincidentally. One such book was *We Pray Thee, Lord* by Roy Wallace Thomas. After having a coffee with a friend in a nearby town, I had a strong intuitive hunch to go into a small secondhand store. I was already driving to the ferry terminal to catch my ferry ride and was concerned about time. I drove for a few blocks and realized that I was having one of those moments where I was not listening to my intuition and was wondering what I had missed. I turned the car around and went back, where I found Thomas' book. I opened it and found the following description of "scientific hunches" arising from the research conducted by Professor Baker back in the 1930s. Thomas describes Baker's work:

"The scientific hunch [is a] unifying or clarifying idea which springs into consciousness suddenly as a solution to a problem in which we are intensely interested. In typical cases, it follows a long period of study but comes into consciousness at a time when we are not consciously working on the problem. A hunch springs from a wide knowledge of facts, but is essentially a leap of the imagination in that it goes beyond a mere necessary conclusion which any reasonable man must draw from the data at hand. It is a process of creative thought.

The general conditions under which these scientific revelations appear were indicated as good health, relaxation, freedom from worry, and from interruption. Many mentioned some form of exercise or manual employment such as shaving, dressing, motoring, gardening, fishing, golfing, walking, playing solitaire, listening to music. ...

Baker found that hunches come to most scientists in that borderland of consciousness just preceding sleep or when the mind is fresh upon awakening or when the mind is occupied with some other matter. Thus the hunch appears when the mental conditions are ripest for the subconscious or deep self to yield its contribution."

If you put away the problem, take a shower, or go for a walk, you may experience a moment of creativity bubble forth in your mind. You may find greater inspiration if you let a decision percolate outside your awareness. This is especially true if the decision you are trying to make is complex. As a decision or problem becomes more complex, it is harder to keep all of the variables in order and in their proper priority. You may unwittingly entirely omit major factors, or overvalue some of the less important aspects while devaluing the most important. With an increase in complexity, you may not be able to clearly see how multiple factors interact, bringing about the common saying, "I didn't see that coming!"

Many times while writing this book, I would be thinking about how to write a particular section or what insight to share. I would put the computer away for a while and go for a walk in the park or sometimes I would do some housework. In a flash of insight, the answer would appear. This also happened when I was stuck with a coding problem when building an app. Putting the problem away for a while and then all of a sudden, the solution would pop into my head unexpectedly!

If you feel stuck at some time, try setting up the above conditions for insight. Gain knowledge, then let go by taking a break or doing something else, and see what your higher self brings you!

Always believe something wonderful is about to happen!

10. Learning about Your Beliefs

"For every problem, there is a solution that is simple, elegant, and wrong."
– H. L. Mencken

While beliefs have been associated with the little inner voice inside your head (that little voice that just said "What little voice?"), I believe that a more complex system of understanding beliefs is needed. First of all, you don't just think in sentences in your mind. Your thoughts and beliefs are actually stored images, feelings paired with those images, and associations. These are also associated with events that have occurred in your life. The old idea of changing a belief by changing just your thinking is no longer valid. What you need to do is change how you feel about certain things, places, and people. In essence, you must replace the emotion associated with something to be able to change a belief.

Your mental images are what form beliefs. It is the association that you have with an image that triggers an emotional response and forms your beliefs. Your past experience has allowed you to form opinions and beliefs on everything from how people will behave under certain situations to complex scientific beliefs. Your images and beliefs contain textures such as strength and weakness, community involvement, darkness and light, the level of struggle involved in doing something, financial implications, and the experience of pain or opportunities for happiness.

When your beliefs are in accordance with what is happening in your life, you experience cognitive resonance. This is the feeling of peace you have when things are going well. When there is a discrepancy between your ideal life and your current life, or a struggle between how you believe you should feel and how you actually feel about something, or a belief is challenged by new evidence that contradicts your belief, you experience cognitive dissonance. This dissonance can bring about behaviors of avoidance. With wisdom seeking people, it brings about growth.

One of the things your mind strives for is consistency. Unfortunately, striving for consistency means that you make errors in judgment and perception. You see what you want to see, and you see what you expected to see unless you learn to accept that inconsistency will occur. We choose our friends based on our search for consistency. If you are told that something will be negative, you will likely perceive it as negative, because of expectations. To be this way is part of the human experience. Overcoming your expectations and cognitive dissonance is to heal and improve yourself. Being open to changing your beliefs will spur you on to action.

I would also recommend making a list of what you do not believe in, as that list can be very revealing as to your actual beliefs about others and yourself.

The Stages of Challenging a Belief

While writing these pages, I attended a talk on the nature of reality, which I found very interesting, not because of the subject per se, but because of the subjective nature of reality itself, and the varying definitions and opinions we hold about it. When the talk changed to a discussion format, many members of the audience began to argue with each other about the nature of reality, fiercely defending their own observations and definitions. Robin Williams once poked fun at the topic by naming one of his earlier comedy records, "Reality: What a concept!"

One of the key points the moderator made was that no single reality is ever totally provable, nor is it possible to have a single worldview with more than one person in the world. It is interesting to note that in the history of humanity, there have been numerous "realities" that were subsequently proven wrong, if not outright foolish, but were sacred beliefs in their time – such as the sun and stars revolve around the earth, and a good bloodletting will help cure a disease!

While the incorrectness of these beliefs is now obvious to us, there are many beliefs we hold today that were not considered possible or reasonable only a few decades ago. For example, until the 1970s, employment ads were divided into two columns – male help wanted, and female help wanted. Such a policy would violate today's laws. The effort required to challenge these policies and get them changed was enormous. Using these changes as a guide for your own personal beliefs, you can see that there is a process through which beliefs get challenged, become unacceptable, and are replaced with new beliefs. I would suggest the following stages as a framework for developing new beliefs:

- An intuitive sense, an opening up, a flash of insight
- Feeling threatened
- Confusion and ambiguity
- Envisioning a new idea or way of acting
- Application of the belief
- Testing of the belief
- Acceptance and affirmation of the belief
- Retesting the belief
- Affirmation that the old belief was incorrect but served its purpose

Changing a belief involves an inward process of asking yourself, "How did I come to believe this?"

To develop new beliefs, you need to gain perspective and objectivity. When you are in the middle of a large city, you only see the skyscrapers surrounding you. However, when you can rise above the skyscrapers, you will see the pattern of city blocks, roads, and the overall picture of the city. Moving even further back, you can sense the map of the state and continent. The same concept holds true with your problems of self-development. Your difficulties often lie in being unable to get an objective perspective. Perspective does not come to us instantaneously but rather with a sense of irritation that something is amiss. Irritation and confusion are usually necessary before insight. Allow the confusion to exist. In your personal life, you need to examine which beliefs you hold that perhaps need to be let go, whether they are societal, familial, or personal. Be willing to question the validity of your beliefs. This is the sign of true intelligence!

Discovering Your Attitudes

Although we have built a strong case for emotional expression, it is a fact that emotional expression by itself is not enough to bring about healing. If you are to resolve patterns and heal emotionally, you need to examine your attitudes, behavior, and self-talk, as well as express yourself emotionally. Fortunately, all aspects are intricately related, and therefore working on one will have positive effects on the others. Too often, one of the aspects will be compromised due to the stress you are experiencing. Just as a drinking habit may numb your emotions, and negative thoughts will affect your moods, so, too, will positive thoughts and emotional expression lead to improved behaviors.

When examining and evaluating your beliefs, you must do so without judgment and self-criticism. You need to create an inventory of your actions and feelings morally and honestly. You need to look at the values and beliefs you hold in the situation and determine if those values are appropriate, valid, and really reflect the way the world works. Examine your first impressions of when you think of someone, a place, or a time in your life. These initial feelings can be the indicators of what may need to change to bring about greater mental health.

Often you have wholly swallowed the values of the role models around you. In particular, this happens in childhood when you have yet to develop your own distinct identity, values, and belief systems. I once heard a minister define democracy as "three foxes and a chicken getting together to decide what's for dinner." Even if you protested, you might not have had the power to change things. Sometimes you were outnumbered. You need to evaluate the values, messages, beliefs, self-talk, "shoulds," level of responsibility, and perhaps how much power you did or didn't have at the time.

Attributions and Subtext

One of the critical aspects of my healing process was the examination of my own attributions. Attributions are reasons you develop to explain why people do and say things. From being a child to living as an adult, we all make attributions. Often these attributions are incorrect. From my own childhood, I remember making assumptions about why my parents did certain things. When I was in Grade 4, my father had major surgery to treat cancer. The surgery changed his facial features. I remember the weeks in the hospital and how I missed him. On the day he came home, we were told to stay in the kitchen. I had missed him so much and wanted to convey this to him, so I broke the rules and went into the living room to welcome him. Both my mother and father got angry with me. I assumed that my father did not want to see me, and my first encounter with him in weeks was painful, and I felt very hurt. Through the logic of a child, I assumed he did not love me. Looking back on how the surgery disfigured him and talking it over with him in later years, he told me how happy he was to be home, how he had missed us, but since we were so young, he did not want to scare us with the stitches and swelling on the side of his face. It now all makes perfect sense. Of course, my parents were not adept at ascertaining my needs, but I could certainly see that my attributions and assumptions were incorrect. This led to my healing of this incident and others.

When things happen that are painful or even joyful, we often attribute the reason for someone's behavior. Quite often, these attributions are assumptions based on limited knowledge. The problem is that later in life, we treat these attributions as though they are facts. Recalling the event to the point where we made the attribution and then studying whether it is true or not can be helpful. The daily use of reappraisal has been shown to decrease negative emotions regarding unpleasant events. Discussing the event with the people involved requires calmness and an openness to being wrong about our attributions. While others may appear to us to be making excuses in trying to explain their behavior, be open to their explanation, for in it lies their truth and their reasoning, and the key to unlocking misunderstanding.

As I examined my attributions in various situations, I began to see how much my father deeply loved me and how he was humanly limited in his ability to show his love. I recently came across some research showing that some fathers stated that they were less responsive to children on days with more job stress and more irritable on days with greater social stress. The children, on the other hand, could not discern the days when their father was experiencing greater stress of either kind. If their father was unresponsive or irritable, they could not attribute it to stress and likely took it personally, perhaps thinking it was caused by something they had done.

In learning to identify your assumptions and attributions, it is helpful to turn to a concept in the field of acting. In every scene, there is what is called the subtext. The subtext is what happens below the surface, or what is conveyed by micro facial expressions, tension, and expectations in a scene. Sometimes what is not said is more important than what is said. Scenes are written to convey certain motivations and tension between the characters. When writing a script, the author has a clear understanding of what is to be communicated. In our own lives, this is not true. Can you really know the true intention of others? It is so easy to err in making assumptions as to why people do things!

Here are some questions that can help you probe the underlying subtext in a situation:

- I expected him or her to…
- I believe his or her intentions were to…
- I think he or she acted in such a way because…
- I felt…
- I wanted him or her to…
- I acted in such a way because…
- The underlying conflict of the situation is…
- I think he or she wants…
- In this situation I need…

Try to stand back from a situation and understand how your mind works. Self-help groups can be very supportive and provide opportunities for insight, as you get to observe and learn how others think and work through issues. In this manner, new ways of thinking and looking at assumptions are modeled for us.

Try to understand what judgments you are making about other peoples' intentions, motives, feelings, and reasons underlying why they do things. It is important to note that, in each situation, others are making assumptions and attributions as well. It may appear to us that they are doing irrational things, but at some level, there is a string of reasoning underlying what they are doing! What judgments are you making about yourself? What feelings do you have that you are or are not expressing? What would you like to occur? How would having answers to these questions change how you feel about yourself and the other person? How would it feel to accept that they couldn't give this to you, not because they didn't want to, but because they did not have it to give?

"The subconscious accepts as true that which you feel as true, and because creation is the result of subconscious impressions, you, by your feeling, determine creation."
– Neville Goddard

11. Learning the Language of Feelings

Part of self-growth and developing self-knowledge involves learning to express the feelings, ideas, and thoughts you are experiencing. To describe how you are feeling is a challenge given the fact that language is imprecise, and at times, it is difficult to translate bodily sensations into words.

While taking some Chinese lessons, I questioned my teacher about the expression of emotion in Chinese culture and language. As mentioned earlier, in Traditional Chinese Medicine, it is a prolonged, excessive, or insufficient emotion that causes an internal imbalance.

I was told that there are seven basic emotions, and the rest are combinations of emotions or impressions we have of ourselves or others.

The seven basic emotions are anger, joy, worry, pensiveness, sadness, fear, and shock (fright).

Other feelings or states such as jealousy and envy are described as impressions that result from your thoughts and beliefs about other people. Some psychologists suggest that your feelings come from your thoughts. Others believe that emotions come from a deeper experience. If we consider the seven basic emotions as soul experience and other emotions as impressions from thoughts and beliefs, we can reconcile the two theories. Recent research using Magnetic Resonance Imaging has shown that your emotional center reacts much faster than your thinking process. Does this mean that the "thoughts into emotions" theorists are wrong? Not really! It means that we need a more complex model to describe the relationship between thinking and emotions. Some feelings arise from your heart center, while other feelings may be triggered by thought processes, perhaps even subconscious thoughts. It is possible, too, that your heart-centered feelings will impact your thoughts. To progress in your growth, regardless of the theory, you need to learn to express and communicate your feelings and examine your thoughts.

In my travels to China, I learned how precise the Chinese language is in this domain compared to the English language. Most Chinese characters that express emotion are usually paired with another character to refine the writer's meaning. For example, the root word *bei*, which means sadness,

Let Go and Heal

can be combined with other characters to mean sad, sorrowful, melancholy, grieved, painfully sad, mixed feelings of joy and grief, compassionate, bitter, miserable, sad and worried, grieved over the death of a friend, grieved and indignant, pessimistic and gloomy, overcome with grief, sad and choking with sobs.

The same goes for the word for happiness, *xi*, which, when combined with other words, can mean outright glee, overjoyed, not feeling tired of it, buoyant, cheerful, fun, pleasure, and contentment. I found that the Chinese language seemed far more subtle and accurate than the English language.

There is also an important phrase, *le ji sheng bei*, which means "when joy reaches its height, sorrow comes in turn; extreme joy begets sorrow." These words of wisdom echo the familiar phrase, "what goes up must come down." Other phrases more completely described concepts rather than just feelings. A word describing bitterness referred to "going through years of suffering, to be full of misery but find no place to pour it out."

Imagine if we could all become more literate and complex in describing our feelings. In reflecting on how you are feeling, you can refine your description by describing not one but many feelings. Also, describe the situation and what you are hoping for. For example, instead of saying, "I am hurt," try to go deeper. You could say, "I am feeling sad and betrayed because I was let down when a promise was broken." This is far more precise and communicative than the words "I am hurt." Learn to be more descriptive!

Each of us gets hurt to varying degrees simply by living our lives. No one is immune to difficulties. How you deal with these emotional challenges greatly affects your future responses to similar events and challenges. I believe, as many others do, that a great deal of mental illness results from the inability to process emotions and the associated events.

One of the concepts taught in my computer business systems courses is the difference between data and information. Data are facts and figures, while information is the processing of the data into meaning, trends, and patterns. While on a subway in Beijing, I was inspired to look further into this concept after noticing a young gentleman seated across from me with the word "wisdom" followed by a clear and precise definition printed on his T-shirt. It defined wisdom as the ability to discern or judge what is true, right, or lasting. Wisdom is insight, the sum of learning through the ages, as well as a wise outlook, plan, or course of action.

Simply knowing facts, without understanding the underlying causes, is not wisdom, yet it is unlikely that you can develop wisdom without knowing the facts. It is important to discern between measurable facts, and your opinions, which are conclusions based on what you have experienced.

To experience emotions is only the data of your experience. Express the emotion, look at their inner meaning, and discover the root cause. Doing this develops your knowledge and insight.

Our Emotional Habit Inventory

To gain an understanding of your emotional habits, you can examine your previous behavior and comfort levels associated with your past levels of self-expression. In a book about adult children of alcoholics titled *It Will Never Happen to Me: Growing Up with Addiction as Youngsters, Adolescents, Adults*, author Claudia Black provides a questionnaire that can help you to learn about your own history and current practices of emotional expression. By answering each question, you can get a better understanding of your own emotional behavior inventory.

Answering these questions may take some reflecting and an effort to remember how things were. It is equally important to ask yourself how you would answer regarding your current behavior. Have you carried any of these past behaviors into your adulthood? While I answered these questions, I realized that in most cases, I was crying silently, even though no one was around. I realized this was a carryover from my childhood: many times as a child, I cried myself to sleep, but silently, so no one would know. With the discovery of this, I gained a stronger sense of vocal expression, which improved my singing range and tonal quality.

How would you answer the questions below? Keep in mind that there are no right or wrong answers:

- When do you cry?
- Do you ever cry?

- Do you cry when alone?
- Do you cry hard, or do you cry slowly and silently?
- Do you cry because people hurt your feelings?
- Do you cry for no apparent reason?
- Do others know when you cry?
- Do others see you cry?
- Do others hear you cry?
- Do you let others comfort you when you cry?
- Do you let others hold you?
- Do you let them just sit with you?
- What do you do to prevent yourself from crying?
- How is your pattern as an adult different from when you were a child?
- What did you do with your tears as a child?
- Did you cry?
- Did others know you were crying?
- Did you let others comfort you when you were crying?

Although the above questionnaire deals with crying, you need to examine your habits regarding joy and laughter too. In addition to repressing crying as a child or adult, you may often tend to repress your joy as well. Many families do not share in the joy of others. Repressing emotions is similar to turning down the volume on a stereo: the full range of sound is lowered. Unlike current stereos, which have numerous controls to shape the sound, you cannot selectively block out only certain emotions. If emotional repression is the norm in a family, it follows that joy and happiness will not be shared either.

The following questions can help you understand your past concerning joy and happiness. Again, there are no right or wrong answers, but these questions will help you identify factors that can contribute to, or detract from, your current enjoyment of life:

- Did you experience joy in your family?
- Did others express laughter?

- Did others share your joy?
- Were you laughed at or ridiculed for laughing or being spontaneous?
- Was depression a major factor in the day-to-day life of a family member?
- Do you feel comfortable laughing and expressing emotion as an adult?
- Were you taught to feel guilty for having fun?
- Were you very quiet?
- Were you spontaneous?
- Were you expressive?
- As an adult, do you express your creativity in some way?
- Are you creative in your work?
- Can you easily have fun or be silly?
- Are you easygoing?
- How do you express anger?
- What makes you sad?
- How do you deal with sadness?
- What makes you fearful?
- How do you deal with fear?
- What makes you happy?
- What makes you laugh?

Fortunately, you can effect change in your personal habits and behavior in relationships once you become aware of your patterns and emotional hurt. Once you are aware, you can slowly change your attitudes and behavior through your emotional healing work. You can change the way you behave in your family and encourage emotional expression in your children. You can do things differently than your parents did. The first step is awareness.

So, What Am I Feeling?

If someone were to ask you, "How are you feeling?", how would you answer? For many of us, it may be difficult to accurately answer this question. In some cases, you may never have actually been asked such a

Let Go and Heal

question. In a society where relationships are built upon communicating, the absence of an understanding of how you are feeling limits your ability to develop close relationships. How can you interact if you are unaware of your feelings? It is difficult to have self-knowledge if you are not in touch with your emotions.

So how do you feel? Here's a checklist to help identify emotions. Take a look at this list often: do a self-check, and try to evaluate which emotions are present or not at a given moment. Which emotions have you experienced recently? Which emotions would you like to experience more often? Try combining words to express how you are feeling. There is no rule that you can only be feeling one emotion at a time!

How am I feeling?

Afraid	Aggressive	Agonized	Angry
Annoyed	Anxious	Apologetic	Arrogant
Bad	Bashful	Bewildered	Blissful
Bored	Cautious	Cheerful	Cold
Confident	Confused	Content	Curious
Defensive	Depressed	Detached	Determined
Despondent	Disappointed	Disapproving	Discouraged
Disbelieving	Disgusted	Disillusioned	Disoriented
Doubtful	Ecstatic	Elated	Embarrassed
Empty	Enraged	Envious	Exasperated
Excited	Exhausted	Exuberant	Fearful
Frenzied	Frightened	Frustrated	Furious
Great	Grieved	Guilty	Happy
Hassled	Helpful	Helpless	Hopeful
Hopeless	Horrified	Humbled	Hurt
Hysterical	Indifferent	Innocent	Insecure
Interested	Irritable	Irritated	Isolated
Jealous	Joyous	Liberated	Liked
Lonely	Loving	Mad	Meditative
Mischievous	Miserable	Morbid	Motivated
Negative	Numb	Offended	Optimistic

Outraged	Pained	Panicked	Paranoid
Pessimistic	Perplexed	Powerful	Powerless
Puzzled	Regretful	Relaxed	Relieved
Resentful	Restless	Sad	Satisfied
Scared	Sheepish	Shocked	Skeptical
Smug	Surprised	Sympathetic	Tender
Tense	Thoughtful	Undecided	Uneasy
Unhappy	Unsure	Useful	Valuable
Vulnerable	Withdrawn	Worthless	Worried

Go through each word and think of a time or situation when the word describes how you felt. Take the time to also imagine how each word makes you feel and how that word would feel in your body. Remember, too, that sometimes you may have no words to describe how you feel. An emotion may be simply a sensation in your body.

Many times, I have encountered people who felt they needed and wanted to cry. They definitely believed it would be helpful and healing, yet no tears would come. In my own healing process, I experienced this several times. I learned that I had to be patient, that there was some lesson I needed to learn to unlock my pain. I trusted that the protective nature of my subconscious would be wise enough to know when I was ready. I was never let down by this process! At other times, however, when very busy and unable to make time to meditate and explore my emotions, the following process helped me. Sitting quietly, I would scan my body for tension. I would ask myself, "What am I feeling at this moment?" Remember that it is not always necessary to find a word to describe how you are feeling. Simply feeling the energy of the emotion is enough to begin the process of release.

12. Beginning to Feel Again

"To remain whole, be twisted.
To become straight, let yourself be bent.
To become full, be hollow
Be tattered that you may be renewed
Those that have little may get more."
– Lao Tzu

Opening Up to Emotions

When you are ready, your mind will allow you to gradually begin feeling the emotions that have been suppressed. Your mind is your own powerful ally, and it will protect you from emotions that you are not yet ready to face. Sometimes you need to learn a few lessons, build sufficient strength, or gain certain skills before you are ready to deal with your issues. Your subconscious mind is smart enough to know when you are ready.

You will likely begin to experience brief or fleeting moments of sadness, anger, or fear. As quickly as the emotion surfaces in the early stages of release, like a wave, it may just as quickly disappear. A reasonable reaction might be to try to hide or to run from these feelings. Try to understand that getting in touch with these feelings and releasing them will bring you greater benefits in the long run. The emotions you touch on may seem intense and frightening to you. You may want to focus on the fact that it must take a tremendous amount of energy to keep these emotions below the conscious level.

At this time, it is important that you do not dismiss or reject your feelings, but rather to validate and take ownership of them. You must remind yourself that, given your situation and events that occurred in your life and how you dealt with them, your feelings are reasonable and appropriate. The first awareness of emotions may involve a state of confusion. Slowly you will begin to understand these signals, identify what the emotions are, and learn to articulate what you are feeling.

In the early stages of awareness, you may also begin to remember certain events in your life that you had long forgotten. These events, like your emotions, may have been kept out of your consciousness due to their painful nature. It can be quite common to find that memories from your childhood, previously forgotten, come back with their associated emotions. If you do find yourself remembering events or incidents, it is because you are now ready to deal with these aspects of your life.

Awareness of your emotions can come to you in your dreams, as well as through events in your daily life. Typically, dreams in which there is water coming up from a sewer, or a river overflowing, indicate that your emotions are a source of concern. On some occasions, you may dream of painful or sad situations that seem so real and emotional that you wake up angry or crying. You may also find yourself waking to find no trace of tears and wonder why. As mentioned, your mind is a powerful ally, and although your dreams may seem disturbing, they can help you to better understand yourself. Dreams are often messages from your subconscious in the form of symbols, trying to tell you something you need to hear or to know.

Although these first stages can be somewhat overwhelming, you need to remind yourself that it is possible to work through these issues and heal from them so that they will no longer have so much power over you and your relationships. You may find it encouraging to trust a higher power to help you through and to provide you with what you need to release and heal.

The Past Is in the Present

While you need to revisit events that happened in the past, there is often a tendency for other people to say, "It happened years ago! Why don't you let it go?" or you may say to yourself, "That happened years ago, so why is it still bothering me?" For some people, it may be a form of denial to say "It's over, get on with it." In any case, the fact that you are hurting is being missed.

If you listen to your heart and acknowledge your hurt, your response might change to "Yes, it happened years ago, and I'm learning to let go. I'm working on it." Some say time is the greatest healer, but that depends entirely on what you have done during that time. If you were numb and did not know how to express your emotions and heal, your hurt will

Let Go and Heal

continue until you learn the process of letting go. Their advice is true: you must let go, but more importantly, you must learn how to let go.

You need to heal the wound, to give your soul the time it needs to heal and to rebuild itself. Your soul will come out well and strong in the end. Acknowledge the wound. Acknowledge the hurt and pain. Let it go, release it, and allow the healing to occur. Doing so will open you up to so many opportunities.

Unthawing Frozen Feelings

I like to use the analogy that suppressed painful emotions are like meat that has gone bad and has been put away in the freezer. When suppressing your emotions, they don't seem to cause any bother until you start to get in touch with the feelings. Then you begin to feel the hurt and the pain. Like the spoiled meat in the freezer, they don't smell until you begin to let them thaw. When you thaw them out, they have to be dealt with. But you can deal with them. When they are frozen, you don't seem to have to deal with them, but they take up space in your compartment. Eventually, the compartment gets full, and you can't put any more in! You can start to heal and get into better emotional health by emptying your frozen emotional freezer.

Beginning to feel again involves several steps and concepts for you to grasp. First, it is not possible to simply flick a switch and begin to feel again. You cannot instantly begin to experience feelings generated in the present. When re-establishing your emotions, you usually must face the emotions you have not dealt with. In other words, you cannot ignore the past when it comes to beginning to feel again.

When you begin to feel again, you are initiating a gradual process. At times I have heard of therapists or individuals attempting to schedule a time to feel their emotions. Judging from what I have experienced and what others have expressed to me, suppressed emotions will come to the forefront when you are ready. They are usually triggered by a scene in a movie, recalling an episode from the past that you had forgotten, or scenarios that occur in your dreams. Often your dreams can have high emotional content, and when going through a catharsis, it is not uncommon to wake up from a dream sobbing.

Many people have expressed that getting in touch with emotions is similar to peeling an onion: it involves peeling away one layer at a time. Eventually, you get down to the core of the onion or the core of your emotions. At this stage, you usually have a deeper understanding of yourself and have achieved a greater sense of emotional health.

Admitting you are numb and hurting is a major and crucial step in getting better. Beginning to feel again requires surrendering and accepting that you are hurting. Even though you may not be feeling all the pain and may not be in touch with your feelings, you are in touch with the fact that your state of mind is one of unhappiness and stress. You recognize your previous behavior of running from your emotions.

For many of you, admitting you are hurting may seem like defeat or failure since you have fought so hard and for such a long time to win this emotional battle. As many recovered people can attest, it is really a victory to admit that you are hurting. It is a crucial step in finally recognizing something about yourself that you may have been denying for a long time. It is a courageous step and your first victory in achieving emotional health!

At the same time that you surrender your fight against your emotions, you must develop a commitment to release your suppressed emotions and to heal. At first, you may be frightened by the prospect of turning on your emotions and releasing them. However, as your work progresses, you will experience immediate benefit from releasing your emotions and begin to anticipate the long-term benefits of your work. If you are not committed to releasing your emotions and healing, it will be easy to slip into old patterns again. Sometimes this will occur, but if you are truly committed to your own healing process, upon the realization that you are repeating old patterns, you will begin to work on establishing new, healthier ways of resolving your past feelings.

In your healing process, it is important to give yourself permission to feel. You must reassure yourself that allowing the feelings to come to the surface is OK and will actually benefit you. It is like gradually turning on a tap. The water comes out slowly at first, but you have control over the rate of flow. If something touches you or moves you, you should let yourself feel it. If someone compliments you and you feel sadness, allow

Let Go and Heal

yourself to feel it. If something or someone brings out some anger in you, you should let yourself feel the anger and the hurt behind it. For a long time, you may have been in the habit of stuffing your feelings down whenever they appeared. You must learn to feel the feelings and let the energy dissipate. Allow yourself the time to focus on getting in touch with what is coming up for you.

At all times, it is very important to accept whatever you are feeling, whether it is anger, sadness, joy, guilt, or any emotion, whether it seems appropriate or not. You may have felt shame for feeling certain ways in the past or have been ridiculed for crying when young. In some cases, expressing joy may also have been considered inappropriate. In some families, numbness and avoidance of expression extend from anger to sadness to happiness and joy as well. You must not be judgmental of your emotional states.

There is a human tendency to avoid pain and uncomfortable feelings, yet my own personal experience has shown that acknowledging what I am feeling without trying to remove it has led to their dissipation and disappearance. It is like a campfire. If you do not add more wood, the fire will eventually burn itself out. Thinking negative thoughts, feeling victimized, and being resentful is like putting more fuel on the fire of emotions. Letting the emotions be and expressing them is like letting the fire burn until it consumes itself. The event that triggered the emotion from then on has no power over you, nor can it be resurrected unless you metaphorically put wood on the fire by reliving the event and giving it more power.

It is equally important to try to not rationalize your feelings. If you are feeling a certain emotion or combination of emotions, it is OK – even if you cannot explain the source of your feelings. Trying to understand or rationalize why you are feeling a certain way usually gets in the way of being in touch with your feelings and expressing them. Feelings do not need to be explained. They exist – sometimes illogically. Feelings are feelings. They exist on their own without rationalizations. They just are.

When unresolved emotions surface, you may not know exactly why they are surfacing or what event in your life caused the original feelings.

Clarity will eventually come to you. The release of emotional pain will allow your mind the freedom to recall events that you buried a long time ago.

The important thing to keep in mind is that the feelings are there and need to be released, regardless of whether you know what caused them in the first place. I often went through periods of release, not knowing why I was experiencing the feelings I was having at the time. Even without knowing their source, I worked on releasing these feelings. Keep in mind that there is an intention of facing the feelings. In the healing section of this book, I will teach you how to release the feelings and, with the new clarity of mind, resolve the original hurt and move closer to emotional health.

13. The Emotional Life Cycle

Releasing your unresolved emotions involves passing through several stages to completely release the energy that you have trapped inside. Often you may not be aware of what originally triggered the emotion: you may only know that you are hurting for some unknown reason. You need to move through these moods and feelings and simply allow them to surface and be felt.

The process of healing is repetitive. It involves becoming aware of certain feelings and releasing them, then becoming aware of other feelings and releasing them as well, and so on until you become emotionally clear. Each time you release, you should also be invoking the inner observer, as described in the chapter on healing.

You can get in touch with your unresolved emotions one layer at a time. When you achieve release, you essentially peel away a layer of the unresolved emotions. You can then move on to the next layer of emotion and become aware of it when you are ready. This process can take some time, but if you are committed to your emotional health and put some effort into changing your ways to achieve a release, you can begin to realize the benefits relatively quickly.

Emotions are processes of energy. This idea can be further enhanced by the idea that emotions have a natural life cycle of energy, which, if fully expressed, results in the dissipation of the energy. Emotions, if allowed to take their course, will come and go of their own accord. The reality about emotions is that if you acknowledge and express it, the energy will fade over time unless it is restimulated. Most of us, however, block the emotional process at one of the four steps in its life or energy cycle.

The Event

The first step that initiates emotion is the event itself. The event may produce sadness or joy or perhaps one of the many other emotions. To start the emotional process, you need to acknowledge that the event occurred. This means letting go of the denial process you may have maintained. If you have a habit of denying that you have been hurt or do not give much weight to the negative things that happen in your life, you shut the emotional process down at that point. Your body may, however, react by moving into a subtle state of awareness involving increased muscle tension and other symptoms. Denying the actual event can often lead to a state of disassociation from reality to a point at which you may not remember certain events.

Sensations

The next stage is having an awareness of a feeling. Again, feelings are a whole body and mind experience. The emotion may be experienced in any part of the body as a gut feeling, muscle tension, or facial expression. With the body experience also comes a conscious tone to the emotion such as a change in mood. Again, if the emotional experience is acknowledged and allowed to flow freely, the stage of expression can occur. Should you try to avoid the awareness by altering your state or using some of the other avoidance techniques mentioned earlier, you will likely end up with physical symptoms or a reduction in your ability to think rationally. You will become more sensitive to similar issues and be less willing to tolerate emotional expression in others.

Expression or Repression

The expression stage can take many forms depending on personal preferences and methods of expressing yourself. There is no one, right, or perfect way of expressing an emotion. Emotional expression is deeply personal and is really an expression of your soul. A few techniques and methods of emotional expression, outlined in a later chapter, will help you to discover your own personal style of expression. Again, many people stop the emotional cycle by shutting down and "swallowing" their emotions. Tears are blocked, anger is pushed down, and even joy is restrained due to self-consciousness. All of these actions lead to the same symptoms of emotional blocking listed in the previous step. In this step, however, since you have awareness, you are doing greater harm to your self-esteem because you deny your own emotional existence. Nathaniel Branden wrote that denying your emotions is one of the main causes of low self-esteem. When you deny emotions, you end up committing a crime against your own soul by disowning yourself.

Let Go and Heal

The Energy of Release

In the early stages of healing, an emotional catharsis may leave you with a great deal of energy or, alternatively, you may feel exhausted. The energy that you may experience is like an unconstrained spring. Think of a spring that has been compressed. It is being held down just as your emotions were. Release the spring, and the energy in the spring causes it to stretch and recoil until it reaches its natural position. A release of emotions can have the same effect on you. You may experience variations in energy and mood fluctuations like the spring being released. You may feel exhilarated, as the energy you have been using for suppressing is made available to you for other purposes. You may find yourself requiring less sleep. You may want to change things in your life. You may seem to be on an emotional roller coaster at times. As you progress through your healing process, the amplitude of the waves usually decreases. You will eventually find yourself in a more stable state where your mood varies by certain degrees, but not as widely as in your early stages of healing.

I believe that it is at this time in the healing process, when variations in mood occur, that many people get labeled "manic-depressive." Manic-depressives are people who have a depressive disorder and experience wide mood swings. Unfortunately, many people consider such a diagnosis a sign of a condition that will last their entire lifetime. While a person who has experienced a substantial loss may experience mood swings, it is important to note that in the process of releasing stored-up energy, the mood swings may, in fact, be a natural process of beginning to recognize and deal with emotions. As the emotions are expressed, the mood swings should decrease.

Returning to a more natural state may take some time. You will discover a new baseline for your consciousness. It is better to put off any major decisions or lifestyle changes until you come to terms with your release and gain an understanding of how you feel after the catharsis. Releasing emotion is very demanding and can take a great deal of energy from your body. Although you may not have exerted yourself physically, the emotional expression can leave you exhausted. I often found that a day or two of rest following a release was very helpful. I would find a place to relax, do some reading, or curl up with my pet. This period was a time for rejuvenation and consolidation. Go to a park, read a book, watch a sunset, or do some other calming activity. Allow your soul and heart wounds to heal!

Achieving a New Emotional Baseline

Completely releasing an emotion may be frightening for you simply because you may have never done this before. You may have never experienced the release associated with grieving a loss and healing. A scar may remain, but the wound can heal. Releasing and letting go of a long-held emotion can bring about a sense of unfamiliarity. Maintaining a daily routine of the same feelings provided a sense of security and avoidance of change, even though the emotions did not serve you. To let go of familiarity opens up new possibilities and awareness. You may find yourself wondering who you really are without all of your emotional baggage. When the pain is gone, you can be more open. Others may feel more open and communicative with you. You will have given up a part of yourself that was around for so long it had become comfortable. You may need to get to know yourself without your depression or anger. Your depression may have actually seemed to be one of the only consistent things in your life, although not a very positive one.

By releasing your deep-rooted feelings, you may find yourself adjusting to a new state of consciousness. At this time, you can reduce your fear and insecurity by reminding yourself that you are in a state of transition and a new beginning. Your life situation and emotions will eventually settle, leaving you healed and better prepared to solve problems and feel joy in your life. If you have become accustomed to depression, feelings of joy may be unfamiliar to you. Welcome them!

14. Five Stages of Deep Release

With the challenges I have faced, I have worked through a great deal of deep-rooted pain. Eckhart Tolle refers to this pain as the "pain-body." I truly believe the pain-body can be healed, and its impact on daily life removed from the present moment. Having completed this deep release when needed, I no longer carry these deep pains, and I am no longer as deeply triggered by similar events. Having successfully worked through numerous issues, I can say with confidence that understanding the following stages were extremely helpful in resolving deep emotional and mental difficulties. Some of the lessons I went through to be able to write this section challenged me to the core of my existence, but the rewards of emerging on the other side were plentiful and continue to this day.

Biting the Bullet

The first stage of deep release is to feel the deep raw pain. The term "bite the bullet" comes from the days of medical practice when the anesthetic had not yet been invented. If a doctor needed to perform an operation, the patient was given a few drinks to loosen them up. They were then told to bite on something very hard, usually a bullet, to distract their mind from the pain. In the case of emotional pain, biting the bullet means to accept the intensity of the pain, but remember that it is only temporary. If you want to let it go and be healed, you must accept that you need to face the pain rather than avoid it. Pain is difficult, but sometimes it takes more energy to avoid it than to start moving through it. We all fear the unknown but resent being stuck. Biting the bullet and facing the pain allows you to get unstuck and begin the process of healing.

Burning through Exquisite Pain

I use the term "exquisite" to describe the emotional pain you are working through because the feeling of this pain is life-changing. You are not feeling the pain out of self-pity or to seek comfort in familiar feelings. You are feeling the pain with the intention of burning through it, of letting it consume itself, so that you may eventually be free of it. I have found when I try to get a sense of what that painful event feels like in my body rather than simply visualizing it in the mind's eye, it becomes more real.

The act of burning through pain is a noble cause: it is the way of burning through locked-in pain that unconsciously impacts your behavior and sense of being in the world. The pain is exquisite when you can envision the transformational effects of your healing work. Let it go by giving it up to your higher power and the universe. The universe is so expansive it can easily take it from you and neutralize its energy.

Surrender

To fully feel your pain, it is necessary to surrender to it, to fully embrace it, to fully feel it, without denial of its existence and strength, without pulling away or running away from it when it gets overwhelming. You may feel as though you won't live through such intense pain, but if you can take care of yourself through affirmations about your worth, goodness, and desire to heal, you can surrender, knowing that you can bring yourself through it. You can experience the fear of change yet also be aware of the joy of your new birth. While you may be fearful of surrendering, you must face your pain fearlessly.

The Death of Pain

In the depths of pain, the time comes when, after the surrender and a feeling of being forsaken, you can let the pain die. There comes the point of stillness in the pain that includes intensity with purpose. You have felt the depths of despair, loneliness, and hurt, and have surrendered to these feelings, but you have not surrendered your will to live, only the will for this pain to continue. You become willing to exist without this pain that has been a faithful but unwelcome companion. You realize it can no longer serve you, but you have been afraid to let it go. As humans, we strive to keep everything alive. Your pain is no different, but this does not help you. You need to let go, to allow the pain to die, and in so doing, allow part of you to die with the death of the pain. It frees you to move on, but since you are often afraid of change, you are usually afraid to let your pain die. We are a stubborn lot sometimes. Be willing to let the pain die, and see who you will become without it. Miracles can happen from completing this process. I know, and you know, because I survived my pain to write this book!

Completion and Awakening

When your pain dies, you may feel exhausted and out of sorts, but this usually is the exhaustion of relief, and a reintegration period occurs during which you gain great insight. During this time, it is necessary to ground yourself to the earth so that you can rebuild on a solid awareness and the sense of your new self that is emerging. With these issues gone from your persona, you can see other people in a different light, perhaps without the anger, and with a little more compassion. Your values may change, and your respect for yourself and others will grow. You will also be able to acknowledge your own courage to face your pain and discover the depth of your resourcefulness. In some Christian circles, this process of feeling pain, the surrender to it, experiencing its death, and the awakening is the metaphor of the crucifixion. It is a powerful healing metaphor that can provide support in difficult times. Remember that emotional expression is not enough. You must change your thoughts, beliefs, behaviors, and expectations. These are the keys to healing and happiness.

> "There came a time when the risk to remain tight in the bud was more painful than the risk it took to blossom!"
> – Anaïs Nin

Part 3 – Healing the Inner Wounds

15. Defining Healing

Imagine your life as a big picture puzzle that has been put together over the years. It forms a picture that represents your life at this point in time. Healing involves taking apart that picture and, while reassembling the picture, repainting each piece of the puzzle before placing it into a new picture. Your subconscious mind, life lessons, new knowledge, and intentions guide you to repaint each puzzle piece. Make sure you have good intentions on your healing journey. Throw away any ideas of revenge or punishment and focus on being a better version of yourself.

In describing the meaning of healing, it is necessary to examine many aspects of your life. Catharsis alone may bring relief; however, if beliefs are not changed, does healing really occur? Similarly, if you alter your beliefs but persist in unhealthy behaviors, you cannot truly claim that you have completed your healing work. Therefore, a definition of healing is complex. Let's examine the major aspects of healing.

First, healing involves the removal of lingering emotional hurt through the resolution of the pain. How you do this may be personal and unique to your own situation, beliefs, and circumstances. It involves identifying and processing unresolved events so that the emotional content becomes information and our personal history.

Furthermore, healing involves resolving the "shoulds" and "musts" that you tell yourself and that others have placed on you. If you are living by someone else's standards and expectations, you are not truly living your own life. You need to recognize these expectations, some of which may be only indirectly implied. When you start to live by your own rules, you will be able to define what your own expectations are. You will achieve a greater sense of self and self-fulfillment.

Healing also involves recovering a sense of worthiness, or perhaps developing it for the first time. Remember that who you are is no longer dependent on what other people told you. Bo Yin Ra writes:

> "Other people's judgment of your value defined the worth that also you saw in yourself. Other people's admiration caused you to

regard yourself as 'admirable.' Other people's recognition of your person taught you, as it were, to recognize what you believed to be your *real* self.

Other people's low opinion of your being you regarded as so justified that even you could only still respect yourself in secret, in your heart of hearts. Indeed, you feared it was sheer vanity if every something in your mind rebelled against your being treated with such disrespect from others, given that you sought to raise yourself out of the depth to which you had condemned yourself in your own view.

You thus derived what you consider as your 'person' from judgments made by others, while from your own experience, you clearly have no concept of your real self.

No wonder that you rather would 'forget' the image representing only your appearance in the eyes of others. No wonder you are trying to "forget" what other people fancied you to be.

Your real authentic self, however, you will surely not desire to 'forget.' You simply caused an image of yourself – a phantom others planted in your head to pass for what you truly are… The image of yourself that you are seeking to forget because it makes you suffer – the phantom you created of your being, formed of other people's judgments – that effigy you truly should forget; indeed, you would do well to exercise it promptly."

You need to challenge other people's beliefs that you have swallowed without evaluation. Do you wish to keep owning and maintain a particular belief? Do you need to recover more positive instincts and beliefs that you abandoned because they were inconsistent with the beliefs imposed on you? You need to integrate the parts of yourself that were disowned or cut off to please others. Often this was done simply to survive in a threatening environment.

A memory I recalled through healing work was that as a young child, I used to love to dance and sing for my parents. I would run from the living room to the kitchen and dance for them, having queued up my favorite

Let Go and Heal

record. One day my mother shouted at me, "Stop being so ridiculous and silly." I ran back to the living room, stifling my tears. From that day on, I stopped dancing, and the process of shutting down my creativity began. Years later, my father recalled how I used to dance as a child and said: "One day, he just stopped." Through my healing work, I have reconnected with my singing voice and joined a choir. I now play guitar, take voice lessons, and, at the time of writing this book, I am recording a CD. Like many others, I have discovered that it is never too late to enjoy old talents you put away and also enjoy newly discovered ones. Another aspect of my healing process, particularly with my music, involved reducing self-criticism and the tendency to be hard on myself.

Healing also involves the acceptance of responsibility for the choices you did have the freedom to make, while accepting that you may not have been responsible or deserving of everything that happened to you, particularly in areas that were beyond your control. Healing is also about setting boundaries and developing the self-respect you deserve but may not have received. Often victims of abuse will feel a sense of shame or guilt. In perpetrating his or her crime, the abuser initiated and then perpetuated a sense of shame, but over time, the victim may internalize these messages. It is necessary to challenge these unfounded beliefs and feelings and learn to consider that you are lovable and did not deserve what occurred. You need to challenge your self-talk and respond with more positive and loving messages to yourself.

As with your self-talk, healing involves challenging your behavior and learning new responses. In the case of addictions, you may need to learn how to share and express your feelings in new ways, rather than numbing them with your addictive behavior. This can be a frightening prospect, but a rewarding action when you learn that you can manage your feelings in more productive ways.

Healing also involves revisiting old issues, challenges, and traumas, and resolving them through the integration of feelings and memories. New feelings may emerge from this process as well as memories long forgotten. Healing may also involve learning to let others help and learning to trust again. Healing is diligently nursing yourself back to health with new behaviors, thoughts, feelings, and actions.

Some changes may be profound. You may choose to associate with a more positive group of people, to become more assertive, or to diminish certain behaviors. In cases of addictions, you may decide to call someone for support, or join an online support group meeting, rather than repeat the addictive behavior.

Healing also involves changing from trying to regain the past to letting go of what was and learning to move forward. You have to stop trying to regain the past, or hoping to get back to where you were before things happened. You can't go back in time. Acceptance, being present, moving forward to a new you should be your focus. Remember, personality, life, and possibilities are all fluid and can flow in many different wonderful opportunities.

Keep in mind that sometimes the healing process can seem overwhelming. You may experience an intense period of awakening, where insight comes quickly and intensely. Friendships change, some friends pick up unconsciously that you have changed, feel anxious, and react in unpredictable ways. You may find people you considered lifelong friends disappearing. You may find that a friend opens up and confides deep issues to you only to find that they then hide from you because they feel they overshared. Do not worry about all these things. I've been through periods of drastic change, and it has always been for the better. When going through one of these periods of upheaval, I felt that my life was being turned upside down, but I came to realize that my life was already upside down, but was being turned right-side-up! Keep that idea in mind!

Finding Your Undamaged Self

Through the development of inner space, you can find that there is a deep inner space that is undamaged – the undamaged self. The undamaged self is a sense of who you are free of your core wounds. It is a sense of unconditional love that you may feel from your spiritual practice, or when you are in nature or looking at the stars, or sitting quietly and meditating. A sense of calmness comes over your body when connected to the undamaged self. You feel a sense of compassion and love for yourself. A common group exercise is to meditate and recall a time when you felt safe and loved, but for many people, there are no memories of such a time. If that is the case, you need to work on creating your own feeling of safety and self-love. If you have no previous connection to your undamaged self, then it is time to begin to develop this connection and sense of it.

Connecting with the undamaged self for the first time is like the signal strength bars of a cellphone. In stressful times you may feel like there is no signal or only one bar. But by developing inner space through quiet time or finding your personal soothing behaviors, you can increase the bars on the signal strength of your connection to your deeper self. Once you know what it feels like when connected, you can begin to notice when you are not connected, and you know where to go to get reconnected.

By developing inner space, you gain the ability to look inward and examine what is going on rather than invoking a reaction to discomfort through the fight, flight, or freeze responses to stresses.

Awareness of Choice and Invoking New Reactions!
Often you try to resolve a behavior pattern by trying to develop new habits intended to counteract the behavior itself. A more appropriate and likely more effective method to eliminate the behavior pattern would be to go to the foundation of the problem by re-examining the event, suppressed emotions, images, and beliefs that generated the pattern. This type of self-examination will bring about a long-lasting solution to the problem better than short-term attempts to change habits to bring about behavior modification.

The ability to change your reaction lies in the gap between the event and your reaction. With an awareness that you have the power of choice over how to react, you can choose to react differently. At first, the gap seems to be an extremely short measurement of time, but once you are aware of the gap between event and reaction, and you stop for a moment and center yourself by breathing and observing. You can learn to be in control and evaluate what you are feeling and choose your response if you choose to respond at all.

The first few times I tried to practice this, I was actually surprised how little control I had over my reactions. I became more aware of that gap between the trigger and my reaction, and as I learned to breathe, I found myself having a greater sense of control. Instead of snapping at someone or responding with feeling hurt or playing the victim role, I could breathe the emotion away and then respond more calmly. I learned to recognize that my emotional body was reacting, but my mind could still maintain control and choose how to respond, often with more kindness even though the ego wants to fight! This helps in the present moment, but if you meditate when there is no trigger, and make a commitment to healing, you can gain self-knowledge and identify your triggers at a time when you are not being triggered and work to heal them.

Since a surprising portion of your behavior can be the result of emotional distress, alleviating the emotion can result in the removal of the distressful behavior. Once the emotional distress is dealt with, you no longer have to resort to obsessive or compulsive behavior in an attempt to block the emotions. You may no longer need to reach for a drink, drug, or other addictive substance to escape from your pain. You may begin to experience closeness as you become more open and genuine. You can take off your emotional masks without fear. You will also likely have a greater capacity for rational thinking once you release and resolve your emotional distress. Habitual patterns of behavior that were a symptom of your distress are removed from your daily life because you have resolved the deeper problem.

The healing of triggers leads to new behaviors, and new behaviors lead to better emotional states as well as more rational thinking. By combining emotional expression and changing your thinking and behavior, the results can often be astounding in terms of healing, growth, and personal development.

Silencing Shame, Guilt, and the Inner Critic

Each of us has an inner voice that can work for us or against us. Unfortunately for many, this inner voice becomes the inner voice of our criticizing and neglectful parent. A major aspect of healing and change is to learn to tame the inner voice and turn it into your best friend.

First of all, you must become aware of your thoughts, especially any that are critical of yourself, especially in subtle ways. It is also important to know the difference between guilt and shame. Guilt is a feeling that you did something that you regret. Shame is a feeling that you are a bad person. Guilt helps you grow and improve, but shame harms you.

Be aware that the inner critic is prone to mistakes. It may equate feeling lost and confused, which happens to everyone at some time, with failure. Your inner critic will say, "I shouldn't feel like this, I must be a failure." You need to counter these words with statements like, "It's a challenging time, but I'm working through this, and I'm OK with how I'm feeling!"

You don't want to completely silence inner speech as the experience of silent thinking has been linked to problem-solving, creativity, and self-regulation. An out-of-control, untamed self-critic is also creative and can create problems for you and deplete your will power.

The secret to taming the inner critic is to learn to accept that no one is perfect and that it is OK to make mistakes. Ask yourself how a good friend would talk to you and begin using a similar, compassionate tone of inner voice with yourself. Give up the need to prove yourself to anyone, including yourself. Thwart the inner critic by asking questions such as "How did I come to believe this?"

Breaking "Loop" and "Spiral" Thinking Patterns

In supporting a few friends through difficult times, I observed a distinctive pattern of loop or spiral thinking, which was hard for them to break out of once they got locked into the pattern. Since I could see this pattern in my friends, it became easier for me to see it in myself. Spiral or loop thinking usually involves a trigger that leads us to a feeling, which leads to a negative thought, which in turn triggers more debilitating feelings, which then feeds thoughts. In one friend I could see the pattern of a date going badly, feeling alone, feeling bad about being single, feeling the criticism of her parents, feeling she hadn't accomplished anything, seeing all guys negatively, losing hope, and then talking about how she disliked the city she lived in. When we talked, and she started with how she was disillusioned with the city she lived in, I would reply, "So the date didn't go well, right?" But, until we uncovered the previous thoughts, our conversation focused on what was not good about the city she lived in.

Once we identified the triggering feeling, we could avoid the loop by balancing any negative thoughts with positive ones. She didn't deny that she felt lonely or that her parents criticized her, but she was able to counter her loop by thinking some positive thoughts and writing out a list of all her accomplishments.

She now is more aware of when she is in a downward spiral. And how she can, with the power of choice, use her imagination positively to spiral up in a positive direction. By writing down your sequential thoughts and feelings, hopefully, you can see the pattern. It is also possible to enter a loop at any point in the circle of thoughts. There may be multiple entry points. However, by being aware of your thoughts, you can also discover multiple exit points out of the loop or spiral and begin to think more positive thoughts towards yourself and your situation.

Ending Defeatist Behaviors

In the introduction of this book, you may recall how I described myself before my healing work. I kept myself extremely busy, took on many projects, and kept myself at a considerable distance from others. I could not slow down, nor could I let people assist me at times when I needed help. I was very independent and unable to let other people know my true self. I believe that many of these issues were the result of not having processed the natural emotions that had occurred due to the losses I had experienced and the beliefs I developed about myself in the course of my upbringing. As I began to challenge these beliefs and to express and resolve the emotions, my self-talk improved, and I gradually learned new behaviors as a renewed sense of creativity and rationality appeared.

In your healing process, you often become aware of various self-defeating behaviors or habits that limit your ability to develop a sense of self-esteem. The development of self-esteem is a crucial component in identifying many of the contradictions and falsehoods that you have erroneously believed about harmful events. Identifying the true nature of the perpetrators and increasing your self-worth brings about release and healing. Self-esteem is a sense of self that develops in small portions, like building blocks, on top of each other. Building a stronger foundation of self-esteem allows you to see the contradictions within hurtful events.

Let Go and Heal

Too often, you may sabotage or undermine your own self-esteem with behaviors that stem from your attempts to get deserved love and attention. You may do one or more of the following:

- Addictively seek approval or validation
- Allow others to determine your worth
- Addictively and dependently seek love
- Set unreasonable goals and expectations for yourself and others
- Avoid setting boundaries
- Give away personal power
- Minimize the positives
- Exaggerate your experiences to make them seem more impressive
- Engage in black-and-white or all-or-nothing thinking
- Generalize your experience using words such as "always," "everybody," or "nobody"
- Use the word "should" too often (referred to as "shoulding on yourself")
- Expect perfection from others and yourself

All of the above behaviors can diminish your sense of self-esteem and can prevent you from developing a spiritual and emotional backbone. Developing a backbone is done by keeping your personal power and setting boundaries with others so that you can choose when you wish to let someone be involved with you. The key to a backbone is the ability to make choices and follow through with them.

Often when you are confronting your own issues, you end up confronting behavior in others; moreover, you may need to decide what your own standards of acceptable behavior are. You can then use this yardstick to measure how you are being treated in relationships. Confronting the inappropriate behavior of others can be a challenging prospect and often requires that you go outside your comfort zone. When challenged to do so, you may feel intimidated and fearful and unable to focus on the whole situation. When you face such a situation, you can increase your chances of success by feeling your breath and your feet on the floor, and by seeing the other person while focusing on the space around him or her. This can help you maintain your sense of strength and accomplish the boundary setting you wish to achieve.

To achieve healing, it is necessary to bring an end to the defeatist behaviors that are contributing to your own sadness. Constantly going over an event without re-examining the context will only serve to restimulate hurt and sadness. Similarly, negative thinking can be a habit that is contributing to your sadness. If this is the case, you need to counter your negative thoughts with positive ones. Recognize what you can change and what you can't. Sometimes the only thing you can change is your thoughts: the past cannot be changed, but you can change how you look at it!

Taking time at the end of the day to note three positive things that happened, no matter how small, will help you develop a sense of gratitude. You may have trouble with this task simply because you have been overly proficient at noticing the negatives. If you struggle to come up with any positives, this is an indication of how underdeveloped your skill is in this area. If you practice noticing the positives, in time, you will become more positive. If you find yourself fighting the idea of stating them, then perhaps this is an indication of anger that needs to be resolved. Noticing the positives does not mean denying the negatives and hurt in your life; it simply means giving weight to both and attempting to achieve a better balance between recognition of all aspects of the events going on in your day-to-day life.

One way to modify behavior is to replace it with new behavior. This more often than not brings about new and different results, moving you towards greater emotional maturity and self-understanding. And, by changing your behavior, you end up changing your feelings. Conversely, by changing your feelings, you end up changing your behavior. Similarly, changing your behavior can change your thinking, and changing your thinking also changes how you feel. In other words, your thinking, feeling, and behavior are interrelated. In your healing process, it is necessary to work on all three, but a change in one area will often lead to changes in other areas. It is a complex process that begins with small changes in the way you manage yourself.

16. The Process of Deep Healing

Applying Your Learning, Insight, and Growth

At this point, you have built a foundation of understanding and are ready to bring about some deep, long-lasting healing. While you may have expressed emotion before and felt some relief, you may find yourself triggered again and still feeling the pain. The keys to healing lie in being open to new beliefs and a new worldview.

Unfortunately, our human wiring leads us to defend beliefs, even though these beliefs no longer serve you. You are emotionally attached to beliefs and often experience the "backfire effect." This is the tendency to defend your beliefs even more strongly when evidence contradicting your belief is presented to you. Keep in mind that beliefs are not simple logical statements. They are more like mental images and impressions of people, places, and situations. They form part of your identity. To change a belief requires allowing your own identity to change. That can seem frightening to you, hence your mind protects you with the "backfire effect" and in doing so does you a disservice.

Keep in mind that beliefs have energy and momentum. Like trying to stop a moving vehicle, it takes substantial energy to stop a belief. Fortunately, there is no need to stop the car or belief, you simply let it keep going and disappear into the sunset, and you get a new car or belief! You need to be willing to let them go and get a new vehicle for living with new features and modern technology!

The Key to Healing – Re-evaluating Your Beliefs

While you have probably heard "You can't change the past," it is important to learn to recognize when your beliefs about the past are impacting the present. Many times, I have encountered people who accused me of "living in the past," but honestly, the emotions I was experiencing were actually happening in the present. They were emotions and issues that I had suppressed and not dealt with. They were clearly impacting me in the present and were easily triggered by similar situations. What I do acknowledge is that simply reliving and expressing the old emotions is not enough to bring about healing. As I did, you must also examine your beliefs and attributions about the original event and the people involved. Insight is the key to dissolving the dark emotions, eliminating negative thinking, and finding freedom and happiness.

When examining an old hurt, it is as if that time and place in which you were hurt are in the present. Likely, your inner child is mentally and emotionally at the same time and place of the past event. This is why it is painful to face your emotions. The fear of pain can be so strong as to cause you to avoid recalling the feelings of the situation.

In *Therapy for Adults Molested as Children*: *Beyond Survival*, John Briere writes: "Most papers and texts on the treatment of PTSD (Post Traumatic Stress Disorder) emphasize the need for adequate emotional discharge." Briere states that this emotional discharge is needed regardless of the type of trauma. Even though trauma often results in a tendency to avoid feelings that are similar to the event, facing the emotions and releasing is necessary for growth.

Recalling the event in present safety and with new insight and awareness allows us to discharge the emotion in a manner that achieves resolution of the hurt. If you simply recall the event and feel the emotion without examining the beliefs and changing your self-talk, you only restimulate the hurt, and healing does not occur.

Therapists often hear of a client's fear of loss of control. You may fear that if you start to cry, you'll cry forever. The idea is to relive the original incident in an environment of safety and to ensure that you know the pain can be escaped if it becomes unbearable. You have become skilled at using your intellect to avoid pain, and you can use these skills at such times to your advantage if the pain is overwhelming. It is important to balance the pain of the original incident with the present sense of safety in re-examining the emotions and to emphasize that you can easily return to the present. This can be accomplished by focusing on objects around the room or by answering various unemotionally stimulating questions relating to your present situation or daily life.

To resolve pain, you need to become your own observer and participant in your pain. In present safety, you can experience the original pain, fear, and threat to yourself and begin to understand its true nature.

Let Go and Heal

T.J. Scheff writes: "When the balance of attention is achieved, the client is both participant in, and observer of, his own distress. Under these conditions, the repressed emotion ceases to be too overwhelming to countenance; the client becomes sufficiently aware of it to feel it and to discharge it." When re-experiencing a hurt, you will feel the pain, fear, and danger of the original incident. You must remind yourself that although the experience from the past is very real, the present is safe, and you are physically removed from the original danger.

In identifying the beliefs that are trapped in the emotional content, it is also necessary to identify the internal conflict that is causing the anxiety. Usually, the conflict is a result of two partially opposing aspects or beliefs.

According to Gestalt therapy, resolving the conflict involves the softening of the self towards the unaccepted belief. This involves being willing to look at the issues that are troubling you. It is a willingness to look inside and to allow the feelings to be felt and acknowledged. When you do this, a point of balance is attained, and you become as much an observer as a participant. Otherwise, a restimulation occurs rather than a healing experience. Being your own observer, you can become more aware of the true nature of the event, your self-talk, and the beliefs that you hold about the event. You can then objectively examine the content and nature of the beliefs and whether they are, in fact, true. With present safety, the assistance of a counselor or a support group, and your own improved judgment and self-value, you can better judge if these attitudes, beliefs, self-talk, and messages that you were given or created ever were, or are, still rational.

More often than not, you will discover irrationally or improperly placed guilt or responsibility. In other instances, you may discover that you made a promise to never be hurt again, never be poor again, or never be ridiculed again. Through the discovery of the underlying cause of your pain, you can learn to practice acceptance of yourself and others. You will learn that you did the best you could at the time. You can then adjust your attitudes and beliefs accordingly. Learning theorists agree that it is easier to replace a negative habit or belief than to try to eliminate it. From this comes the acceptance that it is easier to change yourself by substituting a positive belief. If you believed that you were unworthy and then learn otherwise, if you believed you were bad or brought on the hurt and then realize otherwise, at such moments, you release and heal. You learn that now, in the present, there is a contradiction between the original situation and the truth of the situation. Your newer, healthier belief contradicts your previous belief, causing you to release and let go. With new beliefs about the situation and yourself, you will heal emotionally.

The content and nature of some of these new beliefs and attitudes are numerous. Here are a few examples:
- You learn that you are now safe.
- You learn that you have power.
- You learn that you can do things differently.
- You discover that you didn't deserve the treatment you received.
- You learn that you were and are lovable.
- You discover that you can now make other choices.
- You learn that you can remove yourself from a situation.
- You learn that you are competent.
- You recognize that you were in a no-win situation.
- You learn that you are capable of having a happy life.
- You learn that you weren't responsible for what happened.
- You learn that what happened wasn't fair.
- You see the situation in a different light and perspective.
- You can accept that others make mistakes.
- You accept you did your best with your knowledge at the time.
- You can accept that you do not need to be perfect.
- You learn that you are not useless.
- You accept you have value without having to earn it.
- You accept that life is not perfect and at times, is unfair.
- You learn that "It wasn't about you."
- You learn that you don't need to take things personally.
- You learn that you don't have to be alone.

Over the years, many people had told me, "You have to change your thinking" or "It's all in your thoughts." The concept of positive thinking seemed very distasteful to me. In my training as a counselor, I felt that the counseling theories that only dealt with thinking were lacking in complexity. These theories seemed to reduce issues down to a simple statement that minimized the complexity of the issues. On top of this, these theories seemed to ignore a very important part of my personality – my emotions.

Recent research has shown that there is value in observing and acknowledging your negative thoughts. Also, researchers have shown that trying to pump yourself up with cheerful slogans can make people with low self-esteem feel worse. I believe these slogans reach into the subconscious and highlight your conflicting internal beliefs. The alternative to positive or negative thinking is whole or realistic thinking. With realistic thinking, we observe both our negative and positive thoughts and allow either to occur without judgment.

The positive thinking crowd seems to think that we should always feel great. That is simply unrealistic. You don't have to tell everyone how you are deeply feeling, but acknowledging to yourself that you are not having a great day is purely acceptable! The other value of negative thoughts is that these thoughts may be a calling from your mind to try to heal something. In essence, your brain may be nagging you to do some healing work. Suppression of thoughts you do not want to have actually may result in an increase in their frequency!

Are there other benefits to negative thinking? Yes! Research has shown that grumpy people get details correct. Negative thoughts and emotions bring your challenges into focus and illuminate the need for a solution. Vulnerability, negative thinking, and negative emotions are also linked to greater levels of creativity. Workgroups who feel comfortable expressing negative emotions and thoughts tend to work together better as a team.

Even regret can be beneficial. Exploring your regrets can help make sense of the past, help change behaviors, and increase your level of insight. Regret is to be explored, but at some time, what hasn't been done must be forgiven and let go. Doubt can also be a helpful friend as you examine beliefs. Doubt can be healthy if it leads to expansion, but unhealthy doubt is circular in nature and destructive: it minimizes your potential. Doubt is helpful when re-evaluating beliefs in the process of questioning beliefs and values. Doubting your self-worth is not helpful and even destructive. As a friend Audrey Foo posted on Facebook: "Doubt, it is like a virus that infects our thoughts. Be very careful to notice it, for it can disrupt the greatest patterns, even of love and spiritual connection." Allow a sense of confusion in the re-examination of your beliefs, but never doubt your self-worth or value as a human being!

Although you may have established beliefs and patterns, as a human, you are intelligent enough to learn and develop new beliefs once you receive new information or insight. Often, the discharge of emotion will result in greater clarity of thinking that will allow you to examine your belief systems and behaviors.

Some beliefs you hold may not even be apparent to you, simply because they are inferred rather than explicitly expressed. Often well-meaning parents will make statements such as "If you do not do well at X, you will never be or have Y." "X" could represent school, homework, table manners, being quiet, or any other behavior that they want from us. "Y" could represent any result that they wish, such as going on to college, having friends, a successful marriage, or a job. What "Y" represents is their model of success, which, in all likelihood, will be accepted by you as your measure of success (perhaps unconsciously) as something you should attain.

Statements made to you in such a manner result in an implied "should." For example, a friend told me how his father often scolded him as a child and teenager by telling him that if he did not stop a particular behavior his father found annoying, he would lose all his friends. A statement such as this says several things. For example, my friend felt that he had been told that his friends did not value other qualities in him and would give up on him simply because of one or two minor weaknesses. He internalized other messages from his father's behavior. He realized that he had developed a belief about success: he should always have a considerable number of friends. Otherwise, he would feel unsuccessful. He placed an unconscious burden on himself to satisfy this implied "should." By coming to recognize this implied belief, he was able to resolve these feelings and feel a greater sense of self-acceptance and comfort with being alone.

Altogether, healing involves developing a new cognitive map of yourself and of the world in which you live. It involves challenging your cognition, your behavior, and your emotions, and linking insights with feelings. Insights are essentially useless if they are without attachment to your feelings. If the insights are purely intellectual, they have no effect on your emotions. It is through the combination of insights and feelings that you achieve healing and growth. You may learn a great deal about human nature, about yourself, and about others. You may discover new aspects of yourself, new creativity, and new talents. You will grow in understanding and self-knowledge.

Healing Core Wounds and Triggers

It was at a very painful time late in my healing process that the most profound changes occurred. With the news that a love interest had no romantic interest in me, and feeling the subsequent disappointment, a powerful dream occurred in which I felt tremendous sadness, but in the dream, I avoided showing my feelings to my parents. While dreaming, I confronted them with the fact that they had taken no interest in my daily life and had no idea of the things I was going through. As I awoke sobbing, a great deal of pain and rawness existed in my chest area.

I was deeply sad, and in pain, but in surrendering to my pain, I experienced profound healing over the space of about five days. During those five days, I took very good care of myself, getting massages, and giving my energy to the healing process. I was in great pain but knew that I was moving through a powerful transformation. I chose to see a counselor who could help me move through the emotion, rather than just talk around it. Logically I knew that the level of emotion was out of proportion for the amount of time I spent with her and the very little bonding we had experienced, but something deep had been triggered that needed attention and healing.

Coming out the other end, I managed to release very deep emotional pain as well as profound sadness and grief over not being listened to, being ignored, being isolated, and my lack of friends and family connection during my earlier years.

I had experienced deep release before, but there was something special about this release. I believe I got through to a deep core issue, and in healing this issue, I found that my relationships, friendships, and acquaintances changed around me. It was a physical and emotional shift that produced dramatic, deep results. I had healed a core wound.

Core wounds, frozen needs, and promises create all sorts of internal conflicts. You may find yourself desiring, needing, or even craving attention, love, money, or friends, while other wounds may cause you to repel or repulse the very things that another wound needs or craves.

Some of the symptoms of having an inner wound are having strong feelings of:

- Being unloved
- Needing to belong
- Needing to be special
- Needing validation
- Responsibility for something that happened
- Unworthiness
- Needing to prove your worth
- Being overly critical of yourself
- Shame for giving yourself self-care and love

Another symptom of having an inner wound is having difficulty saying "I am a good person" and believing it.

Challenging Beliefs about Relationships and Purpose

Once you heal a core wound, you may find that your life purpose will have changed. You may realize that it may be time to let go of some friendships with people who were there to serve the purpose of filling your frozen need, or to be the object of your attempts to heal your inner wound. You may have been trying to change someone to make yourself feel better and to make it seem that you matter more to them than to yourself. You can begin building healthy relationships with people who are not unconsciously trying to find love but can give love.

Let Go and Heal

In the process of healing a core wound, you are open to seeing people more objectively through a healthy lens, as Vermin Ennans wrote in this Facebook post:

> "I was in love with an abuser because I believed I saw who he really was. It was actually my ego projecting itself onto someone else to excuse my desire to change them. I had to decide if I wanted to be right, or if I wanted to be happy. That required me to accept that partner for who they were and not who I wanted them to be. I left. And I am far happier for it."

Through the healing of inner wounds, you set the stage for major changes in your life. You may face pain in the process of doing so, but ultimately the process is transformational, leading to greater internal happiness.

17. Getting Unstuck

"No problem can be solved from the same consciousness that created it."
– Albert Einstein

In your healing journey, there will often be times when you get stuck. In these times, you do not see solutions, and you seem to repeat patterns of behavior. Sometimes a lesson or test reappears, yet you make the same mistakes or simply don't know what to do. At times it may be your own behavior or attitudes that get you stuck. You fall into a trap or hole. To become unstuck means to learn to recognize the holes you fall into, to acknowledge them, and eventually learn to walk around them. Some of these holes and traps are:

- Anger
- Depression
- Despair
- Fear
- Fear of failure
- Guilt
- Helplessness
- Insecurity
- Isolation
- Loss of control
- Panic
- Powerlessness

Often these feelings or states arise because you do not understand what your body is telling you about your feelings. You may lack knowledge or feel overwhelmed by the signals. You may fear being wrong or being rejected for showing your emotions. You may also be playing old tapes of a past situation in which you may have been helpless or powerless. Again, you need to achieve a sense of balance that tells you that, in the present

Let Go and Heal

moment, you do have choices and that you can act differently than you have in the past.

Are you living in the past instead of the present? Are you going over events again and again without any resolution? If so, then you must change your thought patterns and address your feelings on the issues. As you become more aware of your feelings and your history, you begin to comprehend how things were around you. You have several options to choose from in the way you can proceed. You can choose to go over your past and remind yourself how tough it was, or you can address the feelings and realize that you survived and that you can heal from those events.

You need to put the past behind you and hold hope for a better, healthier future. To do this, you may need to face some emotions, accept the past, and change your thinking as it occurs in the present. If you do so, you will likely find happiness and the types of relationships you are looking for. The Bible states that what you ask for, you shall receive. If you ask for more pain, you will find it. You may even give it to yourself by beating yourself up over past events and things you wish you had done differently. The other choice is to accept what was and to choose a better path and a better way – now available to you because of the work you have done. If you look for happiness, new friends, support, and kindness, these things will come to you!

You need to recognize that you have options and that you are no longer powerless or helpless. When you recognize these qualities of your new present situation, your fear and despair disappear. You can learn that emotional release and healing can bring an end to the isolation that occurs when emotions are accumulated. Remember that crying due to the pain of hopelessness and despair is different from crying for the purpose of healing.

The Self-Pity Trap

Often when you are sad or grieving, it is easy to fall into the trap of self-pity. Self-pity involves feeling overly sad for yourself as a victim. If you are finding yourself developing a "poor me" attitude, you may need to look into your pattern of being helpless and without power. In your emotional healing, you need to remember that you are not helpless and that you can change your situation. Your goal is to heal and be free of lingering sadness rather than remain a slave to it. You need to realize that you are much more than your pain or your emotional state. Although you may have carried your pain around for a long time, you need to entertain the idea that it is possible to rise up from it and experience a more joyful state of being. Your emotional state is not necessarily part of your personality. It is something that can be resolved and released to reveal a more creative and energetic you!

Temporary self-pity does have its value in our healing process. Identifying that you are feeling pity for yourself can help you discover that there is some hurt to be resolved, or simply that you need to acknowledge that you are feeling sad or unhappy about something. To deny the sadness is to deny your feelings, but to remain in the pity can be a trap that will block your emotional healing. True, it can be part of healing to feel sad, but when this becomes an excuse for the way you are, then you are not healing but hiding. You are avoiding going further along in your healing process.

Imagine a triangle with feeling, pity, and denial, each in a corner, and detachment at the center. In your healing process, you may move from corner to corner of the triangle. However, your greatest healing times can occur when you are operating at the center of the triangle. Denial plays a role in healing by allowing you to deal only with what you can handle. Overwhelming yourself can be harmful and can place a great deal of stress on your mind and body. Pity and sadness allow your mind to acknowledge your sadness and that you have been hurt, but you must eventually move closer to the center position of detachment.

Detachment is a term often used in self-help groups describing a sense of objectivity from others and your problems. Detachment means that you can objectively see the problem in its true light, without the clouds of emotional patterns that have sabotaged your objective thinking. For example, you may have given your power to others or allowed others to be your unofficial parents. As a result, you end up reliving your roles with your parents with these people, thus clouding your understanding of what you really need and desire from them.

Let Go and Heal

Detachment also means being able to differentiate your problems from other people's problems. Through detachment, you learn not to suffer from the reactions and actions of other people. You begin to develop your sense of self-esteem, measured by your own set of judgments and values, as well as a strong belief in yourself. You learn to accept that it is not possible to have everyone like you. By developing a sense of balance between feeling, self-pity, and denial, you can learn about yourself, acknowledge your own feelings, and see issues realistically and objectively.

Holding On

Most of us unsuspectingly become stuck at some stage. For example, you may get to the expression stage and genuinely work on expressing yourself. But to complete the process, you need to be willing to let go of the emotional energy and the associated beliefs. Letting go of beliefs is challenging because you have an emotional attachment to them. Yes, beliefs are your friends, and you form a bond with them that needs to end just like a relationship with another person. You need to be willing to exist with the issue at hand being completed and gone from your life. Sometimes a particular emotion or belief has been around you so long that it feels as though it is a part of you. To let it go may mean rediscovering yourself and finding out who you might be, without the emotion that has defined your behavior for such a long time. You may not be happy with the emotions you are experiencing, but you may feel comfortable having them around. They become a possession with which you are unwilling to part.

Letting go of an emotion or belief involves risk. It means that you will be moving on to a new phase of your life. This may frighten you to some degree, and as a result, you cling to your current emotional state. The cost of not going all the way with your emotional expression is that you hang on to the emotion, and it can then be easily restimulated. Imagine trying to launch a toy boat in a pond with a small string attached to it and tied to the shore. The boat will head off, but it will never be able to sail freely or continue on its journey. Emotions and beliefs are the same in that you must be willing to completely let go of them. Otherwise, you end up in a state of emotional tension that never quite fully resolves itself.

To successfully release the energy associated with your emotions, you must be willing to go completely through the process of release. To simply become aware of the emotion and feel it is not enough. You need to be able to completely express it, and then fully let it go and dissipate. You must be willing to let the emotion leave you and give up any benefit you obtained from having it. If you do not give up the benefit of your emotional state, its expression becomes parasitic. It has served its purpose, but it is now being used to make someone else wrong, to punish another person, or even yourself. Your attitude must be changed. Otherwise, your continued expression without resolution ends up harming yourself and others. It is especially easy to get in touch with anger or sadness, to feel part of it and then back off, without resolving it. When you do this, you simply retraumatize yourself as well as the people around you. You trick yourself into thinking that you are doing well by experiencing the emotions. To achieve emotional health, you must go further. You must be willing to completely express the emotion and completely let it go. You must get in touch with the feelings, feel them, learn what incorrect beliefs you hold, and let the emotions leave you. Your goal is growth and acceptance of what is. If you hold on to old beliefs and feelings, you become addicted to your view of the triggering situation and use the emotions as an excuse for your way of being. You learn to speak the truth without drawing a battle line.

Increasing Your Awareness

To solve problems, it is often helpful to examine and expand your scope and awareness of the problem. Often you become stuck because you fail to see other options. Just as though your problem was confined to a small room, you end up breathing only stale air that surrounds the problem. You need to bring some fresh air in or, as the saying goes, "shed some light" on the problem. This can be achieved by searching for new ideas as well as expanding your range of solutions. It is possible that you may decide to stop resisting your problem. It takes much more effort to resist something than to actually do something about it.

It is helpful to step back and look at others who were involved in the original problem. I always felt responsible for an incident that happened while walking to school in Grade 1. Two of my friends and I were walking

Let Go and Heal

to school with another friend from the neighborhood. As we got a few blocks from home, my friend refused to continue. We were physically trying to drag him, knowing no other option at the time. A car pulled up, and the man inside yelled, "Leave that boy alone!" He looked like one of the boarders at my friend's house, so we continued and left him behind. My friend did not show up at school for a couple of hours. When he did, he had scratches on his face, and he was screaming and crying. He had been kidnapped. I don't know whether he had been sexually abused. The police were called, and an investigation began. One of my friends told me that it was my fault for leaving him. I felt tremendous guilt. In hindsight, it was not my fault that this man did the things he did. It was not my responsibility to get this friend to school, and it was a normal reaction to respond with fear towards the man. Furthermore, there were two or three other people with me who also took no action other than to continue on to school.

Here is another example. A friend of mine told me how, at an early age, he asked his mother why his brother looked different than the rest of his family. His mother responded that his brother was adopted. As a child of five, he was in awe that his parents would take in a child and provide a home. He told his brother how neat he thought it was to be adopted. All hell broke loose. His parents hadn't told his brother that he was adopted. Both children were traumatized by the incident. Reviewing the situation, his parents should not have told him without telling his brother first. They were adults and should not have expected a five-year-old child to keep such an important secret, which, it can be argued, should not have been a secret in the first place. Nor did they convey to the child that it was extremely important to keep this information to himself until they had a chance to talk to his brother.

By objectively looking at these situations, you can realize that the expectations placed on the children were unreasonable and unfair, and it was, therefore, inappropriate to blame them for the outcomes. While you may not have ever been involved in incidents of kidnapping or revealing an adoption, you can look back on other types of incidents with a greater understanding of the roles that others played. Recognizing that others had responsibilities as adults, you can more easily understand the situation and let go of misplaced responsibility!

Facing the Truth

One of the prime rules of healing is that healing cannot occur if you are mired in denial of the truth of the hurtful event. Denial serves the purpose of protecting you from the pain when you are not ready to deal with it, but often you end up using denial without being aware of its consequences. Denial often prevents healing.

In examining any event, you must be willing to accept the truth about it. For example, you may have to accept that you were laid off, that you felt rejected, lonely or isolated, or let down by yourself or others. You may simply have to acknowledge that, indeed, you were hurt.

Healing is a process of telling yourself the truth. You may have felt pain, shame, fear, loss, or helplessness, or you may have felt anger. You need to face these truths and realities of the situation to allow healing to take place. Often you may have to own up to secrets that you have hidden from yourself and others. It is your secrets that cause you the most pain. You may not need to reveal them to others, but you need to at least be truthful with yourself. A big part of healing is self-forgiveness.

Reaching a Crisis Point

Although it would be nice to think that humans constantly strive to solve their problems of their own initiative, it is often a crisis that precipitates an increase in understanding. I have frequently joked with friends that many of the lessons I have learned were affectionately called an "AFGE" – Another Friggin' Growth Experience. It has often been noted in recovery programs that reaching a crisis point, or "hitting bottom," is crucial to the troubled person's recovery and subsequent elimination of the addictive behavior. In the case of career choices, many decisions are made due to a crisis such as a loss of job or health issues. In either case, people often later regard the crisis as a positive event that dramatically changed their lives.

With the case of hitting bottom, many recovering alcoholics will say that the signs of their problem were there all along but that it took a very loud and clear message for them to get that they had a problem. Sometimes you think that admitting you need help is a sign of failure, that you should be able to solve things on your own. Like many others, I have come to realize that trying to do it all on my own can itself be a failure – a failure to accept the help and knowledge of others. To admit you need help can take a lot of courage. It's not a failure but really a victory. Look at yourself and assess where you are. Can you do this alone, or could you make use of the resources that hundreds of thousands of people have used and are using now? I have grown from being independent (dependent only on myself) to being interdependent (dependent on myself and others). This builds community.

It is a sign of growth and of your ability to trust when you reach out to others. It's not easy at times, and at times doing so may be well outside your comfort zone. But because you took the step forward and did something different, it really is a victory. It is the start of healing, and the start towards achieving some serenity.

A crisis point may result from the building of tension and emotional stress due to a financial, relationship, or health problem that finally becomes unbearable with the addition of a new crisis. The chronic stress may have its source in the past, or in the present, or both. It seems that many individuals attempt to ignore a crisis, often leading to behavioral problems and emotional distress.

Since crises often appear to bring about long-term positive change, I believe it is important to recognize that the events that occur in your life seemingly happen for a purpose – to nudge you along to your next level of understanding. In earlier times, I would have run from my problems and feelings, denied them, or told myself I was silly for having them, but now I recognize that the feelings are natural and normal. I also know now that it is far healthier to feel them and release them than to stuff them down like I used to do.

Working on the Real (and Deeper) Problem

Many counselors will attest to the fact that the problem a client presents for counseling is often not the actual problem he or she should be dealing with. For example, if the difficulty is with sleep disturbances, there may be a myriad of underlying causes to account for the symptoms. Similarly, with a family conflict issue, the deeper issues may encompass one or more causes ranging from addiction, family dysfunction, communication styles, a fear-based inhibition of accepting what is, or, at the root of it all, one's self-esteem.

Sometimes what you need to do is face the underlying problem by asking not "Why?" but "How did this happen?" and, more importantly, "What am I afraid of admitting about myself?" A dear friend of mine and I would meet up every couple of months due to our travel schedules. She was having a difficult time getting over her ex-boyfriend. The relationship had ended poorly, and she kept asking herself if he had loved her, or if he was a good or bad person. This type of stuck conversation went on over several meetings, but at one meeting, she appeared lighter and happier. She realized that she had been asking the wrong questions and essentially had been working on the wrong problem. She had been asking herself whether her ex-boyfriend was "good" or "bad" and "Why had he ended the relationship?" She said she finally realized that, when she looked deeper, she was afraid to believe or admit that maybe she had chosen a bad guy. She confided that she had always believed she was smarter than the other girls and knew how to choose a good boyfriend. She could see other people making bad choices and had made a promise to herself that it would never happen to her. She admitted to herself with self-compassion that she had failed just like other people do. She practiced self-acceptance and accepted that it is normal to make mistakes. This resolved the confusion, and she no longer felt such a strong need to know why he ended the relationship. She began to move even further forward, realizing that there was no need for judgment about whether he was a "good" or "bad" person. She recognized that he had chosen to be with her just as much as she had chosen to be with him.

Clearly, facing your fears – for example, admitting you have broken a rule, a contract, or a promise you made to yourself – can feel painful at first. Combined with self-compassion, you can get to the real issue at hand, become unstuck, experience a great deal of growth, and lighten up your soul! You have to stop searching for an answer you may never find.

Let Go and Heal

"A mistake repeated more than once is a decision."
– Paulo Coelho

Confusion Can Lead to Innovation

It isn't surprising that most of us have an aversion to confusion. It is an unpleasant state of doubt that arises from trying to understand our old beliefs while considering new ones. Confusion is necessary, though, if you want to move forward in your thinking, attitudes, and feelings. By allowing confusion to be present, you open yourself to new ideas.

Moving into a new realm of being requires a degree of innovation. While the term "innovation" has usually been used solely in the business world, it is a key consideration in personal growth. Göran Ekvall did some pioneering work in the concept of innovation over twenty years ago. He suggested that several relevant dimensions contribute to innovation. The first is how motivated you are for change. Second, you need some freedom to make a change. How attached are you to personal and family attitudes? Can you make changes in your environment that have a chance of succeeding? The third concept involves how much time you can set aside for creativity and evaluating ideas and plans. The fourth requirement for innovation involves safety. There are certain people I don't bother talking to about issues, but I do have several friends with whom I can share on a deeper level in safety. Ekvall's fifth requirement is to allow for playfulness and humor. To satisfy Ekvall's sixth requirement, you need some kind of conflict and debate. Unless we are suffering from a victim attitude of helplessness, conflict moves us to act! Innovation requires that you are willing to take risks to solve a problem.

"To know when one does not know is best. To think one knows when one does not know is a dire disease. Only he who recognizes this disease as a disease can cure himself of the disease."
– Lao Tzu

Creating Creativity

I recently read an article authored in the 1960s that is still relevant today. Frank Barron was a pioneer in the area of understanding what factors facilitate creativity. One of the most important factors is the motivation to create meaning in one's life. The second is a sense of intuition or trusting one's inner judgment. Also, creative people tend to like a challenge and are more likely to admit to others that they have troubles. A further characteristic is what is called ego strength or resiliency. Like innovation, a willingness to take risks is necessary. Fortunately, these are all traits that you can develop and make choices about.

You have the power of imagination to visualize yourself possessing these traits. That is the first step towards developing them! While you may have learned some negative uses of your imagination, it is necessary to practice developing the positive side. It becomes necessary to stop the heightening of suffering through imagination and to begin to use it wisely. You can choose to use your imagination positively, envisioning a positive future.

Invoking the Power of Hope

Whenever you undertake a project or task, it is usually with a sense of hope that there will be rewards for your efforts. In emotional healing, there will be times when you are making progress. At other times you may seem stuck and feel that you are making little progress. In revealing your pain to yourself and releasing it, it is easy to lose sight of the fact that things will get better. In times of trouble, you must remind yourself of the progress you have made.

Often you may feel overwhelmed by your problems. At times some people may even feel suicidal. If these thoughts occur, it is helpful to try to alleviate the feelings of being overwhelmed. This can be accomplished by trying to identify the issues that are causing the greatest amount of stress in your life, discovering alternative ways of dealing with distress, reducing the amount of self-criticism and "shoulds" that you generate, and breaking problems down into their smaller components. You need to remind yourself that these problems shall eventually pass.

Let Go and Heal

You must make an effort to notice that although you may have a lot of work to do and things may seem bleak, there is a light at the end of the tunnel. You can recover from your past injuries and begin to feel joy again. When times get tough, you can reach out to a friend, or if necessary, call the local distress center. There is always hope, even if you must look for it. Others have gone through difficult processes such as yours and are willing to help.

Healing and growth are possible when you maintain a sense of hope. Hope gives you strength in dealing with stress, motivates you to overcome difficulties, and lessens the burden on your mental health when you go through difficult times. Hope allows you to stretch beyond your current situation. Hope for the future is the most powerful thought you can have, next to being present and knowing you have the freedom to choose how you react to unfavorable circumstances. Hope is usually a protective factor, allowing you to look positively to the future with the expectation that, while things may not necessarily be perfect, they will somehow improve.

Many people talk about hope and its power, but what exactly is hope? Reading through many articles on hope, I noticed numerous definitions. It seems that hope is part emotion, constructed belief, faith, and intellect. It is also perhaps simply a visceral sense of a future in which things will get better, or at least that life will have some purpose and meaning. Despite many rejection letters for this manuscript from publishers, I always had hope that it would be published. Without my having hope you would not be reading this book. Hope also involves a sense of persistence despite rejection and setbacks.

From a logical point of view, hope is a correction in your thoughts. When you start to have thoughts such as "Maybe it won't happen," you can change your thought pattern simply by saying, "It can happen. I have hope!" Hope allows you to weather setbacks and, in times of discouragement, pick yourself up and keep on going.

Another aspect of hope concerns the time frame for the manifestation of the things hoped for. There are actually different types of hope. The first type that you should understand is daily hope. Daily hope provides meaning and a sense of purpose to your day. It motivates you to get up in the morning and enjoy your day through simple daily pleasures.

The next type of hope is goal-oriented, such as completing a course or program, finishing a project, taking up a new hobby, or planning a future trip. This type of hope helps pull you through challenges and routine work that needs to be done to obtain a reward shortly. This hope is similar to the character-building practice of delayed gratification, where a good thing is postponed so that you can do what is necessary to make the deferred reward possible.

Long-term hope is a type of hope that is life-sustaining and helps you to understand that despite difficulties, your life has meaning and purpose. It helps you to make sense of, and smooth out, the peaks, valleys, downturns, and upturns that you have encountered along the way. It is a deeper soul feeling that gives you the power to effect change over an extended period. It takes a long time to turn a heavy, slow-moving ship around. When faced with tremendous challenges, long-term hope gives you the courage to work hard, knowing that individual steps and effort will lead to long-term benefits.

Now we turn to the possible dark side of hope – false hope. As many have said, there are two sides to any coin, and the same can be said about hope. Hope can be used as a tool of denial when you refuse to believe the facts and cling to an idea that something different will happen. Even then, sometimes, what you hope for does come true against all the odds! This is what is called miraculous hope. The factor that distinguishes miraculous hope from other types of hope is the probability of the event happening and the emotional investment in wanting the event to occur. If a loved one has a terminal illness, you can hope for a miraculous cure. If you are unprepared for the possibility that the cure does not manifest, then the loss of the loved one can bring much greater pain and a sense of betrayal. Still, there are many cases of miracles occurring, of astonishing recoveries, and triumphs of the human spirit. If you have hope, don't let anyone take it away from you!

Another dangerous type of hope is expectational hope. Expectational hope refers to developing a belief that an event or person will complete you

Let Go and Heal

and make you happy. You may believe that meeting your soulmate will bring you lifelong happiness or that getting married will bring a joyous life. This kind of hope usually brings disappointment when the ultimate happiness does not occur after the event occurs, or you feel temporary joy that diminishes into depression, arguments, and dissatisfaction. Looking back, try to evaluate whether you have developed any expectational hope and let it go.

Finally, a powerful type of hope that I have experienced is phoenix hope. It is a hope that motivates you to rise above your current situation, to begin and endure a path of recovery, and to strive for a better life. As you may recall, the phoenix legend from Greek mythology tells of a bird consumed in a fire, to be reborn as a greater spirit. Many of us, after getting a sense of this type of hope, are compelled to move forward and to make things better. It is often not an easy journey, but the image and legend of the phoenix and its rebirth will keep you moving forward on your path.

You may now be asking yourself, "How can I develop hope?" I think the answer is quite simple. First and foremost, hope is a choice. It is a desire to have positive thoughts. There are times when it is healthy to have a yearning for something better, for happiness, even though we realize that happiness comes from within. You can choose to start to have the smallest of hopeful thoughts, such as "I will wake up in the morning" or "I will hope to make positive choices." You can also blend your hope with a feeling of being realistic and not discouraged when things don't go your way or when you have a setback. In observing my own progress with developing hope, I noticed that a willingness to feel inspired was always the first step. Inspiration is the keyword for developing hope and overcoming despondency. While inspiration can mean "being drawn into high levels of feeling or activity," it also refers to "drawing air into the lungs." You can instill consciously accessible hope by drawing it in from others or from your inner spirit. Hope can be instilled by visualizing a compelling future, recalling uplifting memories, or inspiring movies, leaders, speeches, or music. One good thing about hope is it is contagious. Find the things that help you hope, and that inspire you. Put these reminders around you where you will often see them – on your desk, on your bathroom mirror, on your fridge. Make sure you have daily reminders of hope. Make time for hopeful inspiration!

> "I can lay bare her troubles because I have not lost hope."
> – Lin Yutang

18. To Forgive or Not Forgive?

"Growth in wisdom may be gauged exactly by the diminution of ill-temper."
– Friedrich Nietzsche

In your healing process, you may ask yourself whether it is necessary to forgive those who have harmed you. But first, it is important to also ask whether there is anything to forgive. Stating that you need to forgive someone implies that they did something wrong. This may be the case, but is important to evaluate whether your pain is a combination of what they have done and your own belief system. It is important to evaluate both. You must evaluate whether the issue is a serious one that requires forgiveness or whether it is just a misunderstanding or difference in viewpoint that caused the disruption in the relationship.

Is Forgiveness Really Necessary?
There is now some healthy debate about whether forgiveness is necessary to heal and move on. You may find that you can move on by restoring self-worth, self-esteem, and self-compassion without going through the process of forgiving. Many people repeat the sentence "you have to forgive to heal" as a cliché, but perhaps a deeper understanding needs to develop. I came across this posting by Devin Graham and was given permission to include it here. Devin did a great job of summarizing the "forgiveness debate":

"Healing is not contingent on forgiveness, and it would be wonderful if we put an end to shaming those who choose not to forgive. Those who have truly healed themselves by facing and releasing their rage, their shame, their helplessness, their guilt, and their sadness in a regressed state as the child (not the adult) might understand that forgiveness is not a necessary step for ALL. We might say we have forgiven yet have not yet worked through our repressed rage and anger (this was my case). We might have skipped that stage and have forgiven prematurely. This might not be true forgiveness; it might be a form of spiritual bypass. Sometimes, it is an empty gesture done to avoid having to deal with unpleasant repressed rage that so many of us unconsciously hold on to. I know; I've been there."

Part of the problem with the research articles on forgiveness lies in the definition researchers have used. Some researchers define unforgiveness as a harmful and cold emotional complex characterized by bitterness, anger, fear, and unhealthy rumination. Wiser researchers have identified that these negative aspects do not occur with unforgiveness if it is a cognitive, awareness-based position of the victim. The victim may actually feel empowered by choosing not to forgive. If negative emotions are not at play and rumination is not present after choosing not to forgive, then perhaps forgiveness is not necessary. It is an ending to the anger and rumination that is required to be healthy.

Defining Forgiveness

If you decide that forgiveness is the process you wish to follow, you need to evaluate and clarify your understanding and definition of forgiveness.

First and foremost, forgiveness is something you do for yourself. It is also for the good of all the people involved. It is an act that restores your sanity by changing your attitudes and feelings. In forgiveness, you do not condone the actions of others, nor do you minimize the impact those actions had on you. It is not a process of wiping the slate clean. It is a process of acknowledging what occurred, the impact of those actions or events, and the work you have done to cope with and resolve the problems.

Secondly, forgiveness does not always mean reconciliation. Forgiveness can occur without reconciliation or an apology from the offender. It is also important to note that forgiveness is not necessarily or even probably something you do only once. It is an ongoing process. If you do not forgive, you end up living with resentment and bitterness. If you are unable to forgive, you are more likely to avoid certain people and situations and have unhealthy thoughts of revenge. It appears that revenge is a purely human trait, not present in the animal world. Being prone to revenge correlates with a higher degree of depression. Even if you succeed in being revengeful or adopting an avoidance stance, these strategies rarely, if ever, bring you long-term happiness.

Forgiveness brings about continuity in relationships and eliminates any sense of self-righteous indignation, contempt, hostility, and thoughts of retaliation. It also impacts the frequency of recall of troubling incidents. Forgiveness results in improvements in many measurable aspects of well-being. If another person knows that you have forgiven them, they, too, experience a greater degree of wellness. Furthermore, while it has been suggested that people are more likely to forgive those with whom they share close rather than distant relationships, making an effort to forgive those who are more distant can also benefit your own well-being.

On the other hand, by not forgiving, you end up harming yourself. Most definitions of serenity include not only acceptance and empathy, but also forgiveness as a fundamental means by which to attain it. Others have seen a lack of forgiveness as an imprisoning of the soul. Terry Waites, upon release from his hostage ordeal, said that he felt it had been necessary to forgive his captors. Otherwise, he would have remained captive forever.

In my own path of forgiveness, I found there was a very spiritual dimension to the process. In doing forgiveness work, I discovered a greater sense of being human and learned more about others. I learned about the frailty of the human condition and the difficulties other people had faced. I also learned not to judge, to be mindful of my own limitations, and to maintain a spiritual practice of love for myself and others.

Still, it was a difficult process, as I needed to examine the nature of my anger, attributions, and self-doubt. With situations of abuse, it became necessary to move towards seeing the abuser as a human being with weaknesses and someone who was not totally evil or bad. It is often easier to hate than to forgive. Naturally, I was very angry with several people who had treated me poorly, and verbally, emotionally, or physically abused me. At times I felt I would like to confront them and hold them accountable for their actions. To heal, it is necessary to gain understanding beyond these feelings.

Should I Confront?

While moving forward in your healing process, you may consider confronting the offender. In such cases, it is extremely important that you understand your expectations regarding the confrontation. It is important to stop further incidents, so one must be mindful that additional pain may arise from your expectations of the offender. You may expect them to apologize and dramatically change their behavior, but this may not occur. Some people will deny the offense. Others may admit to it and apologize, yet continue with offensive or abusive behavior due to their own difficulties and problems. Others may begin their own process of healing, while others may still be resentful. In your quest to forgive, you need to give up the notion that the offender owes you something or needs to make up for what they did or did not do. Only when you give up this notion can you have truly forgiven them.

While you may feel that confrontation is necessary, it is often ill-advised, as it never goes as planned. Forgiving involves the lack of a need to retaliate. It also involves accepting an apology if one is given. One of the most difficult things to do is to accept an apology when you are still very angry. You may not be at the same healing place as the other person, and as a result of the timing, healing may not occur if you do not acknowledge the apology and modify your thoughts accordingly. You may be still invested in being angry and judging the other person. To heal and forgive, you must begin to see the good in others. Remember that apologies come in many forms. Sometimes a gesture of goodwill, special eye contact, a hug, or other body language will suffice when words are hard to speak.

One of the most difficult types of forgiveness to achieve occurs when there is no acknowledgment of the incident or hurt. In this situation, you need to discover for yourself what you need to forgive. Essentially, you need to master your own healing process.

The Mask of Pseudo-Forgiveness

Another challenge for many is what is called "pseudo" or "false" forgiveness. You may go around saying, "I've forgiven," but it is really only a state of denial in which the deep work of forgiveness has not been done.

You have moved from anger directly to pseudo compassion without having gone through the process of true and deep forgiveness.

I have learned that going from anger straight to compassion does not bring about authentic forgiveness. In most cases, the shortcut backfires. You have only repressed your anger and denied it. While you maintain an air of forgiveness, you may find yourself easily triggered when speaking of the original event, or you find yourself reacting emotionally when the issue is raised.

You haven't really done the required work and are blocking out the feelings. Forgiveness involves a full acknowledgment of the consequences of what happened, and you may be in fear of those feelings and acknowledging your anger. If you have truly forgiven, then you should be able to discuss the issue, consequences, and your old anger feelings without any residual triggering.

Facilitating Forgiveness

According to the latest research, forgiveness actually is a learned skill that comes with age and is developed over the total life span. According to a French study, adults are more likely to forgive than adolescents, and seniors are more likely to forgive than younger adults. There are also several factors that facilitate forgiveness or make it more difficult. The first consideration is the degree of harm that was experienced. Obviously, a simple mistake made by another person that has little impact on our lives is much easier to forgive.

Secondly, if you have been adequately compensated in some way, such as through an apology or kind deed, you will be more likely to forgive. Also, strong emotions regarding an incident tend to make it more difficult to forgive. It is necessary to work through the emotions to bring the incident into a process of forgiveness.

Finally, if you have a reason for why someone did something, or you can gain insight into why something happened, it is much easier to forgive. In a forgiveness study, college students were told that a dog had bitten another person. One group was told the dog had been abused, while the other group was not given any reason. The first group exhibited far more compassion for the dog than the second group.

By viewing the other person as a person with flaws just like yourself, it becomes easier to forgive. A technique that seems to help facilitate the process of forgiving is to write down your story. I remember an incident that happened years ago that I was angry about. I took some time and wrote out what happened. As the details flowed out, my ability to see other aspects of the incident expanded. I developed a much deeper understanding of the dynamics of the situation. Forgiveness became easier!

Blocks and Catalysts to Forgiving

Of all the factors that stop us from forgiving, age is not one of them. Study after study has shown that forgiveness is a learned skill and habit that seems to increase with age, not diminish as do so many other aspects of living. It seems that as you get wiser in your older years, you learn to forgive and increase your sense of well-being. As mentioned previously, another factor that helps you forgive is the closeness of the person you wish to forgive. You might find it more difficult to forgive a colleague than a close family member. What helps you forgive is a desire to restore the relationship, especially when the other person is a member of your close community.

From the studies I have read, there appears to be very little difference between genders in willingness to forgive. The mood is, however, a factor in willingness to forgive: it is easier to forgive when you are in a good mood. Also, generally speaking, people find it easier to forgive if there was no intent to harm, or if there was no negligence. The more severe the consequences, the more difficult most people find it to forgive.

There are other blocks to forgiveness that we can examine. First of all, some people want revenge or punishment. This is clearly a block to forgiveness. Others want to cancel the consequences and return to the state that they had before the incident. Often this is not possible and therefore blocks people from forgiving. Many people believe they cannot forgive if they have not received an apology. Correspondingly, many people find it easier to forgive if there are repentance and remorse on the part of the offender.

In some situations, people will forgive only out of social, peer, or authority pressure. This type of forgiveness is not as effective in reducing anger and generating healing between the offender and the injured person. Forgiveness out of obligation is less effective than forgiveness derived from a sense of love and compassion for yourself and others.

Finally, some people find it easier to forgive after some time has elapsed since the event. Perhaps as you acknowledge and healthily express emotions, and the event fades into the background, friends, family, and colleagues will realize the value of the relationship and will be willing to make amends or let go.

Seven Steps to Forgiveness

I have found that the following steps bring about lasting forgiveness when implemented and practiced daily. I've had many things to forgive, so I've had practice. I've noticed that it is easy to fall back into the trap of unforgiveness and resentment unless you make it a daily habit to forgive. Why forgive? You forgive so that you can stop harming yourself through resentment and begin to move into a state of happiness and gratitude.

Stage 1 – Admit You Are Angry!

Many of us will echo the thoughts, "What? I'm not supposed to get angry! I've done all this healing work!" I've learned that it is harmful to get angry, but it is more harmful to be angry and not admit it! The way to check if you are angry is to observe your inner dialogue about how you are relating to yourself and others. Are you finding yourself being negative, critical, or frustrated? Do you find yourself being impatient with people and critical of how things are done? Are you constantly blaming others for your troubles, wishing that others would change? If so, then you are likely angry. Try to recognize what you are angry about. It may not be recent little things, but something that happened months or years ago. Look back in time to what might have triggered your anger and where your expression has been blocked. Bitterness is anger with no outlet to be heard or a feeling that you cannot change anything. It is a form of helplessness. Try to discover what you are bitter about. Make a list of resentments. Don't hold back or edit your thoughts. Being honest with yourself is the first step in healing anger.

Stage 2 – Acknowledge the Loss and Consequences

To fully forgive, you need to look at the consequences of the event. By consequences, I do not mean just emotional pain. Look at the past and the present, and honestly note any changes. Were you physically injured? Were you emotionally hurt? Did you suffer financial loss? What other types of losses occurred? Was there harm to other relationships? To achieve lasting forgiveness, it is important to acknowledge all of the losses. Otherwise, forgiveness will have to be revisited. When listing the losses and consequences, try to look objectively at the incident without investing in the emotions around the losses at this time.

Stage 3 – Softening Your Stance and Being Vulnerable

The next stage in forgiveness is to open yourself up to change and dissonance. You cannot spread butter when it is hard and cold. Forgiveness does not come easily when your ideas or thoughts of revenge and justice are hardened. You must retreat and re-examine your approach. Just like a pound of butter, if you want to forgive and heal, you need to let your ideas thaw and be molded into a new perspective and combined with other ideas and views. You need to admit that harboring anger and resentments violates the laws of kindness and compassion. Harboring anger harms both yourself and other people. You must realize that, by not forgiving, you are now betraying the person with whom you are angry. This is not an easy step. It can be painful to realize that it is you who needs to change and that it is you who has the poison of anger and resentment. It is easy to build up a wall of justification around your thoughts, actions, and feelings regarding the harm done to you. To heal and forgive, you need to break through this wall and tear it down completely!

This stage of forgiveness also requires you to look at whether there was any responsibility on your part. In some cases, there was none; in others, you may have taken action that contributed to the problem. In the latter case, it may be hard for you to admit that you caused part of your own suffering since it is easier to blame others than to take any responsibility. This stage requires an honest, fearless, kind, and moral inventory of your own actions and behavior. Sometimes you may not like what you find, but

Let Go and Heal

facing your shadow can be one of the most powerful healing experiences. See if you can find some common ground.

Stage 4 – Stop Punishing

One of the common impulses of people is to try to punish those who have harmed us. Most studies have shown that punishment rarely teaches anything other than to promote resentment in the person doing the punishing! Some of the ways you may punish are by withholding companionship, giving the silent treatment, or even giving compliments but then taking them back with an insult. You may try to go further with legal action, or by damaging things the other prizes, or by gossiping about them. To truly forgive, you need to give up the expectation that the other person will be punished. You can ask them to make amends for their harm, but if they refuse or are unable to make amends, then releasing them from the idea of punishment frees you from lingering resentment. You need to stop invalidating them.

There is great wisdom in the following Buddhist teaching: "Should one person ignorantly do wrong, and another ignorantly becomes angry with him, who would be at fault? And who would be without fault?" It is far better to try to forgive and reintegrate your friends back into the community than to ostracize them through punishment. Try to practice compassion, work at developing a deeper understanding of how and why people behave the way they do. It seems that we prefer a simple explanation of things, yet we need to understand that human beings and the relationships between them are complex. Understanding the ways of the world and the people in it requires wisdom and self-control. Use the opportunity to forgive as a means of growth.

Stage 5 – Identify Some Good in the Other Person

This step involves finding some good in the other person. It is probably the most crucial step in bringing about lasting forgiveness. It can also be the hardest, depending on the severity of the event you are trying to forgive.

According to Francis Bacon, the key to forgiveness is in "not expecting the other to change, to give love, to be kind and develop the ability to see that in everyone else's eyes and heart there is some good." In forgiving, you try not to think of yourself as being good and the other person bad. You can find it easier to forgive if you can understand that the other person also has difficulties and was harmed in the past.

If you do not practice this step, forgiveness will be futile because it will be done with a sense of contempt. If you cannot find good in the other person, then at least pray for them. A wonderful technique for developing your vision of good in another is to imagine a seed of goodness in their heart, and in prayer, imagine that both you and God are watering it to make it grow stronger. Better yet is to imagine that each person already has this great flower of goodness in them. Admit that it has been obscured from your view because of your anger, resentment, and justifications. Learn to look for the good. At first, like developing any skill, it is challenging. You will become better at it with practice.

Stage 6 – Develop Genuine Neutrality

Hopefully, in the process of forgiveness, you will come to resolve any negative emotions and thoughts about yourself and the other person or organization. To do so requires that you do not expect or demand any payment or restitution after forgiveness. You must assume that there is no debt owed to you. Mother Theresa once said, "It is between God and myself, it was never between them and me anyway." This must be practiced daily. It is easy to slip into anger and resentment if you do not cultivate the practice of neutrality. Depending on the severity of the event, you may choose to not have any further contact with the person, but if you meet them by chance, you want to have a sense of neutrality and calmness instead of avoidance.

Stage 7 – Stay in the Present

"Bury the hatchet" is a phrase you may have heard many times. There is wisdom in this phrase if you understand its original meaning. The phrase comes from the spiritual traditions of North American Natives who would put all weapons out of sight while smoking a peace pipe. For your own forgiveness work, you must keep the original wound out of sight or out of the present mind. It is necessary to acknowledge what happened, to not forget it, but also to not drag it up again like a fresh wound. Resurrecting

Let Go and Heal

the event and bringing it up again with the person who harmed you will cause you to feel the associated feelings again. Balance your memory of the event with your memory of the forgiveness work you have done. Practice loving those you don't spontaneously feel warmth towards.

All of your forgiveness work can be undone, and the resentment rekindled if you begin to dwell on the event again. If you rerun your mind's movie of the harm, you may find yourself back in a hurt and angry state. It is the nature of your mind to ruminate, and therefore, you must develop self-discipline and remind yourself that you have completed forgiveness work around this issue. Thank your mind for the intrusive thought, and send it off into the far reaches of the universe! Refuse to bring the past into the present again. Continually rise above the injury. Practice compassion and unconditional love towards all people.

Making Amends

There is great wisdom in one of the most critical steps in recovery programs in which you make a list of all the people you have harmed and make amends to them as long as doing so will do no further harm. I believe this step is a very powerful example of doing unto others what you would have others do unto you. It is also a powerful step in self-healing, respecting others' boundaries, and taking ownership of your own behavior and issues. We have all hurt someone some time in our lives. Examining the impact it had on yourself and others, and looking at how your own character may have negatively affected someone else, requires self-love and a degree of caring for other people.

While attending a dinner, I bumped into a woman whom I dated briefly after completing my master's degree. At the time, I was physically and emotionally burnt out and wasn't warm and accepting of her kindness. I told her how bad I felt about how I had treated her. Although I conveyed that I was not in good shape and that I wasn't really capable of giving at that time, she was not the one who had a problem. I said I was sorry for not recognizing the gifts she had to offer. I could tell from the sense of relaxation that came over her and the unspoken reduction in tension between the two of us, that my words meant a lot to her.

Clearly, this was a case in which contact between the two of us would not harm her, however, in some situations, an apology can bring about more harm than good. When a secret has been kept from someone, and then you tell him or her and also apologize, you have to wonder if the apology is meant to help them or yourself by appeasing guilt. For this process to work, I would suggest that the apology must address some event of which both people are already aware. In apologizing, you may be bringing up old wounds for the other person that they are not ready to deal with. It is best to ask whether it is OK to talk to them about it. If they say no, then their wishes should be respected. If you apologize for something you did that the other person was never aware of, you may end up hurting that person with new information, dumping your problems onto them, and causing pain over a closed chapter of their life.

Making amends can entail other methods, too, if necessary. For example, if there is someone you cannot contact and you wish to be forgiven for some deed, create a simple ceremony in which you do something for a stranger, and in silence, release yourself from owing the apology. You are still accountable for your actions, but in some way, you are giving out the energy of health by completing the issue for yourself. If you are fortunate to have that person come back into your life at some time, you can tell them of the ceremony you conducted for them.

Self-Forgiveness

In my healing, it was very important to forgive myself as well. There have been times when I have let myself down, regretting the things I had not done or wished that I had acted differently. Self-forgiveness is needed just as much as forgiving others, yet it is just as difficult. Self-forgiveness is accepting yourself for the things you did with the knowledge you had at the time. It is accepting your limitations, yet not limiting your capacity for change. Self-forgiveness requires that you look at your shadow, or the secrets you hold that you hope no one will ever discover. It is about acknowledging your deepest fears.

I was twenty-three when I was told that my mother was terminally ill. I simply could not accept that she was going to die. I was also quite busy with starting my undergraduate degree and was playing in a rock band. I postponed going to visit her at the hospital. When I finally did, she was unconscious. I never got to say goodbye to her. It was always difficult to forgive myself for this until I realized that there was no way I could have held my life together other than to deny my fears and to rationalize that she had bounced back at other times, and she would do it again this time too. Being gentle with myself, accepting the place I was at during those weeks, as well as sharing these feelings with a counselor, has helped heal this shadow. I have come to accept that my mother knew far more about me than I realized. At the moment she passed away, I was setting up my drums for a high school dance. As she departed this level of existence, I felt her presence sweep down on me, hug me, and then move off towards a great expanse of freedom. I knew that she was gone and that she loved me deeply enough to say goodbye. She wouldn't want me to feel remorse, and she certainly wouldn't want me to punish myself.

Try to discover which events in your life you have regrets about. Practice self-acceptance, forgiveness, and self-compassion.

"Does a true hero have to be heartless? Surely a real man may love his young son. Even the roaring, wind-raising tiger turns back to look at his own tiny cubs."
– Lu Xun

19. Resolving Anger and Resentment

The Nature of Anger

In writing this chapter, I must first admit that I had a very deep change of heart in the way I believe people can heal from anger. Over the years, I had heard of many methods for releasing anger, and I tried many of them. Most of them were exercises that involved punching a pillow, screaming or some similar expression of anger energy. I found that over time, none of these solutions to dealing with anger energy really worked, as later, I still found myself being angry. Fortunately, with some Buddhist teachings, some insight, and a combination of challenging experiences, I learned to heal my troubles, and thereby reduce my anger. I've learned that anger isn't the problem. My thoughts, habits, and views of other people and myself were what needed work.

I recently came across a new way to classify emotions without using the term "negative emotions" in a comment on Facebook by Caryn Brooks Coleman and subsequently in a book by Everett Worthington Jr. called *Hope-Focused Marriage Counseling: A Guide to Brief Therapy*. The idea is that the emotions we label as negative are actually protective emotions. Anger is often a signal that you feel threatened. The need to emotionally protect yourself gives rise to anger when dealing with a perceived threat, trying to defend your beliefs, or feeling you are not being loved.

Clearly, anger is one of the most destructive emotions you can experience, whether it is occurring internally, or you are the recipient of someone else's anger. There are some misconceptions regarding anger that I hope to clear up in the coming pages. For a while, people thought that venting anger would help resolve it. Buddhist leaders, however, suggest that solely venting anger tends to train people to maintain their anger. Furthermore, venting exercises such as screaming and yelling can do damage to your vocal cords. In the coming pages, I'll describe some more myths about anger, as well as provide personal examples of how I worked through and resolved my anger.

I believe that the term anger is often used incorrectly to describe a diverse range of emotions and states that encompass aggression, rage, and resentment. While anger can often lead to aggression, it is possible to experience anger and resolve it without becoming aggressive.

I have also learned that rage appears to be fear-based in that it usually results from an overwhelming sense of being unable to control your situation or to effect any change. Researchers have found that perpetrators of violence usually do so when experiencing a strong fear of losing control. Rage can be simmering and smoldering beneath the surface, erupting when control is threatened, or a state in which someone is actually already out of control yet is trying to re-establish it ineffectively. Studies suggest that people who are filled with rage are also filled with shame or a deep-seated resentment regarding oppression and silencing.

Resentment, on the other hand, is a slow-burning anger of choice, and a self-fed poison that eats away at your soul. Resentment does considerably more harm to the person doing the resenting than to the one being resented. Refraining from resentment-driven anger requires a great deal of repressive control and may be maintained unconsciously.

Anger and Timing

I would like to differentiate between three possible anger states that can occur. Two of them deal with timing. The first state occurs if an event has already occurred, and you have not practiced self-control. You are already angry. In this case, your body's chemical mechanisms have already produced numerous hormonal and muscular reactions. These need to be calmed and taken care of, and their energy reduced in a healthy way.

The second state occurs when you are truly angry but won't admit it to yourself. This can be a severely draining state as the energy is present, but not acknowledged and deeply repressed in muscle tension. Your body has already reacted, but the mind refuses to acknowledge it, leaving your soul in poor health and low spirit.

The third state happens when you are fully aware and in control of yourself, and an anger-provoking incident occurs. In this situation, you can practice various exercises and self-control to not get angry. This is the power of prevention.

Developing Self-Control

I am now of the firm belief that getting angry is not a resource that you or I should draw on repeatedly. It is a state in which you are often dangerously out of control. To get angry is to be human, but not necessarily humane. Through simple chance and synchronicity, I met a martial arts and Qigong teacher who helped me to understand the true meaning of martial arts, anger, self-control, and compassion. I asked him, "How do you deal with anger?" His reply was very insightful:

> "The people around the world don't get the real meaning of martial arts. It is not to attack or to kick other people. It is just to kick and attack our own anger. With Qigong, you learn how to attack and control your anger. When you get up in the morning, you listen to some calming music and do some practical and corrective Qigong exercise so you can kill the negative energy or the negative thinking that maybe you are going to do a bad thing. So when you do some Qigong, you can have internal balance, self-confidence, and self-control, which leads you to be flexible in your life and strong with yourself. When you are in some hard situation with others in your life, you can control yourself so that if someone gives you bad energy, you can give back goodness."

Of all the emotions, anger seems to be the one that you can easily feed and build upon. Like adding wood to a fire, your thoughts can easily increase the heat and intensity of your anger to the point at which you are in a rage. Become aware of how you feed your own anger. Notice the shallow breathing. Invoke your inner observer and take deep, slow, calming breaths.

Regarding anger, there are some valuable lessons to be learned from the world's religious leaders. In researching this book, I searched the Bible for references to emotion and anger. The one phrase that came up over and over again was that Jesus "was slow to anger." There is great wisdom in these few words. From Buddhist teachings, I have learned a great deal about anger. In *Making Your Mind an Ocean*, Ven. Thupten Yeshe writes:

"I encourage people not to express their anger, not to let it out. Instead, I have people try to understand why they get angry, what causes it and how it arises. When you realize these things, instead of manifesting externally, your anger digests itself. In the West, some people believe that you get rid of anger by expressing it, that you finish it by letting it out. Actually, in this case, what happens is that you leave an imprint in your mind to get angry again. The effect is just the opposite of what they believe. It looks like your anger has escaped, but in fact, you're just collecting more anger in your mind. The imprints that anger leaves on your consciousness simply reinforce your tendency to respond to situations with more anger. But not allowing it to come out doesn't mean that you are suppressing it, bottling it up. That's also dangerous. You have to learn to investigate the deeper nature of anger, aggression, anxiety, or whatever it is that troubles you. When you look into the deeper nature of negative energy, you'll see that it's really quite insubstantial, that it's only mind. As your mental expression changes, the negative energy disappears, digested by the wisdom that understands the nature of hatred, anger, aggression, and so forth."

Needing a Voice for Your Needs

I have come to the conclusion that anger often arises because your needs require a voice. When anger is calmly expressed as needs and requests for change, meaningful communication can occur. Communicating your needs is important, but if you do so in anger, the other person will likely become defensive and retaliate. Then you may find yourself in a more difficult situation. The other options are to let go of the issue, change your expectations, forgive, practice mindfulness, or simply walk away from the situation.

The Need for an Apology

Often you may trick yourself into thinking that the only way you can resolve your anger is to receive an apology. While an apology often helps, if the person you are expressing your needs to does not listen or does not adjust their behavior, you end up remaining angry and possibly getting angrier unless you look at your unmet needs. You will also end up with a greater degree of anger if the other person becomes defensive or even retaliates rather than listens.

Anger and "Who You Remind Me Of"

Resolving anger often demands that you develop new insights or change your expectations of the other person or organization. Perhaps it may require that you adjust your own behavior. Or, it may require you to consider that your anger may be out of proportion to the actual event due to your unresolved issues. For example, you may transfer anger towards a person when they remind you of someone else with whom you are angry. This type of transference occurs with other feelings as well, but more frequently occurs with anger. In a situation like this, you need to step back and observe your own issues. You need to gain insight as to why you are really angry with this person or if the anger seems unreasonable. Your anger may be part transference and at the same time, also be a reaction to someone's inappropriate behavior. Develop the art of discernment.

Anger Expression Styles and the State-Trait Anger

It is also a good idea to gain an understanding of your anger expression style, as your expression style can have a major impact on your health and well-being. An anger-in style is defined as anger directed inward or suppressed. "Anger-out" is defined as expressed, as directed outward away from yourself and possibly towards others. "Anger control" refers to the ability to control anger feelings. The "reflective anger" style involves considering the cause of that anger. A person with "trait anger" has a tendency to frequently experience anger. Anger expression styles can either be constructive or destructive, depending on the situation. In a study of grade school children, children who used the reflective style had fewer instances of rage and trait anger, while the high users of anger-out style had the highest trait anger for all grade levels. Anger expression is linked to interpersonal conflicts, negative self-perception, and decreased self-esteem. Anger-out has been linked to somatic complaints and unhealthy behaviors. While anger can temporarily make you feel stronger, anger-in has been linked to long-term emotional inexpressiveness. Your anger style may not always be consistent. You may vary according to who you are angry with, using one anger style with a spouse or close relationship, another with someone in authority, or another still with someone to whom you are not close.

Anger styles obviously have an impact on your relationships. For example, it has been shown that the constant use of the anger-out style can damage your love life even twenty years later, while an anger-in style is known to cloud relationships and dull emotions.

Developing a state of trait anger has, arguably, the most extensive ramifications. It is known to impact your cognitive abilities by promoting cognitive biases. If you have developed a higher trait anger state, you likely have a predisposition to more frequent anger and anger of longer duration. You may also be more ready to detect aggression, even when it is not there, leading to a sense of unintentional defensiveness. The evaluating of social situations in this manner has been identified as a predictor of anger, aggressive behavior, risk-taking, diminished self-control, road rage, and revenge.

While the reflective style seems preferable when compared to the other styles we have discussed, what you should be working towards is dissolving the anger. Doing this requires additional knowledge about the self, others, the nature of the provoking situations, and perhaps some acceptance and letting go.

The Four Pillars of Undoing the Anger Habit

Many people realize that their needs may be expressed without shouting or yelling. Once you start to yell and shout, the other person becomes defensive and effectively stops listening. Think of a time when someone has yelled at you. Do you listen carefully to each word he or she is saying? No, your listening skills are turned off almost immediately when someone yells at you. By speaking in a firm, self-respecting, and confident tone, you emphasize what you are trying to get across, and the other person is more likely to listen. Once voice levels start to rise, the other person usually responds in the same manner until you are in a shouting match in which no one wins. By keeping your voice calm and not matching someone else's yelling, you can effectively communicate your thoughts and feelings.

Once you have expressed your needs, you will usually uncover the hurt that created the anger in the first place. This hurt will usually manifest itself as sadness that can be released through acceptance, writing, and crying. Remember that anger does not need to be acted upon. It only needs to be acknowledged and to have its energy dissipated through changes in your thinking and expectations.

A perspective that I have worked on developing is that if I am expressing anger negatively, then I am disrespectful with myself! This amazing lesson taught me to become more aware and to be more responsible. I try to be patient while driving and refrain from honking my horn, or "giving the finger," and getting upset at how everyone else is a bad driver!

Driving and other situations can help reflect back to you how centered and calm you have trained yourself to be. For a while, I was constantly noticing how resentful and angry I had become and how I was responding to challenging situations with complaining and negative behavior. I made a conscious effort to improve my attitude and exert more control over my reactions. I learned that there are four pillars to the development of non-angry behavior and put them into practice.

These four pillars are:

- Compassion
- Control
- Wisdom
- Cheerfulness

I know now that all four must be present: the first three begin with me and are more internal, while the fourth pillar, cheerfulness, is an external expression to others, so that my kind, compassionate attitude can be shared.

Let Go and Heal

To deepen my experience of this concept, I have utilized the auto-response training that was popular in the 1960s and 1970s. The auto-response training technique involves placing yourself in a desired state of mind and then associating a word or phrase with that state. When feeling challenged, impatient, or sensing a loss of kindness, I simply repeat to myself the phrase "CCWC" to remind myself of my practice of compassion, control, wisdom, and cheerfulness. The sense of calm, focus, and purpose returns instantly!

In *Anger: Wisdom for Cooling the Flames*, Thich Nhat Hanh says that anger is like a fan that has just been turned off in that, even though there is no longer power, the fan keeps spinning. Eventually, though, it loses momentum and slows down. Our anger can be very similar to the energy of the fan blade: it may take some time for your body to recognize that you are no longer angry and cleanse yourself of the physiological remnants that anger generated.

Again, practicing firmness with compassion will prevent the development of an anger habit. However, like me, many have developed an anger habit. We need to resolve the fact that we are already angry, and our body has responded with muscle tension and chemical changes. I found this anger more difficult to deal with, but I learned that forgiveness and compassion were the tools that helped me. I had to recognize that when I responded to being betrayed by becoming angry about it, I had become a betrayer as well. My anger at people in my life was the result of an underlying judgment. By realizing that I had been betraying their goodness, too, and subsequently working to see the good in them and forgiving myself for betraying them, I was able to heal a great number of relationships.

I have learned that to heal anger, I must sever the injury from any contempt, recognizing the hurtful incident as ignorance, misunderstanding, fear, or passion. The way to end anger is to become wiser, to plan your thoughts and reactions, to not expect the other to change, to give love, to be kind and develop compassion, and see that in everyone else there is some good. Anger, if useful at all, is only useful if it is short-lived.

Changing Your Expectations

It is a fact of life that people often let us down. When this occurs, the untrained mind may feel disappointment, resentment, anger, or a range of other emotions. Although it is reasonable to expect people to keep appointments and promises, you must remember that others, being human, are subject to their own strengths and weaknesses. By continually placing expectations on others, you are likely to be more often disappointed and angry. This is especially true if your belief system and expectations do not allow for the occasional failure. To be happy, it is necessary to accept that there will be disappointments in your life. You cannot change others, but you can change yourself. You want to maintain standards in your friendships and relationships, but if your expectations are unreasonable, you are bound to end up disappointed at times unless you become more tolerant.

An example that comes to mind is the fact that I used to have an unreasonable expectation that friends would be around forever. It is a fact of life that people grow and, as a result, sometimes you outgrow your friends or your friends outgrow you. Because of my unreasonable expectations and my inability to let go, I found myself constantly fretting and getting angry over the friendships that had faded away. By recognizing the nature of these friendships and acknowledging that one or both of us had moved on, I was able to change my expectations and therefore reduce and eliminate my anger.

Healing Rage

If you have ever felt totally out of control and in a fit of anger done things that you would not normally do, you have experienced very strong rage. At the other end of the rage scale lies a chronic, underlying state of rage that makes it easy for issues to trigger anger, or even trigger depression if the rage is not acknowledged. Rage can manifest as an explosion of unexpressed anger, or an ongoing state of anger often referred to in psychological research literature as "high trait anger" and commonly captured by the description of a person who has "a very short fuse!"

In reviewing episodes of customer rage, researchers identified commonalities such as strong negative emotions, fury, wrath, disgust, contempt, scorn, and resentment. Feelings of being cornered and out of control were present. Rage was often manifested through physical, verbal, nonverbal, and displaced expression. The displaced expression occurs when anger is taken out on people who have no connection to what caused the anger. These anger expressions were harmful to all involved. In an attempt to prevent the infliction of such harm on their employees, some call centers have installed voice measurement software to detect significant levels of anger in customers so that appropriate interventions can be used to calm down callers.

In searching for studies and journal articles using the keyword "rage," I discovered there was actually very little information on the topic. I found this surprising since rage is one of the most damaging states of being for relationships and for society. It is the emotional state that we rarely admit to.

While completing my training for my master's degree in counseling psychology, we participated in counseling sessions with other students. The sessions were videotaped, and we would view them in class. I certainly felt vulnerable during the times that my sessions were being viewed by other students as my classmates got to see a side of me that I rarely showed. Our teacher would provide comments about what was going on at a deeper level, and she commented that underneath my calm demeanor was an underlying rage. For years I did not understand what she meant, but finally, with some personal exploration and understanding, I was able to see what she had observed.

My search for information about how to deal with rage left me empty-handed until I discovered Ruth King's book *Healing Rage: Women Making Inner Peace Possible*. In this book, Ruth King describes the concept of an inner rage child. This is a distinct inner child who is having a temper tantrum, wants to be acknowledged, listened to, heard, and calmed down. The first step in dealing with inner rage is to acknowledge the existence of this inner rage child. By acknowledging my own inner rage child's existence, I could move to the next stage of talking to this little child and having a conversation with him or her. I was able to calm the child down by listening to the child's concerns and imagining the energy being calmed.

Using this process could calm my mind and emotions whenever I found myself in a strong emotional state. Of course, the first step in calming anger was to acknowledge the anger, and I could easily do this once I had learned to be my own observer. I would enhance the rage healing process by utilizing the Buddhist purification exercise of having the inner rage child breathe in black air and breathe out pure white air.

Instead of shunning rage, you can refrain from acting on it. You can acknowledge its existence, treat it like a child, and give the inner rage child the empathy and understanding that he or she so badly needs.

Anger Resolution Exercises

Jump Forward in Time

This exercise comes from Rebbe Nachman, an eighteenth-century teacher of Kabbalah mysticism and founder of the Hasidic movement. He suggests, "When you feel yourself getting angry, stop! Imagine yourself as having already exploded, and you now feel wasted. For that's what happens when you are angry. Your soul leaves you. Do this, and your anger is sure to dissolve."

Breath Purification Exercise

At times when I am angry, I have found that meditation has helped reduce my anger. I imagine breathing in a dark coal color of air and breathing out white light. The breathing in the coal-colored air acknowledges your anger while breathing out white light transforms it. I have found this exercise to be extremely helpful in calming anger (even calming rage, which I discuss later in this chapter) and regaining control of my emotions. This exercise is a powerful de-escalation exercise that helps transform anger into more positive energy.

In many cases, the root of anger comes from your frustration in your desire to love and be loved. Through this purification, you can connect with your deeper desires. Remember, anger is usually a secondary emotion resulting from unmet needs.

Let Go and Heal

Give Your Anger to Nature

A Native American exercise to dispel anger energy is to go to a riverbank and pick up six small rocks. In quick succession, throw the rocks out into the water as hard as you can, imagining the anger energy leaving your body with each rock. Watch the river cleanse and wash away your anger in the ripples created by the splash of the rocks. It is a Native American tradition to speak to the earth to heal yourself. This is also reflected in the Bible in Job 12:8 – "[S]peak to the earth, and it will teach you."

Practice Random Acts of Kindness

If you learn to take the emphasis off yourself and have compassion for others, you can reduce your anger. I remember a friend telling me how a person she was driving with was in a very angry mood. As he pulled up to an intersection, a squeegee kid ran up to the car. He rolled down his window, and instead of yelling at the kid as my friend thought he would, he gave the kid a couple of bucks. Turning to my friend, he said: "It's amazing what a charitable deed can do for your spirit!" My friend said that he was calm and relaxed for the rest of the trip.

Regain Control

Should you be in a situation where you find yourself very angry, it is important to tame the anger by lowering its energy level. There are two techniques I can recommend. The first is to breathe deeply. When filled with anger, your breathing is usually quickened, shallow, and in the upper chest, or in some cases, you may completely restrict your breathing. Breathing is one of the easiest things to control. By slowing your breathing and breathing deeply into your belly while telling yourself to relax, you can give yourself a few moments to regain control, process the anger, and think about a calm response.

The second method is to imagine your anger as a man running. You can imagine the man gradually slowing down his pace, to the point where he is walking, and then eventually have him sit down and meditate. This mental exercise has been very helpful in calming both my thoughts and emotions.

Express Your Energy through Creativity

On a day that I felt particularly frustrated and angry, I sat down at my electronic piano, put the headphones on, and called up all the percussion sounds I could find. My keyboard became a complete drum set through which I could make lots of sound and noise, and express my anger and frustration. It is now rather humorous, but I remember as a teenager being asked by a counselor how I let out my frustrations. I replied, "I use my drum set." All of a sudden, he became very quiet and serious and said: "Are you planning to use it on anyone?" I looked at him rather quizzically and said, "Well, I plan to make some noise, you know, like bang, bang!" He seemed to become even more perturbed and said: "Are you thinking of using them on yourself?" By now, I thought he was really acting strange. I sarcastically replied, "What? Hit myself over the head with a drum?" Immediately he slumped in his chair with a look of total relief as he exclaimed, "Drum set? I thought you said gun set!" It took a few moments for him to recompose himself! He stopped looking at the phone as if he was anxiously preparing to call the police to report me!

Obviously, there is humor in the above story, but, sadly, some people do resort to violence, thinking it will resolve their anger. In their clouded state of mind, they have rationalized that their actions will bring about change. It never works that way. They end up leaving a trail of people victimized and traumatized by their actions, and no healing occurs. Find a safe way to deal with your emotions. Never harm any person, any animal, or anything through your expression of anger.

Reclaim Your Soul

A helpful exercise to regain a sense of control, reduce victimization, and strengthen your sense of self is to perform a ritual or a visualization in which you recover the parts of your soul you feel you have lost from those who have harmed you. It is not necessarily a physical exercise, but is spiritual in nature. Simply close your eyes and imagine yourself feeling grounded in your body. Imagine traveling to the place where one of these people is and imagine yourself spiritually recovering what you lost. Wish them well, and then return to your present moment and place. Sense the renewal in your body!

Let Go and Heal

Change Your Reaction and Behavior

In many cases, anger arises from not accepting "what is." When our needs are not met, the combined frustration leads to resentment and more frustration. At a talk by vegetarian author John Robbins, I was deeply moved by the words of a man in the audience who spoke of his anger as "love with no place to go." His wife had divorced him and had started a relationship with a new man. She had custody of their children. He described how he admitted to himself that he was angry because he missed his sense of family. He decided to let go of the relationship and communicated to his ex-wife that he accepted the divorce and that she was now with a new partner. He forgave her and expressed his wish for her to be happy. In the end, he became friends with all of them, and the flowing nature of his love was restored. By practicing forgiveness and acceptance, he gained a larger family to love.

Separate the Person from the Event

One of the most difficult sources of anger for me to forgive was anger that arose from an injury that caused a great deal of physical pain. A friend jokingly stomped on my foot, causing painful arthritis in the joint that lasted for over a year. Every day I was reminded of the pain, yet had to learn to forgive in some way. It was easy to forgive on one level, but on a deeper level, it required a constant effort, even though my friend had apologized. The difficulty came from the fact that, although she had apologized, I was still suffering. I realized that when my foot hurt, a picture of her would pop into my head, and I would feel anger towards her. It became much easier to deal with my anger as I learned to visualize the event as being separate from her. I imagined a cloud forming over her that represented the event. The cloud then moved away from her, allowing rays of sunshine to illuminate her in love. I would visualize the cloud floating off, and dissolving into a distant rainstorm, nurturing the plants and animals. This meditation has helped me to understand that anger results from the event, but it turns to resentment when it is directed at a person. I now believe that there are no justifiable resentments. Love the person, but challenge the behavior.

Mark Linden O'Meara

Learn to Listen Deeply without Judgment

My healing process has helped me to increase my ability to love unconditionally the people who trigger me the most and to understand that I may have incorrectly assumed that others are conscious of what they are doing. I often quote to myself the words attributed to Jesus: "Forgive them, Father, for they know not what they do." Instead of reacting angrily, first, try to understand what it would be like to be in the other person's shoes. By understanding how someone would come to take such an action, you will be able to respond firmly and challenge inappropriate behavior, yet in a manner that is calm and tactful.

20. Healing with Creativity

"I've hundreds of things to say, but my tongue just can't manage them, so I'll dance them for you."
– Nikos Kazantzakis, Zorba the Greek

My own healing journey would not have been possible without the writing, singing, dancing, drawing, and drumming that I did to express my feelings. Of course, at times, speaking with a counselor was also integral to my growth, as it provided an opportunity to reflect and examine my worldview. In counseling, your therapist becomes a witness to your process and facilitates your growth. Both counseling and expressiveness are valuable, and one should be neither encouraged nor discouraged over the other.

In my own counseling training, we were encouraged to use tools that helped the client. In some cases, a block of clay was provided for the client to mold. I was amazed at how some clients would create beautiful images while talking, seemingly unaware of how their hands were creating metaphors for their inner world. I distinctly remember one client shaping the clay into a vulnerable newborn while talking about herself, yet changing the clay into a round metallic-like cylinder when talking about her mother. Examining the perspective that her mother had also been a vulnerable child at one time opened new pathways to healing for this individual.

In using the expressive arts, you can come to realize that you do not have to be a professional artist or musician to show your gifts for being creative, although you may be surprised to find a hidden talent. Though many have been discouraged, many have also persevered in recovering their artistic abilities. Gradually as you create, you learn to become vulnerable and to share your thoughts, works, poems, and voice. The process of writing and sharing this book began with baby steps of writing a few words, taking singing lessons, then eventually sharing my creativity.

Musical Expression

Musical expression can be very helpful in the release of emotional energy. In *Care of the Soul*, Thomas Moore writes: "One of my own forms of expression is to play the piano in times of strong emotion. I remember well the day Martin Luther King, Jr., was killed. I was so overwhelmed that I went to the piano and played Bach for three hours. The music gave form and voice to my scrambled emotions, without explanations and rational interpretations."

As reported by Judith Ginzberg in *In Search of a Voice: Working with Homeless Men*, music, ritual, and dance can help the men to enhance self-esteem, establish trust, reduce tension, and promote group interaction.

As a singer myself, I have often noticed how singing lifts my spirits. Many singers claim that they often experience a singer's "buzz" – a sense of joy and elation from singing. At one point, I participated in a sound healing workshop with Jonathan Goldman that focused on overtone singing. Overtone singing involves concentrating the sound you make to generate overtones in the resonance cavities in your head. Anyone who has taken singing lessons will know that it isn't just the vocal cords that determine a sound, but also the muscle tension, sinus cavities, nasal cavities, mouth, and throat that greatly influence the sound you make and that others hear. In this workshop, we were taught how to make the overtones. While practicing overtoning, I experienced an incredible sense of joy. It was so strong that I felt I was becoming ungrounded and had to stop. Jonathan came to me and asked why I had stopped, and I explained what was happening. He instructed me to send the energy through the roof of my head, which allowed me to continue.

I often do a minute or two of overtoning in the shower in the morning. It is surprising how quickly it raises my energy level. When you think of it, the sound bouncing around in the cavities produces waves of vibration. It has been theorized that cats purr because it generates a frequency of sound waves that promote bone strength and healing. Perhaps the sound waves being generated are stimulating the amygdala or some other part of the brain that promotes healing, thereby explaining the unbridled joy I experienced in the workshop and the boost of energy.

Let Go and Heal

Keep in mind that you do not have to be a professional musician or singer to enjoy these benefits. The key is to accept whatever sounds you make without judgment. I have often found that I could relax a great deal simply by playing whatever came to mind on my guitar. As the famous Beatles' song goes: "While my guitar gently weeps."

For many, the artistic world is what keeps people connected and sane. Musician Bill Henderson writes:

> "When I was young, I was very shy and had a rough time talking to people… there can be heavy duty pressure in school when you are growing up. Music was the only way that I could communicate with the world that actually worked. Music saved my life. When you create music, you are finding something that makes you feel better, and when you give that to someone, it's a wonderful thing. It helps our culture become saner. The artist's viewpoint is one our society needs more of."

A comment added by Dave DeHaan to an article on Facebook describes the importance of expression through music. He wrote:

> "I was around 3, my father had just died, and one of the people who came over to pay their respects gave me a plastic trumpet. I made noise, I 'expressed' my feelings in that noise and I've been doing it ever since. Then and now, I have my own 'language' and connection to the world through my music, and I feel more 'real' because of it."

Even if you do not play a musical instrument, the listening process can have powerful effects on your mood. Listening to music can increase or decrease your heart rate, dilate your pupils, raise your body temperature, redirect blood to your legs, and stimulate the part of your brain that controls body movement. The brain is good at listening and anticipating peak moments in music, causing dopamine release. Studies have shown that familiar music, i.e., when we know what comes next, can evoke the most powerful chills, and that sad music actually evokes positive emotions. Make sure you have a playlist ready and restore yourself with music!

Express Your Traits and Talents

While not everyone feels a calling to become a singer or musician, it is important to discover your own medium for expressing your soul's nature. This can be done through your hobbies, through your career, or even through your family life. We long to enrich people's lives. In reading the next few pages, try to think of what you would like to do to express yourself. Try a few new things. Sing in your car! Buy a sketch pad and some crayons, or buy a children's drawing app for your phone or tablet. Learn to play and express yourself again! Creative activity has been demonstrated to positively impact the experience of recovery and has indirect and direct effects on performance-related outcomes. The more you engage in creative activities, the more likely you will be able to come up with creative solutions in other areas of your life, both at home and at work.

While much of the research on creative expression has focused on the arts, it is important to express your traits. In career counseling, you may have encountered the concept of Holland Codes. As discussed earlier, these categories of work were developed by John Holland in the early 1970s and have helped many people understand their career choices. You will recall that there are six codes in total. Usually, the top three are listed in an individual's profile. The codes are R: Realistic (Do-er), I: Thinkers (Investigative), A: Artistic (Creators), S: Social (Helpers), E: Enterprising (Persuaders), and C: Conventional (Organizers).

My top three Holland Codes are SAR: Social, Artistic, and Realistic, which meant that as a programmer analyst, I was missing out on my top two codes of Social and Artistic. Switching from programming to teaching meant greater career satisfaction because I was now utilizing all of my traits. Expressing myself through activities such as creating funny videos, writing, and recording songs greatly increased my happiness.

Understanding your Holland Codes helps you discover how you can express yourself. Some people are helpers, persuaders, and organizers. Following through on these traits might mean organizing social groups, volunteering and mentoring, or serving on a committee. Being a connector of people may give a great deal of satisfaction. Painting, renovating, or fixing things may give the same satisfaction that the artist experiences in creating a painting. I recommend reading *What Color Is Your Parachute?* by Richard Bolles to discover more about your world of work and enjoyment. Keep in mind that satisfying your traits does not have to be your choice of work, but could be a hobby or passion afterwork hours. You can also change your attitude about your work, making your goal to serve people, or to create the best work for someone to enjoy at a later time.

Discover Hidden Talents

In times of healing, many people rediscover a talent they have abandoned. Others may discover a talent they never knew they had. In many high schools, we see a great deal of artistic talent that falls by the wayside upon graduation. Perhaps it may be time to try things you always wanted to or were afraid to do.

In reading *The Importance of Living* by Lin Yutang, I learned that in the 1600s, three Chinese brothers started a school called the "School of *Hsingling*." Lin writes:

> "*Hsingling* translates to self-expression, but in the true sense, it means *hsing* 'personal nature,' and *ling* 'soul' or 'vital spirit.' The School of Self-Expression demands that we express our own thoughts and feelings, our genuine loves, genuine hatred, genuine fears, and genuine hobbies. These will be expressed without any attempt to hide the bad from the good, without fear of being ridiculed by the world and without fear of contradicting the ancient sages or contemporary authorities."

The key to immersing yourself in the creative arts is to accept whatever you create and avoid judging it as good or bad. You may wish to start your own "School of Self-Expression," where you are both the teacher and the student! Taking up knitting, gardening, painting, or even volunteering your time can lead to a greater degree of self-satisfaction.

Artistic Expression

Pablo Picasso was quoted as saying that "art washes away the dust of daily living from the soul." Art of any form has been known for ages to have tremendous healing powers when used to express the feelings and creative center of the artist. In referring to artists, we wish to include all forms of art – dancing, music, painting, sculpting, or any other form of expression. When using art as a healing medium, it is important to create expressive art. If you place an object on a table and paint it, the exercise of painting will be relaxing but not as healing as using a canvas or other medium to express your feelings and emotions.

One of the greatest healing tools is a sketch pad and a package of crayons, or an Ipad with a drawing app. You can draw the emotions you are feeling by picking colors that represent the emotions you are experiencing. Shade in areas of the paper to express your emotions. You might add in lighter colors such as yellow and sky blue to express more joyous states. You can create two or three drawings, resulting in a progression of expression that would lead to healing the emotions. This technique reduces stress because it externalizes the emotions you are feeling.

Dance and Drama

A common saying is to "dance like no one is watching," but a true measure of how comfortable you are with your self-expression is how you feel when you dance when someone *is watching*!

Artistic expression is, of course, not limited to the visual arts. Meditation, visualization, chanting (a form of meditation in some cultures), role-playing, and dance can all play an important role in the healing process.

Lou Heber, in a study entitled *Dance Movement: A Therapeutic Program for Psychiatric Clients*, presented findings that, when using dance therapy, patients reported an increase in self-esteem. Fern Leventhal and Meg Chang, in "Dance/Movement Therapy with Battered Women: A Paradigm of Action," concluded that "by motivating female victims of domestic violence to act, dance/movement therapy addresses patterns of helplessness, ambivalence, and inactivity. Dance/movement interventions help women (and men) internalize a positive self-concept as well as gain physical and emotional control." Dancing is also known to help people with mild or moderate depression improve their moods, while improvisational dancing, in particular, is known to help people break out of rigid patterns of thinking and promote creativity.

Keep a Diary or Journal

Writing can be a great way to release emotional tension and promote healing. Even the *Journal of Experimental Psychology* supports the notion that journaling can improve your health and psychological well-being. It is a great technique that helps clear the mind of its cobwebs by getting thoughts out of your head and onto paper where you can look at them more objectively. If you are afraid of someone reading your writing, find a safe place for your journal, or keep it under lock and key if that helps. Writing out your thoughts may seem strange at first, but with practice, it will become easier and easier. Most of you wish you could faithfully keep a journal, but realistically, few do. Simply be content to write whenever you feel like doing so. It is unwise to create an expectation of writing faithfully. Be content with whatever and whenever you write.

Writing also has a second benefit as it allows you to look back and measure progress over weeks, months, or years, noting the issues you have resolved. If an issue is still in your mind, you can continue to work on it. Problems are often resolved and forgotten. The absence of a problem needs to be acknowledged as a success. Go out and purchase a journal. Pick one that has a cover that you like. Many stationery stores carry books with empty pages. Even if you do not plan to write today, purchase a journal so that it will be ready for you when you are ready. In journaling, try to describe what happened, how you feel about what happened, what you would like to have occurred differently, and what you need now.

Write Letters of Letting Go

There are times when you would like to express yourself to someone, yet conversations don't always go the way you want them to. You may also find that the other person will not listen, or perhaps they are no longer around you to hear the communication: they may be miles away, you may not even know their address, or they may have passed away.

Too often, you have unfinished business with someone and need closure. What you want to communicate may vary from relationship to relationship. You may be angry and hurt, or you may wish to tell someone that you love them but never have. Writing a letter to that person can help you express your feelings and give closure, even if you don't send it.

More often than not, you never end up sending the letter, but, like keeping a diary or writing your story, writing a letter is an excellent way to get your thoughts and feelings out of your head. It helps greatly if you write the letter using the words "I feel…" in the letter rather than the finger-pointing "You…"

Whether you ever send the letter is not important. What is important is the expression and release of your feelings. You can write the letter and then, with a clearer head, decide whether to send it or not. Keep in mind that the purpose of writing a letter is to provide a release for your thoughts and emotions, not to try to change someone else's thinking or behavior. What seems to be unfinished emotional business with someone is often an indication that you need to face something in yourself.

Write and Rewrite Your Story

One of the most powerful writing tools available is to write your story and then edit it, expanding your version of what occurred. We often get stuck in a narrative of what happened in the past. Writing it down can help you see how you view the event. Stepping back and seeing the story on paper, you can begin to revise your wording to shift your focus. This kind of writing has been known to improve health, but only if the content of your writing expresses your emotions. In one study, those who wrote about their thoughts and emotions around job loss found employment more quickly than those who wrote about untroubling issues, or those who did not write at all. Problems evoke strong and challenging emotions. Putting pen to paper seems to help focus the emotional energy and extract common themes and personal meaning. Writing about emotional topics has even led to fewer visits to the doctor, improved immune function, and lowered heart rate.

Rewriting your story with a focus on changing the story from negative to positive can be healing, empowering, and result in cognitive change.

Let Go and Heal

The following prompt has been used in numerous studies and can guide your writing. This process requires people to write for fifteen to thirty minutes, on each of three to five consecutive days:

> "For the next X days, I would like for you to write about your very deepest thoughts and feelings about an extremely important issue that has affected you and your life. In your writing, I'd like you to really let go and explore your very deepest emotions and thoughts. You might tie your topic to your relationships with others, including parents, lovers, friends, or relatives; to your past, your present, or your future; or to who you have been, who you would like to be, or who you are now. You may write about the same general issues or experiences on all days of writing or on different topics each day. All of your writing will be completely confidential. Don't worry about spelling, sentence structure, or grammar. The only rule is that once you begin writing, continue to do so until your time is up."

In my own inner work, I have found that sometimes I needed to tell a particular story more than once. I would suggest that there are different stages of telling a story, and therefore going through it a few times may be helpful, especially for more traumatic events. The first time you tell your story, simply acknowledge the event. The second time, you may be more ready to acknowledge your feelings and emotions. As you become more aware of the emotions and can express them, you may want to begin to talk about the impact and consequences of the event. From this point, you can move into an evaluation phase where you look at all perspectives. Finally, you can develop a new paradigm and integrate the story into your personal history.

Although many people do benefit from writing, only do it if it feels comfortable and is bringing about benefits. In one study, when people wrote about their trauma, their anxiety increased. The writing was not helpful for those who were not accustomed to being emotionally open and increased their risk for PTSD. A few years ago, I took The Artist's Way course in which we were expected to write for about fifteen minutes each morning. I was going through a very difficult time and found that the free flow of thoughts onto the pages actually increased my level of depression. The course and book were still very beneficial, but I realized that writing the morning pages was not for me. It was helpful to know that, as mentioned, there is research that backs this up. Again, while most people benefit from this process, it is important to recognize that not every healing practice is beneficial to everyone. Sharing thoughts that have never been expressed can help relieve a heavy heart, but we need to be aware of what works and what doesn't.

Create Poetry

While I am more inclined to write in my journal or to write stories, I have met many people who can communicate far better through poetry. Like a painting or piece of music, poetry can express deep feelings, wishes, and desires, or anger. Yet poetry can present your thoughts in images with rhythm, metaphors, and in some cases, a wry wit. Try it! You never know what you will come up with! During a period of creativity, numerous poems in the form of prayers came to me that led to the creation of my book *Prayers and Meditations for Daily Inspiration*. This book is a collection of prayers drawn from various sources from around the world and includes about forty prayers that I wrote myself as I was inspired on my journey to create the collection. I also discovered my ability later in life to write and edit song lyrics. In high school English class, we were required to write poetry based on a set of rules. I found this blocked my creativity as every poem was analyzed based on rhyme and rhythm rather than creativity and expressiveness. When writing poetry, you can do so without rules, allowing your mind to freely express what you are feeling, thinking, and sensing, without any judgment.

Read Fiction

You may find that getting absorbed into a book is a great way to relax and improve your sleep and well-being. Reading fiction allows you to expand your experience of imaginary situations, and research shows that this helps create new mental models with which to try out ideas. In a test designed to measure empathy, readers of fiction scored higher than nonreaders. In measurements of social reasoning, short story readers scored highest. Another study showed that the exposure to literature decreased the need for closure while, finally, another demonstrated that the more emotion a person experienced while reading, the more they changed in character traits and personality. Fiction opens up new possibilities.

Write the Letter You Would Like to Receive

Along with writing letters that you may never send, you may wish to write the letter that you would like to receive from people you are no longer in contact with. The letter you write could be the words of an apology you wish for or the words that you need to hear to obtain closure and let go. After writing the letter, you can read it back to yourself and have a ceremony of completion.

Create a Vision Board

Gathering magazines, pictures, pens, and paper to create a collage of what you desire and hope for is a powerful exercise to help you visualize your goals. Cut out pictures and words that remind you of a healthy life and arrange them on a piece of poster board. This is a great exercise in creativity that fosters images of hope and direction.

Create Ceremonies of Completion and Letting Go

In some cases, it may not be possible to send the letter you have written, and often you may not want to. Keeping the letter in a drawer can result in a lack of closure or a sense of holding on. To complete the unfinished business, you can have your own ceremony of completion. By ripping the letter, shredding it, or burning it safely in a fireplace, while saying a phrase to yourself such as "I let go," you can create completion for yourself.

Talk to an Empty Chair

It is often very healing to place an empty chair in front of you and imagine that the person you wish to communicate with is sitting in that chair. Proceeding to tell them exactly what you would like to say to them and how you are feeling is a technique often used in therapy. Your mind will become clearer through this opportunity to express yourself. The next step is to imagine hearing them say what you would like to hear from them to help you heal.

Graveyard Visits – When Someone Is No Longer with You

Many of us have lost family members or friends. Again, you may have unfinished business. In some cases, you may want to express your love; in other cases, you may want to express your anger over their leaving. Just because someone has passed on does not mean that you should not be angry with him or her. Going to a graveyard and saying what you want to say can be a tremendously healing experience. Dr. Wayne Dyer described how going to his father's grave and expressing his anger, disappointment, and forgiveness was a catalyst in creating his highly successful book, *Your Erroneous Zones*. Go to a graveyard and say the things you want to say. Remember to forgive!

Make Use of Emotional Movies and Other Media

Often you can bring about healing tears by making use of emotional movies or music. If you find that some sentimental movie, a piece of music, or a poem helps you to cry, then, by all means, use it. Sometimes all you need is a little extra help to get the release started. Sometimes a movie or song will trigger a memory or release for reasons that may be unknown to you. Seize the moment as an opportunity to let go and be free of whatever has been bottled up. Keep a box of tissue handy and let go! I clearly remember a time when some painful memories were triggered while watching a movie with a friend. I became aware of a deep-rooted sense of loneliness and pain that had long been forgotten. I asked my friend to stop the tape, and she held me as I cried. As I took deep breaths, the crying came from deep within my chest. I could feel a knot of energy being released from deep inside of me. Although painful and exhausting, I had acknowledged a deep sense of pain that my friend reflected back to me when she said, "You've really been hurt." After resting, I felt a sense of calmness and serenity, and a stronger connection with my friend for supporting me through this.

On the other hand, remember that you can also use various forms of entertainment to help you laugh.

Let Go and Heal

Visualize a Different Outcome

Creative visualization is a powerful technique that can help you move into the type of lifestyle you wish to have. It can also help you develop a more positive attitude and assist you in the development of a sense of competence and serenity in dealing with others.

There is some sound wisdom in the words "whatever you tell yourself and believe is then true for you." Using techniques of visualization, you can work on your beliefs and begin to train your mind to operate with new beliefs about yourself. Visualize yourself as being successful, and so you will become. If you imagine yourself being relaxed around others, you will likely become that way. There are numerous books on creative visualization, meditation, and affirmations. You may even want to create your own affirmations!

The Birth Order Exercise

A wonderful technique for promoting understanding of family issues and discovering the humanness of your parents and family members is to guide yourself through the following exercise. Imagine your parents as they were when they met. Imagine the conditions they were living under when they married. Go on and imagine what it would have been like if you had been born in the order you wish you had been born. With each birth, imagine the circumstances and stresses on the family. Then imagine the way it actually happened. What were your parents' emotional states? What would the state of each of the other family members be? The purpose of the exercise is not to release others from responsibility for their actions, but to gain a better understanding of what your parents were dealing with while you were being raised.

Draw Your Life Timeline

As an exercise to help you understand yourself better, try drawing a timeline of your life so far, from your birth to the present. Include major events as well as the things you did each year. It is also helpful to map your happiness level at each stage in your life, as well as your spiritual satisfaction, emotional health, and community.

Cultural and Religious Healing Practices

Except for Native American people, North Americans belong to one of the few cultures that lack healing ceremonies. Native Americans practice and participate in various healing rituals such as sweat lodges and talking circles. As a participant of a healing circle, I was invited to partake in a sweat lodge, which is a very spiritual and sacred ritual, led by an elder. While I remained skeptical about the possibility of experiencing a vision as others had described, I was open to receiving guidance in this sacred ceremony. Participating in a sweating ceremony involves going into a covered dome that represents the mother's womb. In the ceremony, rocks (heated in their own ritual by a fire maintained by a designated fire keeper) are brought into the sacred space. Fully describing the depth and sacredness of this ceremony is beyond my ability, but I can describe the beautiful message I received from images that appeared to me during this ceremony! At one point, the image of a wolf placing its head in the palm of my hand and looking up to me vividly entered my mind. What struck me was the look of the wolf's submissive eyes. A moment later, the same wolf reappeared, staring deeply and lovingly at me at eye level, conveying a sense of equality between myself and others. Improving my self-esteem by beginning to live among others as an equal was a key lesson I needed to learn and begin practicing! I was very thankful, grateful, and humbled by this experience.

Other cultures have numerous beliefs and practices that promote healing. Various religions have services that are related to healing. Learn more about what your culture or religion may have to offer you. Again, your healing is a personal adventure, so what you choose may be different than that selected by another. Discover what works for you while respecting the traditions of others.

Research Your Family Tree

Researching my family tree has provided me with a greater understanding of my roots and what my parents and grandparents experienced. It can give you a sense of the large clan, beyond your immediate family, to which you belong. The Internet has made searching easier and the resources of The Church of Jesus Christ of Latter-day Saints provides access to numerous databases of genealogical information. In researching my family tree, I discovered that my father had lost his father unexpectedly at the age of twenty-one. I learned that his parents lost their parents early as well, and one of my great-grandmothers lost her husband when her children were only four and seven. On this side of the family, several children died young. All of this provided me with a greater sense of compassion for these people who had endured a tremendous amount of suffering and helped me to understand some of the key events that shaped their lives. This type of research can also help you to forgive your parents as you come to better understand their circumstances.

Let Your Healing Be Personal

Your path is unique and belongs to only you. There are many things each of us shares, but your circumstances are unique in some way. Your healing process is the same. What works for someone else may not be what you would choose. Some of you are artists, while some are writers. Some may use massage, while some may use alternative methods. Learn to share with others and to listen, but develop your own set of tools for healing. You are unique, and you can develop a sense of what works for you.

Mark Linden O'Meara

Part 4 – Transforming Your Life

21. Invoking Personal Power

Developing a Healthy Attitude

As I began exploring the ideas for the contents of this chapter, I came across a tattered sheet of paper that my father had typed out years before. It was a summary of his notes on character formation and developing a happy disposition. My healing felt complete as I acknowledged the source of my notes for this topic being guided by the help of my long-deceased father. As I reviewed his notes, and also studied the works of Emmet Fox, founder of the Unity movement, I formed a picture of the concepts that I needed to learn myself, as well as how they should be presented in this book.

While I had shied away from solely pursuing positive thinking as a healing method, I have learned that the power of a healthy outlook has profound effects on health, both mental and physical. There is a subtle difference between positive thinking and a healthy attitude. With positive thinking, the negatives are often ignored and go unacknowledged. With a healthy attitude, you can acknowledge what appears to be negative, while keeping a vision of positive outcomes in your mind, and instilling hope for a better future. With a healthy attitude, you eventually acknowledge the negative things as gifts to help you learn.

Part of this healthy outlook is not only to be focused on yourself but also on the good of others. While others may disappoint you, and while you may be discouraged at times by any number of things, including events reported on the news, it is important to train your mind to be humble, kind, and diligent. It is easy when depressed and angry to resent others for their successes, to envy others, to become discouraged from working harder, or to solely see the dollars in work rather than the joy in serving. By being humble, kind, and diligent, you learn to stop finding fault in others and see their good qualities, to praise others rather than criticize them, and to stop attributing their actions to negative intentions you conjure up in your mind. If events of the past are healed, but you still continue to think and act in negative ways, you will not be modeling any kind of healing to others, nor will you be experiencing the benefits of healing work.

Finally, in developing an outlook, you need a sense of purpose. For this, I turn to the words of Emmet Fox, who writes:

> "There are certain key tasks in which we must attain at least some degree of mastery in this life if we are not to waste our time. These are:
> - Making personal contact with God.
> - Healing and regenerating our bodies and demonstrating health.
> - Getting control of ourselves and finding our true place.
> - Learning to handle other people, both wisely and justly.
> - Perfecting a technique for getting direct personal inspiration for a general or a specific purpose.
> - Letting go of the past completely.
> - Planning the future definitely and intelligently.
>
> To have made some real progress on each of these points, even though you may still be far short of mastery, is a true success. Of course, you will advance farther in some of these directions than in others, but some progress must be made in each of them."

These words of Emmet Fox can provide you with a sense of purpose and what to do during your lifetime. Easier said than done, but a great journey of discovery.

Accepting Personal Responsibility

Many times, I have observed people who strongly believe that they are solely responsible for mastering their reality and destiny, yet when things don't work out, they say, "It wasn't meant to be." They imply that a higher order of consciousness was responsible for it not happening, but take credit when things do work out. I have also observed people who are down and out claiming that what someone did to them has ruined their life, even though that event was long ago.

Which is the correct belief to follow? Should you follow the idea of 100 percent responsibility for creating your reality, or turn it all over to a higher power? Or at the other extreme, do you remain stuck in the role of victimization? I think we would all agree that the victimization platitude is not a viable option, leaving us with the first two aspects of the question. The answer is that it is both and neither. It is a process of co-creation in which you always try to do your best.

I remember a story I heard about the conflicts of Native American culture with the justice system. The story goes something like this: A judge told the defendant to be at the court on Tuesday at 9:00 a.m. The judge asked, "Will you be here?" to which the defended replied, "I'll do my best." This annoyed the judge because he wanted a 100 percent commitment from the defendant that he would appear before the court. The defendant was wiser than the judge because he knew that he could only do his best. There are things in life beyond our control that might interfere with the desire to be at the courthouse at 9:00 a.m. on Tuesday.

A wise person understands that there is a time for action and a time for just observing. Sometimes we can exert influence. At other times, having control is an illusion, and sometimes it is an illusion that we cannot control things. For example, many people think that once you find your calling, everything will begin to flow and become easier. Wise people know that things can often become more difficult. The illusion of overnight success is usually preceded by years of work and preparation.

A few months before the publication of this book, I set some personal goals that included playing my drums and guitar more and taking up the violin. Unfortunately, we had a flood in our apartment, and the flooring was damaged. While repairing the floor, I accidentally hit my left index finger really hard with a hammer; I had been momentarily distracted when my wife came around the corner of the hallway. My finger was badly injured and required numerous trips to doctors. At the time of the injury, I had just met a new friend to practice guitar with, and a guitar player I had just met when selling a drum throne had invited me over to play drums. All of these goals and opportunities fell through for at least the next couple of months. I experienced some disappointment, but with the wisdom I had gained, I accepted "what is." I let go of my immediate plans to play music and instead focused on writing. I did not ruminate on the lost opportunities, nor did I act like a victim. I believe that a key to happiness is being flexible with goals and intentions and letting go of outcomes. However, with my increased foundation of wisdom, next time, I will be far more attentive when using a hammer!

What Is Your Life Sentence?

The above section title has two possible meanings. The term "life sentence" normally refers to a lengthy punishment for a crime. "Life sentence" can also refer to a phrase, sentence, or statement you continually say to yourself that reflects your life beliefs. A "life sentence" statement often becomes your "life sentence" or determinant of pain or happiness. How you talk to yourself imprints on your subconscious. What you tell yourself ends up being a "life sentence," a prison term, or an empowering statement that promotes wellness, personal responsibility, a positive outlook, and the freedom to be happy regardless of what is going on around you. Be careful about choosing your phrase. With the power to choose new beliefs and a more positive outlook, you can change your destiny and, ultimately, your level of happiness. You can be released from the prison of your own mind's misgivings and faulty negative beliefs, leading to the freedom to help yourself and to help others!

Make up a "life sentence" or mantra such as "I bring about health, friendship, and abundance for myself and others" will do much more for your life than any grumbling about how your day is going.

It is your attitude and motives that seem to determine happiness, not the amount of money you have or the things that you have acquired. Some workaholics work excessively out of a desire to gain power, show off, and in general, overcome self-doubt and win at the game of social comparison. They are generally less happy than workaholics who work because they like the job they perform. The difference between the two groups is enthusiasm! Enthusiasm should be part of your life sentence! If it is lacking, try to nurture yourself and understand what can restore your enthusiasm. Choose to become passionate about something and develop a sense of curiosity. Both of these traits are known to lead to increased happiness. If you are too tired, perhaps rest is needed, but most often, it is attitude and what you tell yourself about your work and playtime that will restore you. If you get

Let Go and Heal

your energy moving by starting something and overcoming the initial inertia, the energy begins to flow and restores you.

Try developing a personal vision statement for yourself. It should be a statement that you can live up to on good days and bad days, and one that will help correct your outlook. It can change and evolve as you go through life and expand your knowledge and views. It may even grow into a paragraph, or you may have many life sentences that will help you correct your behavior, thinking, and emotions, and deal with challenges. Ultimately it will help you build better relationships. My friend Stephanie tells me: "Stay positive, it's your best defense and one of the things I've always admired you for." Practice the habit of using your imagination positively. Take risks, hope for something better, and expect miracles!

Giving Up the Victim Role

So many of us have, at times, been truly victimized. You did not ask for what you got, and although you may have tried to change things, you may have had limited success due to the enormity of the problem. Learned helplessness is a recognized pattern that develops when you are unable to effect solutions to a problematic situation. For many children, the ability to implement solutions to their problems is hampered and restricted by the behavior of the adults and the organizations around them. As a result, many adults carry around the belief that they cannot help themselves. You do not recognize that you can find your own voice and personal ability to change some aspects of your life. People who have been victimized sometimes remain in the role of victims. Some go so far as having a vested interest in being sad and being victimized, thereby becoming the perpetrators of their own unhappiness.

Here is a list of symptoms of being stuck in a victim role:

- Not taking responsibility for your present mental state
- Blaming others for your troubles
- Claiming your life was ruined by what happened
- Pretending to be powerless over your actions and reactions
- Resenting being made aware that you are playing the victim
- Unconsciously repeating the trauma on others through anger

- Feeling shame for the trauma happening
- Incorrectly believing you were responsible or the cause of the treatment
- Feeling that you are entitled to mistake-free treatment
- Constantly justifying your mood and anger
- Ruminating about the event and the people who harmed you
- Feeling powerless to take action or make decisions
- Reacting with a fight, freeze, or flight response

What goes along with being a victim is that you have been conditioned to not stand up for yourself. As I mentioned in the chapter on masks, my high school counselor, Mr. Arrand, told me, "You were clearly conditioned to not stand up for yourself." I had to work hard to undo that conditioning.

Moving from playing the victim role to being empowered involved accepting that I had been victimized in the past, but also accepting and taking responsibility for creating my own happiness. I acknowledged the difficulties I had been through but worked diligently to heal them and create happiness in my life.

Moving out of victimhood involves perspective-taking. I had two nasty whiplash injuries, but as a result, I ended up going to China numerous times for treatment. Those trips greatly enhanced my life through friendships, exposure to music that inspired some parodies, and many of the songs I've recorded. I recognize that, even though the childhood I experienced was painful, if it had not happened, I would never have developed the knowledge and insight to write this book.

Sometimes a life-changing event is needed to shock us out of our complacent reality and spur us on to growth. While driving down a street, a man darted out in a crosswalk causing all the cars to slam on the brakes. I was rear-ended. The man started laughing at the accident he had caused. Instead of yelling, I calmly in a loud voice asked the man, "Why would you find humor in someone else's suffering? Is that what you have become?" His jaw dropped, and he was clearly embarrassed by his behavior. The lady who rear-ended me apologized profusely. In some ways, I was grateful for the accident as I felt a "wake-up jolt" of energy that resulted in committing

Let Go and Heal

to a period of personal growth and change. Hopefully, you don't need a car accident to renew your commitment to healing and getting out of the victim role!

The time has come for you to break free from the narrow view of being an abused victimized person. You can expand to your true and full potential when you realize you still have the power of choice regarding how you react. No one can ever take the power of choice away from you!

When you give up the victim role, "How could you do this to me?" becomes, "How could you do this?"

"Freedom is what you do with what's been done to you."
– Jean-Paul Sartre

The Art of Self-Evaluation

"Most men would rather deny a hard truth than face it."
– George R.R. Martin

In learning about other cultures, I came across the Japanese practice of *hen sei*. While this has often been translated as "self-criticism," the correct translation is "self-evaluation." Children are taught from a very early age to reflect on their efforts and take note of their personal performance. A teacher may guide them in practice, but ultimately, it is up to the individual to figure out how they can improve. Another aspect of the practice is being humble. It is considered highly inappropriate to boast about one's achievements.

In North America and Europe, self-criticism is considered a sign of depression and poor mental health, yet in other cultures, it is considered a positive function. The difference lies in the fact that the Japanese self-evaluation is devoid of shame. As mentioned earlier, shame is a feeling you are a bad person. Self-evaluation holds no shame.

To be observant of your strengths and your weaknesses can be a powerful facilitator of personal growth. However, most likely, your defensiveness and fear of being shamed prevent you from evaluating your weaknesses. It takes emotional strength and vulnerability to evaluate yourself. It is important to be aware that your ego – your strong sense of identity – will often feel embarrassed and reactive when you are presented with feedback. You know the feedback deeply feels true, but the ego feels threatened. Hopefully, you will become skilled at ignoring the ego. You will learn that being honest with yourself can bring about change.

How do you do the searching and fearless moral inventory advocated in the recovery groups? It begins by taking inventory. The Big Book of A.A. says that most businesses will fail if they do not regularly take inventory. In business, the inventory process is a fact-finding and fact-facing mission. Damaged goods are identified and disposed of. You need to do the same to evaluate without judgment your issues that need work. Begin by taking note of the progress you have made and the good things in your life, but also courageously make a list of all the people against whom you hold resentment and all the things you fear. These resentments and fears hold the clue to healing and moving forward. Be specific, noting the time and place, person or organization, and the reason for your resentment. Revisit the section in this book on forgiveness, and begin to forgive people and yourself.

As you go through life, be willing to admit it when you are wrong. Understand that there is no shame in doing so. Instead of making excuses, empower yourself by recognizing mistakes and not attaching shame or regret. Everyone makes mistakes: you are no different. When admitting a mistake to yourself, you are honoring your humanity.

Don't Feel Ashamed When Insight Comes

I remember one particular day when I was working as a computer consultant and had a payroll issue. I went to talk to the accountant, and she pulled up my file on the computer screen. She started offering suggestions to help me, and I criticized every suggestion she made. I could see she was trying to help, and all of a sudden, it hit me like a lightning bolt! "Holy shit!" I thought to myself. "This is how my dad behaved when I asked him for help with a problem." I was doing the exact same thing, except Lynne was genuinely trying to help. I felt really embarrassed that I was acting out of a learned habit, the same dysfunctional behavior of my

Let Go and Heal

father, which resulted only in frustration for our accountant. I stopped my behavior and told her I appreciated her help and would consider her suggestions. I started to head back to my desk. She could see that I was embarrassed. She was a kind soul, and as I left, she gave me a nod indicating that she understood that I was in the process of evaluation and change.

Another example of personal realization occurred years ago when I had an argument with a roommate. She angrily shouted, "You always make a point and then walk away!" This was very valuable feedback. It's what my dad also used to do, and I realized I was doing this too. From then on, I stayed present, both physically and mentally. My roommate wanted to win the argument, so when I stopped walking away and stood there ready to discuss, she got really defensive and angry. Sometimes people get angry when they see you have the ability to change and don't behave as they would predict.

Being honest with yourself without judgment and the defense mechanism of denial can have a powerful effect on your life. It can free up mental energy and send you in a direction you might not have considered. Such feedback can help you change behaviors that impede communication.

Another aspect of getting feedback is that many people often assume the feedback is meant as criticism and is taken very personally when, in truth, another healthy person may be stating something that is obvious to others but not obvious to yourself. One of the things that I have known about myself from a very early age is that I am terrible at sports. I was the weakling in my family and in school. I could not run fast due to asthma, had a weak eye muscle, and I was very uncoordinated. The key thing I learned was that my sports aptitude had no bearing on my value as a human being. I accepted it, and pursued other interests such as music, singing, writing, organizing events, and being a good friend. Instead of being a volleyball player, I got involved in helping organize a tournament.

When describing my weakness in sports, most people would reply with a statement of denial. They'd say things like "All you need is practice!" or "If you work at it, you could be a good player!" or even "If you believed you were good at sports you would be!" In high school, I did try very hard and kept up a positive attitude, but when talking with a friend, at one point, he said, "Mark, just admit it... you're no good at sports!" At the time, I felt offended and hurt, but looking back, I can see there was no mean intent in his comment. He was just reflecting back to me what he could see and challenged my denial.

Denial seems to be a common trait in our culture to the detriment of our own good. Children are pumped up to believe that they are the best. All children are considered by their parents to be above average, which is mathematically impossible. It would be better for children and adults to develop the process of self-evaluation.

Keep in mind that pointing out other people's issues will not usually enhance your friendships! As they say in recovery programs, "Keep the focus on yourself!" Be willing to learn about yourself. Sometimes gaining self-knowledge can feel painful. Balance the pain with self-compassion.

> "To regret one's own experiences is to arrest one's own development. To deny one's own experiences is to put a lie into the lips of one's own life. It is no less than a denial of the soul."
> – Oscar Wilde

> "And now that you don't have to be perfect, you can be good."
> – John Steinbeck

Parenting Yourself and Healing the Inner Person

To heal and become fully functioning, you need to find in your inner space, a connection to your inner child. Each of us has a child-like quality that needs nurturing. I believe it is from this inner child, with adult knowledge, that much creativity springs forth. When you think back to yourself as a little child, how do you feel?

While much focus has been placed on just the inner child, I found great healing in holding my vision of myself as a teenager and young adult. I recalled the social fears I experienced, the pain I held, and my reaction to it.

I remember the start of high school being extremely traumatic. The first contact I had with my Grade 9 classmates was very awkward and, in

Let Go and Heal

the end, very embarrassing. I had little opportunity for socialization in grade school and was thrust into a full social environment with little social experience and no guidance. I experienced a lot of rejection and was told I was weird. People stayed away from me. I experienced severe ostracism.

To heal, I recalled how I had behaved – repeating things I thought were cool that a friend had told me about his interactions. I was not being myself and was trying to be someone I was not. I ended up keeping to myself and being a loner out of fear of rejection.

I came to realize later in life that, yes, I had behaved in a way that appeared weird to other people. Looking back with compassion, I give love to that young boy who had no guidance and was doing his best to fit in but with disastrous consequences. By becoming my own parent in the present, I give myself compassion and hold my image of myself at that time in kind regard.

A common Buddhist metaphor is that people are like saltwater. The odd or unvirtuous behavior or dysfunction is the salt, but the water, being the individual, remains pure. Hold your inner child, inner teenager, and inner adult with this same compassion towards the water that has had the salt removed. Do this with other people as well.

While you may want to be nurtured, you can develop the skills of being your own parent and talk to the inner person (child, adult, and teenager). Realize that no matter what age you are, your inner person needs care and attention. Listen to your inner person when it calls out for attention and embrace the person within. If there are tears, let the tears flow, being mindful of the ever-present adult parent you have become.

My dear friend Cathy once shared a book handwritten by her sister Elaine Bilmer. Cathy told her sister how much I enjoyed her book. Elaine very kindly hand-copied her book for me. Here is a beautiful excerpt from that book that tells of her pain, healing, and becoming her own parent.

The Lost Child
I want to be that little child all over again,
fun-loving, impish, and full of life.
But this time, things will be different. I will be the new parent.

Mark Linden O'Meara

Go ahead and play, laugh, don't stop. You've only just begun.
I promise I won't scream at you and make you
feel bad or shamed because you want to play.
I'll hold you, stroke you, caress you
and set good boundaries for you.
You will be the one to teach me what your needs are,
I will just be there to help you follow them through.
If you think life is unfair, let me know, and I will validate that feeling. I won't brush you away or disown your thoughts.
If you are mad as hell and want to scream, tell me, go right ahead, I will have you embrace that anger and make your anger your friend, not your enemy.
I will tell you in words that I love you,
not once but many times over.
I know how you clung and begged to have
your mother say she loved you.
It must have hurt so deep that you must have felt
like a slithering snake, crawling on the cold floor, grabbing onto your mother's skirt so you would not go unnoticed.
But then like most people, when they see a snake, they look appalled and scared of it and quickly try to run away from it.
As a small child, I once again felt unwanted and continued to slither and use the vibrations of the cold floor
to make contact with my mother.
Even if I was wet, cold, and the floor was damp, I was mesmerized by that beautiful Goddess known as my mother.
I was constantly reminded and laughed at for being
so needy and a pest to have around.
Like a homeless battered worn-out lost soul,
I would crawl to the nearest corner and bang my head for hours. It didn't matter if I hit my head on hard wood or soft furniture, I never felt the pain. It could have been that I felt so dead inside, this head banging made me feel alive.

Let Go and Heal

My friends are the couch and the wall,
they never brush me away.
The slithering snake crawls down and doesn't give up, maybe this time
it will be different, she might even tell me
I'm beautiful, a lovely, normal, happy, playful, loving child.
In my fantasy, she reaches down, gently grabs me in her arms, and
looks in my eyes and tells me she does so dearly love me.
I fall asleep in her arms, and never want to wake up
for fear she'll think it will be the snake.
Wake up, little one, wake up! I'm here, as I promised. Your new parent
is here. I love you, I love you, I will never get tired of letting you hear
whatever you want and need.
Rest now, hush little precious one, you've worked so hard,
now let me take care of you.
Here's a lullaby to soothe your pain…
My precious little one
Go to sleep… Go to sleep.
You are safe and warm here,
And I do so love you.
Go to sleep… Go to sleep.
For when you awake
I promise I'll be here,
with you in my arms and
me humming to you
I do so love you, I love you,
Go to sleep… Go to sleep.

L. Elaine Bilmer

This poem and story beautifully describes the need of every child to feel loved. Of great importance is that by the end of the poem, Elaine actually moves into being her own parent. It is often a painful but powerful realization to come to the conclusion that you are actually the one in charge of your healing and level of happiness. You might gather information from this or other books and other sources of inspiration, but ultimately it is you who does the work and challenges yourself to rise above your current situation and begin creating inner peace and self-love.

According to Bo Yin Ra, one of the teachers that Eckhart Tolle studied:

> "The inner world experienced by the individual must be transformed into a world of peace, and quiet joy, and here alone can mortal man encounter happiness that will endure. Become your own parent and give yourself the love you deserve. It is your birthright to feel loved. Looking outside yourself for this love can bring heartache because everything in the world is impermanent except for your ability at any moment to choose to love yourself."

"Have a good inner support network. Teach yourself how to be the best voice inside your head."
– Little Woo

22. Changing Directions

"No matter how far you have traveled in the wrong direction, you can always turn around."
– Author Unknown

Unloading Your Freight Train

As I was reviewing my present situation and wondering how I could lessen the impact of the various serious stresses I had been through, I heard the news of a freight train derailment. A video of the derailment had also been posted which showed how the powerful weight of the numerous freight cars contributed to the energy of the derailment as the train sped around a curve in the track. I thought of the freight train as a perfect metaphor and solution to reduce my stress. I realized that I had built up a freight train in my mind with a very heavy boxcar for each of the traumas or stressful life incidents I had been through. The cars were coupled together, forming a long train with significant power, weight, and energy. The weight and inertial energy of the train were following me wherever I showed up and were draining my own energy. Each time a life stressor occurred, I was adding a new car to my metaphorical "life train." It takes approximately a mile and a half for a freight train to stop. In my mind, I imagined myself naming the cars and then uncoupling them and unloading them on a side track, or just leaving them behind. I also added new cars to the train that represented positive things that happened to me and also added cars to represent future opportunities that I was optimistic about. I've repeated this train metaphor exercise numerous times to bring closure and help reduce my stress level.

Focus on Gratitude, Kindness, and Compassion

Sometimes learning things the hard way teaches you very deep lessons. A lesson I needed to learn was that of gratitude, and to not focus on what is lacking, but on my blessings and opportunities and the opportunities that could be ahead of me. Deeply in debt for student loans and with significant medical expenses, at the age of forty-five, I was single and in poor health, while almost all of the people around me had recently bought or upgraded their houses, purchased new cars, and were living a lifestyle that seemed beyond me. I felt continually depressed, seeing the financial and family achievements of others.

It was at this time I began to focus on rebuilding. Countering each thought of what was lacking with positive statements about new friendships appearing, my accomplishments, or sometimes simply by telling myself that I was where I needed to be in my life, brought renewal. Slowly pulling myself out of a slump, I began creating some fun in my life and recommitted to enjoyment. I was in a period of rebuilding and needed to be patient, trusting the process of life itself, volunteering, and finding places to contribute heartfelt connection with others. By focusing on gratefulness, and adapting the strategy of searching out, noticing, and feeling good about the positives, I began to feel a greater sense of happiness with what I had in my life, while still recognizing that this was the first step in moving towards improving things. Feeling sorry for myself or ruminating about the things I lacked did not help me gather them into my life. Some things could not immediately be changed, but over time, I could develop a plan to improve these areas of life that were lacking. Very quickly, new opportunities began presenting themselves as I developed my attitude of gratitude!

There has been a great deal of research that affirms the benefits of developing a deep undercurrent of gratitude. Rather than a superficial or occasional feeling of gratitude, you need to develop it as a deep sentiment. "Sentiment" is a deeply rooted habit or feeling. If we have deep-seated feelings of anger, resentment, or hurt, we can learn to replace them with a deep sentiment of gratitude and positive emotions.

One of the new interventions developed to treat depression is called "Positive Activity Intervention" (PAI). This type of intervention focuses on encouraging random acts of kindness, practicing optimism, counting blessings, writing letters of gratitude, meditating on positive emotions towards others, and focusing on your strengths. You can apply the same form of treatment to yourself by increasing your frequency of positive thinking and action. In a study looking at PAI, the benefits lasted for six months. Feeling positive for just a few moments can have a lasting effect throughout the day. These types of intervention disempower the negative emotions, thoughts, and images one has been experiencing. MRI studies show that generating compassionate feelings activates a part of the brain responsible for contributing to soothing, calming, and feelings of safety and contentment.

Healthy emotions and gratitude protect us in times of crisis. Those who practice gratitude tend to have lower incidences of depression after a traumatic event or crisis. Grateful people tend to be happier and have better health and friendships. It is also a booster shot for romantic relationships. Gratitude lowers stress levels and promotes better sleep by modifying pre-sleep cognitive processes. It reduces the responses to suffering and increases self-esteem. It truly bestows happiness. Gratitude is not something that happens to you but is something that you can create. Everyday gratitude is a choice!

Increasing your kindness and compassion also has a positive impact on the soul. Giving always restores the soul and opens us up to even more gratitude. Compassion leads to being healthier and contributes to longevity. Try to give without expecting anything in return. If you feel you have nothing to give, then just give a smile. In a recent study, students in one group were asked to make someone smile while those in another were asked to do something else to make someone happy. Those in the group that made someone smile were happier and more confident that they had achieved their goal of making someone smile. If seeing the gratitude in others does not lift you up, at least be grateful for your positive qualities and your gift of life!

"Gratitude makes sense of the past, brings peace for today, and creates a vision for tomorrow."
– Melody Beattie

Look Outward with Empathy!
There comes a time as you move through your healing work that you begin to notice the things outside of yourself more than the things inside. You stop looking back and start focusing on looking forward. This means

that you no longer need to focus on yourself as much, and you are ready to give more to others. As I healed some deep emotions and moved out of depression, I became more aware of the emotions of my friends. I began to pick up emotional cues and to listen more empathically. I became a better listener by learning to ask questions. Essentially, I moved from being self-focused to being a more empathic person.

Researchers have identified key elements of what makes empathy so valuable. Empathy is an emotional response to other people's emotional states. It is a capacity to understand another person's perspective, the ability to regulate your own emotions, and increased awareness of self and others. Empathy reduces everyone's sense of isolation and improves the self-image and well-being of the person being listened to. Empathy can be emotional or rational. With emotional empathy, you experience someone else's emotions. Rational empathy occurs when you intellectually attempt to understand someone else's situation.

We all have the hardware for empathy. Sometimes it just needs to be developed and refined. Research suggests that to be more empathic, you can:

- Develop a curiosity about strangers
- Challenge your prejudices and discover commonalities
- Try to participate in the activities and lives of others
- Listen well and open up about yourself
- Inspire action and social change
- Develop your imagination

If you have not worked through and experienced your own feelings, it is difficult to have empathy for others. Looking for emotional cues can develop empathy. The eyes reveal a great deal of emotion as people can only hide so much. Emotions are frequently not put into words, but if you can sense what others are feeling, your simple statement of "I understand" can go a long way. When you consciously commit to developing your empathy, you are committing to forming community and friendship.

Let Go and Heal

Practice the habit of empathy to build your empathy skills. The skills will come naturally to you.

Activation of the Love Voice

One of the biggest traps in the healing process is to get caught up in "us" versus "them" thinking. It is so easy to think of yourself as the harmed individual and to lay blame and judge others who may have harmed you. While it may be true that you weren't treated properly, or perhaps don't like the way others behaved, it is very important to practice compassion and try to see the good in others from the earliest point possible in your healing journey. Granted, this may be difficult, but I, like many others, can attest to how powerfully one's negative judgment of others can get in the way of healing.

Rebbe Nachman says: "The highest peace is the peace between opposites. If you remember this, the next time you meet someone who makes you uncomfortable, instead of heading for the nearest exit, you'll find ways for the two of you to get along."

If you really want to change others, become the change yourself. That means being nonjudgmental and allowing others to be themselves. As the poet Rumi says: "Many want love, few will be willing to become it." Leading by example and showing positive regard for others, rather than contempt, will do more to heal your relationships than any long, deep talk about what troubles you. When presented with two opposing choices, try to find a third alternative!

23. Transformative Living

Redefining Success

One of the important lessons I learned was how to define success for myself. I've come to realize that much of the motivational literature pushes us to be our best, and that is a good thing, but as human beings, there certainly are days when our level of best changes. In writing this book, I have been through health issues and work challenges. I had to take time to work on my marriage, and sometimes, I have been just too tired to do any writing or my creative projects. Finding time to rest and achieving that rest is in itself a success.

After publishing the first edition of this book, I experienced severe financial difficulties even though the book was selling well and had glowing reviews. One evening I attended a healing circle and afterward offered a ride to two of the participants. I had a copy of my book in the car; however, they did not know I was the author. The two guys started talking about how they had seen it in the bookstore earlier that afternoon. They commented to each other that the guy who wrote the book must be very rich from writing it. I got a great chuckle because their perception was so different from reality. I was so broke I could hardly pay the rent.

A few weeks later, I attended a motivational seminar as a volunteer and took the opportunity to talk to the three speakers who were presenting. All were very successful speakers and wealthy. I explained my circumstances to them and told them that I was considering bankruptcy. All three asked me the same questions and offered the same advice. The question was, "Have you done everything possible to resolve the financial situation?" My answer was, "Yes." Each of the speakers agreed that I had done my best, and confided that they, too, had gone bankrupt. They told me that constantly trying to avoid bankruptcy was my biggest block to getting ahead. They advised me that in the end, it was my decision, but that I could eventually get a fresh start.

Most people do not admit to their failures. They will talk about successes, but business failures and personal failures are not normally mentioned at social events or even motivational events, but they probably

Let Go and Heal

should be. Everyone fails at something at some time in their lives, but the true meaning of success is to be able to pick yourself up, brush yourself off, and start on a new journey. The result of my personal failure and picking myself up is the fact that you are reading this new and vastly improved book! Perhaps a new definition of success is to have the courage to make and follow through on a difficult decision.

Success can also be defined as doing the best with what you've got at any given time. It is not about how much money you made, how many businesses you started, or how big your house is, nor is it about how many friends you have. Success is an internal measure of how you are doing at this moment, given your situation, and what you are doing to improve yourself. It is a sentiment of peace that comes from self-compassion and acknowledging that you are willing to grow and increase your understanding of yourself and others. According to John Wooden's definition of success: "Success is a peace of mind which is a direct result of self-satisfaction in knowing you did your best to become the best you are capable of becoming."

Keep in mind that we can control only our actions, thoughts, and feelings, but not the results of our actions. The Upanishads, a collection of Hindu texts, state that we cannot control other peoples' reactions or behaviors, although I believe we may be able to exert some influence on others by modeling healthy behavior.

In modeling healthy and kind behavior, we live a life that treats people well. There is an old saying that people will not remember what you did, but they will certainly remember how you made them feel. If you recall people who are no longer with you, or with whom you worked in the past or even people you interact with currently, you will call up an image that includes a sense of feeling of how they made you feel. If you want to be successful, treat people fairly and supportively so that you become a positive image and memory. Anushree Baikerikar, in her blog post, writes:

> "What if success was measured by how well you've loved instead of what you've earned or how many people know you? What if success was measured by how much joy you've brought

to the table and how much better or worse you left the place than when you arrived? What if success was measured by how kindly and sincerely you've treated those around you?"

This definition is especially important to authors like me. People, and sometimes I myself, believe that because I have written so much about healing, my own life should be easy and filled with warmth and healthy perfection. Life always presents challenges, and although my life has been greatly improved by what I have learned, I still have to practice the lessons contained in this book. Whenever challenges arise, I accept that I'm moving through something powerful and can parent myself through the process.

Regardless of the challenges you are going through, follow these words of Bo Yin Ra in his book *The Book on Happiness*:

> "Secure within yourself a cheerful certainty, convinced that happiness is yours by right, and let no setback ever drive you from the stronghold of your firmly anchored faith. Rest assured, there are at times, energies at work that offer you their help in the moment you are truly willing to create the happiness you seek, instead of longing for it, full of hopes and wishes...
>
> Calmly go the way on which you have been placed on earth, and always guard your inner peace, no matter how the 'blows of fate' might thunder all around you...
>
> Trust instead, your own good right – indeed, your moral duty – to experience lasting happiness; and strive, with firm resolve and confident serenity, truly to create it in your life; so that you, too, may one day find yourself among this planet's happy guests."

This doesn't mean that I ignore emotional pain, but that I embrace it with the confidence and certainty that I can work through it and move into happiness. Happiness is having inner peace in times of difficulty.

Let Go and Heal

Developing Self-Compassion

Many books have been written that try to help you improve your self-esteem, yet new research has revealed something far more important to help deal with feelings of inadequacy and low self-esteem.

One of the valuable lessons I learned early in my teaching career came from a teacher who taught a course on teaching. The lesson was about motivational efforts to boost self-esteem and performance. The teacher and I had a chat during one of the breaks, and we ended up discussing motivational seminars and the long-term impact on participants' mental health and performance. He confided that he had previously been a motivational speaker. He was a very ethical trainer and wanted to make sure that his workshops had a positive impact. He did surveys and consistently found that his participants performed better and had higher self-esteem for about two weeks after his training, but long-term results showed that performance declined to their previous levels and subsequently actually dropped even further. There was also a decline in participants' self-esteem and a higher incidence of depression in some participants. As a result, he stopped doing his motivational training because he knew it wasn't working. He discovered, through his network of motivational trainers, that other trainers had observed the same effect. The key goal of the workshops was to convince the participants that they could maintain a high level of performance. But in the long run, as human beings, it is difficult, if not impossible, to maintain the heightened state if it lacks a foundation. As humans, we sometimes fail and make mistakes, and a simple failure of any kind could pull the rug out from under the motivational training expectations.

Research has shown that the foundation for feeling good about ourselves is not necessarily high self-esteem but behaving compassionately towards the self. Self-compassion is being kind to yourself in times of success, but, more importantly, in times of difficulty or when we aren't feeling our best. Practicing self-compassion, you treat yourself kindly, accept that failures, difficulties, and hardships are common human experiences, and maintain an awareness of pain in a mindful and nonjudgmental way. You can accept that, at times, you will not be able to perform your best and that others are the same way. You can accept yourself for doing the level of work you are doing right now, and that is good enough. Self-compassion is empathy for yourself. To be self-compassionate, talk to yourself as though you were talking with and offering advice to your best friend.

The Key to Feeling Good – Developing Worthiness

One of the topics that intrigues me is resiliency. Resiliency is how some people bounce back quickly from adversity and life challenges. In attempting to understand the concept of resilience, I began focusing on developing a deeper understanding of resilience and its related themes. As usual, life events uncovered some interesting answers.

A few months before a vacation, I was doing some repair work in my apartment. Suddenly distracted, I accidentally clobbered one of my fingers with a hammer. Over the next few months, I had various treatments, but three days before my flight, my hand specialist told me that the finger was likely still infected and needed minor surgery. After the procedure, my finger was now bandaged up again and needed delicate care. I also needed about five days of intravenous antibiotics. It was not going to be safe for me to travel in case of further infection. As a result, I had to delay my trip for two weeks.

When I eventually boarded the plane for my trip, two synchronistic things happened. First of all, I ended up talking with a lady who was traveling to Beijing to meet a friend and travel to other parts of China. We instantly hit it off and, for a while, became good friends. Secondly, on the same flight, I also ran into someone whom I had dated thirteen years earlier. That relationship did not end well for me. I ended up briefly speaking to her and left it at that, but this event left me wondering why the dating situation had troubled me so much and why I often thought about her. After I arrived in Beijing, I spent time in self-reflection. In that process, the key to the cause of my own suffering was revealed.

I had forgotten that this key to unlocking suffering had actually been revealed to me years earlier. After the publication of my first book, I embarked on a promotion tour, which included book signings, newspaper articles, reviews, and being a guest on radio talk shows. One particular show stood out. It was a late-night show, and the topic was healing. The switchboard lit up with callers who expressed their opinions. There seemed to be a division among callers. Some were working through healing, but another group of callers echoed a theme similar to "I went through abuse, but I moved on and just let it be what it was." I had a hunch at the time that this group of callers had one thing in common. Somehow their sense of self-esteem or self-worth remained intact, which seemed to me to be the key to healing from difficult times. They also did not perpetuate being a victim.

I realized that the barrier to healing from this past relationship was my level of worthiness and the mental image I held of that event. Understanding why I thought of her often became clear when I came across research showing that people think of ex-partners when their spirit is low. Reminiscing about past partners is a common characteristic of couples who are experiencing a downturn in their own self-esteem or relationships. In this dating situation, I had been encouraged to be open, honest, and vulnerable, but then got rejected for it. Personally, I realized that my feelings of low self-worth had been triggered by the feeling of rejection. With part of the puzzle solved, I began to look for research on worthiness and self-esteem to truly understand the dynamics of these states and to further my knowledge. What I found greatly increased my understanding of the dynamics and interplay between self-esteem, worthiness, and resilience.

Worthiness involves developing a relationship with yourself and stopping any negative self-talk and replacing it with positive talk. Ask yourself whether statements you are making about yourself contribute to your sense of worthiness. It's OK to say you need to improve. That should not equate with unworthiness. Dysfunction does not equal unworthiness. Give up the idea that you need to love yourself before someone can love you. Although loving yourself is helpful, you can be loved even if you do not love yourself. Watch out for doubt as it is an opposing, sabotaging force in the development and maintenance of self-esteem and worthiness.

Be aware that the human mind has a tendency to believe we are not enough. Most of us need some outside valuation through friendship and relationships. Make sure you choose friends who validate you. You may have had people in your life who have abandoned you for speaking up or conveying your feelings. Give more value to those who have accepted and nurtured you. Uncover your themes of unworthiness in your life or situations where you believed you had to prove your worthiness. Begin to increase your self-efficacy in assessing and building your sense of worth.

Who Can I Be? – Accepting the Fluid Personality

People change a lot more than they predict they will change! Realize that your personality is fluid and changing over time. There is no such thing as a fixed personality. Often after a loss comes an identity crisis during which you re-evaluate yourself and realize that your self-identity is no longer tied to what you do or who you associate with. Research has shown that throughout their lives, people change significantly. The idea that you have already become the person you will be for the rest of your life is not really true.

You can learn that you can be much more than you currently are and that your history does not necessarily determine who or what you can be, although you do recognize your personal limitations. I think this is a sign of good mental health. You don't get angry with yourself or disappointed when you realize you don't have a particular talent. I know I am not good at sports, but I am a good listener and have a good singing voice. More importantly, by learning about and acknowledging your past, your personal traits, and the choices you have made, you can grow into the person you really can be, regardless of the messages you may have received as a child or young adult. Essentially, you begin to accept the past and begin coaching yourself in the present.

One of your life challenges is to rise above the narrow view that you can easily develop when you are immersed in your own culture and family upbringing. There is a Chinese phrase *zuo jing guan tian* which means "Sitting in a well and looking at the sky, you will have a narrow perspective." The definition and wisdom of these words go on to say that "you need to see the trees and the landscape. Otherwise, you will be restricted in what you see."

Your process of personal growth involves trying to discover those things that you are blind to and that are unknown, and also in some cases to uncover your hidden talents. You also may wish to develop your ability to put things into the hidden category by setting boundaries. In personal relationship building, you may need to learn to disclose more to yourself as well as to others and learn about other people.

You can learn to identify the behaviors that occur when one person begins to see patterns that others do not wish to disclose or are simply still blind to see. Being the first person to notice a problem of alcoholism can threaten the stability of other peoples' knowledge of themselves. The denial will be strong because the concept is still hidden to them. There are numerous conflict dynamics involved, especially when one person increases their self-knowledge as they move from hidden or unknown to disclosure with others. When you see what others don't want to see or vice versa, there is a threat resulting in conflict and irrational behavior. Part of your journey involves learning to accept that others may not wish to uncover their hidden information. You need to respect this, manage to continue a relationship with them, and continue on your journey of growth without developing resentment and frustration.

What your family treats as problematic to them may, in fact, be your greatest gift to people.

24. Conclusion

In the process of reading this book, I hope that you have been able to develop some new attitudes and skills for dealing with and accepting emotions in others and yourself. Emotional work is a lifelong commitment. It is something you do for yourself and for your relationship with others in the world. Many of us have had a difficult family upbringing or have experienced difficult times in our lives that, unless resolved, will continue to affect our behavior in subtle and sometimes not-so-subtle ways. Through the healing and acceptance of your feelings, you can break the cycle of how you respond to your emotions and thoughts. Fortunately, you now have tools to gain a greater understanding of yourself and others. As an adult, you can do a better job of ensuring that your unhealthy patterns of behavior and attitudes are not passed on to your children. You can become more loving and responsive to their needs and your own needs as well.

To work on your emotions and to resolve them brings you freedom – freedom to enjoy life more, to have closer and more trusting relationships, and, most importantly, to have clarity of thinking when resolving problems and issues. All of these benefits will allow you to become better friends, teachers, and parents. You are allowing greater opportunities for yourself and for others, lifting yourself above habitual patterns. You can bring about change, greater awareness, and can accept emotional expression in others. All of these benefits will allow you to foster creativity and more effectively nurture others.

Finally, to end our journey together, I wish to quote from Yogi Ramacharaka. I hope that you will be able to practice what he describes – a world of kindness:

> "It follows that one who has grasped the fundamental ideas of this philosophy will begin to find fear dropping from him – for when he realizes just what he is, how can he fear? There being nothing that can really hurt him, why should he fear? Worry, of course, follows after fear, and when fear goes, many other minor

mental faults follow after it. Envy, jealousy, and hate – malice, uncharitableness, and condemnation – cannot exist in the mind of one who 'understands.' Faith and Trust in the Spirit, and that from which the Spirit comes must be manifest to the awakened soul. Such a one naturally recognizes the Spirit's guidance, and unhesitatingly follows it, without fear – without a doubt. Such a one cannot help being kind – to him, the outside world of people seem to be as little children (many of them like babes unborn), and he deals with them charitably, not condemning them in his heart, for he knows them for what they are. Such a one performs the work which is set before him, knowing that such work, be it humble or exalted, has been brought to him by his own acts and desires, or his needs – and that it is all right in any event, and is but the stepping-stone to greater things. Such a one does not fear life – does not fear death – both seem as different manifestations of the same thing – one as good as the other. The student who expects to make progress must make his philosophy a part of his everyday life."

These words are powerful! They summarize what you can accomplish and the state of mind you can live in when free of your past burdens. You can live mindfully and with an awareness of the world around you. Buddhist teacher Lama Yeshe writes:

"If you can understand the psychological aspects of human problems, you really generate true loving kindness towards others. Just talking about loving kindness doesn't help you develop it. Some people may have read about loving kindness hundreds of times, but their minds are the very opposite. It's not just philosophy, not just words. It's knowing how the mind functions. Only then can you develop loving kindness; only then can you become a spiritual person. Be as wise with your mind as you possibly can. That's what really makes your life worthwhile."

Reading this book has likely challenged your ideas and beliefs. It, hopefully, has also provided some comfort and insight. Through the process of reading and practicing the ideas presented in this book, I hope that you and others can become more enlightened and inspired in your journey. Hopefully, these ideas will remain in your heart and daily practice! With an enlightened mind, you can walk your path without fear! Happiness is an outcome, not a goal! It is a by-product of all the things we think, say, feel, believe, and do.

"I am not afraid of storms anymore, for I am learning to sail my ship."
– Louisa May Alcott

25. Bibliography

Aaker, J., Drolet, A., Griffin, D.W. (2007) Recalling Mixed Emotions: How Did I Feel Again? Social Science Research Network

Akinola, M., Mendes, W. B. (2008) The Dark Side of Creativity: Biological Vulnerability and Negative Emotions Lead to Greater Artistic Creativity. Personality and Social Psychology Bulletin, 34(12), 1677.

Albrecht, K. (Apr 21, 2014) The Real Reason We Believe What We Believe, Psychology Today

Algoe, S.B., Gable, S.L., Maisel, N.C. (2010) It's The Little Things: Everyday Gratitude As A Booster Shot for Romantic Relationships Personal Relationships, 17, 217–233

American Journal of Dance Therapy (1991) Dance/Movement Therapy with Battered Women: A Paradigm of Action, Fall-Win Vol. 13(2) 131-145

Artz, S., Jackson, M.A., Rossiter, K.A., Nijdam-Jones, A., Geczy, I., Porteous, S. (2014) In Harm's Way: A Special Issue On The Impacts and Costs of Witnessing Intimate Partner Violence. International Journal of Child, Youth and Family Studies (2014) 5(4): 493-587

Aureli, F., Schaffner, C. M. (2013) Why So Complex? Emotional Mediation of Revenge, Forgiveness, and Reconciliation. Behavioral and Brain Sciences, 36(1), 15-6

Ayar, A. (2006) Road Rage: Recognizing A Psychological Disorder. Journal of Psychiatry & Law, 34(2), 123-150,119

Ayduk, O., Mendoza-Denton, R. Mischel, W., Downey, G. (2000) Regulating the Interpersonal Self. Journal of Personality and Social Psychology. Vol79, No 5. 776-792

Baikeriaker, A. (2015) What If Success Was Measured by How Well You've Loved? Tinybuddha.com

Barbic S.P., Durisko Z., Andrews P.W., (2014) Measuring The Bright Side of Being Blue: A New Tool for Assessing Analytical Rumination In Depression. Plos ONE 9(11)

Barton, A. (Jan 13, 2013) Believe It: Your Personality Is Always Changing. Here's How, Globe and Mail.

Bass, E. & Davis, L. (2008) The Courage to Heal: A Guide for Women Survivors of Child Sexual Abuse, 20th Anniversary Edition, William Morrow Publishers.

Bentall, R. (1992) A Proposal to Classify Happiness as a Psychiatric Disorder, Journal of Medical Ethics; 18:94-98

Bernhardt, B., Singer, T. (2012) The Neural Basis of Empathy, Annual Review of Neuroscience 2012.35:1-23

Bernier, L., (Jul 13, 2014) Ostracism, An Often-Overlooked Form of Workplace Bullying, Finds Study. Canadian HR Reporter 27.13 : 3

Bernstein, E. (Jul 30, 2013) After Divorce Or Job Loss Comes The Good Identity Crisis; Experts Say Most People Should Give Themselves A Good Two Years to Recover From An Emotional Trauma. Wall Street Journal (Online)

Beutler, L. (1986) Inability to Express Intense Affect: A common link between depression and pain, Journal of Consulting and Clinical Psychology, Dec Vol 54 (6)

Bhasin, R. (Dec 1994) Battling Burnout. Pulp & Paper, 68(13), 37

Black, C. (1982) It Will Never Happen to Me: Growing up with Addiction as Youngsters, Adolescents, Adults, M.A.C. Printing and Publishing, Denver Colorado

Black, C. (1989) It's Never Too Late to Have a Happy Childhood, M.A.C. Printing and Publishing. Div. Denver Colorado

Blasi, Anna et al. (2011) Early Specialization for Voice and Emotion Processing in the Infant Brain. Current Biology, Vol 21, (14) 1220 - 1224

Bolles, R.N. (2016) What Color Is Your Parachute? 2016: A Practical Manual for Job-Hunters and Career-Changers. Ten Speed Press, Berkeley, CA

Borquist, A. (1906) Crying, American Journal of Psych., 17, 149 -205

Bo Yin Ra, (1994) The Book on Happiness, Kober Press, Berkeley, CA

Bo Yin Ra, (2000) Spirit and Form, Kober Press, Berkeley, CA

Bridewell, W.B., Chang, E.C. (1997) Distinguishing Between Anxiety, Depression, and Hostility: Relations to Anger-In, Anger-Out, and Anger Control. Personality and Individual Differences, Vol 22, No 4. 587-590

Briere J., Conte J. (1993) Self-reported Amnesia for Abuse in Adults Molested as Children, Journal of Traumatic Stress, 6, 21-31

Briere, J. (1989) Therapy for Adults Molested as Children - Beyond Survival, Springer Publishing Company, New York, NY

Brown University Long-term Care Quality Letter (1980) The Release of Tears: The first phase in the psychotherapy of a 3-year-old child with the diagnosis: Symbiotic Child Psychosis, International Review of Psycho-Analysis. Vol 7 (3)

Buboltz, W. C. Jr., Johnson, P., Woller, K. M. (2003). Psychological Reactance In College Students: Family-Of-Origin Predictors. Journal of Counseling and Development, 81(3), 311

Burns, D.D. (1990) The Feeling Good Handbook, Penguin Group, New York, NY

Bylsma, L., Vingerhoets, J., Rottenberg, J. (2008) When Is Crying Cathartic? An International Study. Journal of Social and Clinical Psychology. Vol 27 No 10. 1165-1187

Campbell, J., Moyers, B. (1991) The Power of Myth. Anchor Press, Norwell, MA

Campbell, R., Pennebaker, J. (Jan 2003) The Secret Life of Pronouns: Flexibility In Writing Style and Physical Health. Psychological Science. Vol. 14 no. 1 60-65

Canadian Mental Health Association (Sept 14, 2017) Moral Injury, www.camh.ca/en/camh-news-and-stories/moral-injury

Cardaciotto, L.Herbert, J.D., Forman, E.M., Moitra, E. Farrow, V. (June 2008) The Assessment of Present-Moment Awareness and Acceptance, Assessment, Vol 15 (2) 204-223

Carpenter, S, (Feb 2001) Different Dispositions Different Brains, APA Monitor, Vol 32 2

Chogyam Trungpa (2001) The Lion's Roar, Shambhala. Boston, MA

Chung, C. Pennebaker, J. (Feb 2008) Revealing Dimensions of Thinking in Open-ended Self-Descriptions: An Automated Meaning Extraction Method for Natural Language, Journal of Research in Personality. 42(1): 96–132

Clay, R.A. (Sept 1997) Researchers harness the power of humor, Monitor, American Psychological Association Monitor

Cloitre, M., Cohen, L., Koenen, K. (2006) Treating Survivors of Childhood Abuse, Guilford Press, New York, NY

Coates, D. (Nov 1997) The Correlations of Forgiveness, Dissertation Abstracts, Section B Sciences and Engineering, Vol 58(5-B) 2667

Colgrove, M., Bloomfield, H.H., McWilliams, P. (2006) How to Survive the Loss of A Love, Prelude Press, Los Angeles, CA

Cong, Y.J., Gan, Y., Sun, H.L., Deng, J., Cao, S.Y., Xu, X., Lu, Z.X. (Feb 4, 2014) Association of Sedentary Behaviour With Colon and Rectal Cancer. British Journal of Cancer. 110(3):817-26

Cook, A.F., Witte, I.A., Morgan, E.A., Abrams, M., Leuchter, M. (Jan 2002) Changes in the Brain Function of Depressed Subjects during Treatment with Placebo. American Journal of Psychiatry, Vol. 159 Issue 1, 122

Cousins, N. (1976) Anatomy of an Illness, New England Journal of Medicine, 295(26): 1458 – 1463

Cummings, E.M., Hennessy, K., Rabideau, G., Cicchetti, D. (1994) Responses of Physically Abused Boys to Inter-Adult Anger Involving Their Mothers. Developmental Psychopathology, 6, 31-41

Davidson, R. (2012) The Emotional Life of Your Brain, Plume Publishing, New York, NY

Davidson, R.J., Kabat-Zinn, J., Schumacher, J., Rosenkranz, M., Muller, D., Antorelli, S.F., Urbanowski, F., Harrington, A., Bonus, K., Heridan, J.F. (2003) Alterations In Brain and Immune Function Produced by Mindfulness Meditation. Psychosomatic Medicine 65:564-570.

Davis, P.J. (1988) Physiological and Subjective Effects of Catharsis: A Case Report. Cognition and Emotions, 2, 19-28

De Jong G. J., Van Tilburg, T., Dykstra, P. (2006) Cambridge Handbook of Personal Relationships / A.Vangelisti and D.Perlman, Eds. Cambridge: Cambridge University Press, P. 485-500

Djikic, M., Oatley, K., & Moldoveanu, M. C. (2013) Opening the Closed Mind: The Effect of Exposure to Literature On The Need for Closure. Creativity Research Journal, 25(2), 149

Djikic, M., Oatley, K., Zoeterman, S., & Peterson, J. B. (2009) On Being Moved By Art: How Reading Fiction Transforms The Self. Creativity Research Journal, 21(1), 24

Downey, G., Freitas, A., Michaelis, B., Khouri, H. (1998) The Self-Fulfilling Prophecy in Close Relationships: Rejection Sensitivity and Rejection by Romantic Partners. Journal of Personality and Social Psychology. Vol 75, No 2. 545-560

Dumont, T.Q., (1920) The Solar Plexus Or Abdominal Brain, Reprinted 2007 by Cosimo Classics. New York, NY

Dyrbye, L. N., West, C. P., Shanafelt, T. D. (2009) Defining Burnout As A Dichotomous Variable. Journal of General Internal Medicine, 24(3), 440-440; Author Reply 441

Ekvall, G. (1996). Organizational Climate for Creativity and Innovation. European Journal of Work and Organizational Psychology, 5 105-123

Ekvall, G. (1997) Organizational conditions and levels of creativity. Creativity and Innovation Management, 6

Eisenberger, N. I. (2012) A Neural Perspective On The Similarities Between Social and Physical Pain. Current Directions in Psychological Science. Vol. 21 No. 1 42-47

Eisenberger, N. I. (2012) Broken Hearts and Broken Bones: A Neural Perspective On The Similarities Between Social and Physical Pain. Current Directions In Psychological Science, 21(1), 42

Eisenberger, N. I., Lieberman, M. D., Williams, K. D. (2003) Does Rejection Hurt: An fMRI Study of Social Exclusion. Science, 302, 290–292

Enevoldsen, Christina (2014). The Rescued Soul: The Writing Journey for the Healing of Incest and Family Betrayal. Overcoming Sexual Abuse

English, T., John, O.P., Gross, J.J. (2013) Emotion regulation in close relationships. In J.A. Simpson & L. Campbell (Eds.), The Oxford handbook of close relationships (pp. 500-513). Oxford University Press

Eres, R., Decety, J., Louis W, Molenberghs, P. (Aug 15, 2015) Individual differences in local gray matter density are associated with differences in affective and cognitive empathy NeuroImage Volume 117, 305–310

Federal Child Abuse Prevention and Treatment Act (2010) 42 U.S.C.A. 5106g as amended by the CAPTA Reauthorization Act of 2010 http://www.childwelfare.gov/topics/can/defining/federal/

Feiring, C., Taska, L., Lewis, M. (1998) The Role of Shame and Attributional Style In Children's and Adolescents' Adaptation to Sexual Abuse. Child Maltreatment, 3, 129-142

Fernández-Serrano, M.J., Lozano Rojas, O., Pérez-García, M., Verdejo-García, A. (June, 2010) Impact of Severity of Drug Use On Discrete Emotions Recognition In Polysubstance Abusers. Drug and Alcohol Dependence, 109, 57-64

Fernández-Serrano, M.J., Pérez-García, M., Schmidt, J., Verdejo-García, A. (Sept, 2010) Neuropsychological Consequences of Alcohol and Drug Abuse On Different Components of Executive Functions. Journal of Psychopharmacology. 24: 1317-1332

Fernández-Serrano, M.J., Pérez-García, M., Verdejo-García, A. (Jan, 2011) What Are The Specific Vs. Generalized Effects of Drugs of Abuse On Neuropsychological Performance? Neuroscience and Biobehavioral Reviews. 35(3):377-406

Flach, F.F. (2009) The Secret Strength of Depression, Hatherleigh Press, Hobart, NY

Flook, L., Smalley, S.L., Kitil, M.J., Galla, B.M., Kaiser-Greenland, S., Locke, J., Ishijima, E., Kasari, C. (2010) Effects of Mindful Awareness Practices On Executive Functions In Elementary School Children. Journal of Applied School Psychology, 26:70–95

Flynn, G. (1995) Negative Feelings Have An Edge On Positive Emotions. Personnel Journal, 74(8), 22

Forward, S. (1989) Toxic Parents, Overcoming Their Hurtful Legacy and Reclaiming Your Life, Bantam Books, New York, NY

Frewen, P.A., Evans, E. M., Maraj, N., Dozois, D. J.; A; Partridge, K. (Dec 2008) Letting Go: Mindfulness and Negative Automatic Thinking. Cognitive Therapy and Research 32.6: 758-774

Frey, W.H., DeSota-Johnson, D., Hoffman, C and McCall, J.T. (1981) Effect of Stimulus on the Chemical Composition of Tears, American Journal of Ophthalmology, 92(4), 559-67

Gable, S. L., Gonzaga, G., Strachman, A. (2006) Will you be there for me when things go right? Social Support for Positive Events. Journal of Personality and Social Psychology, 91, 904-917

Garzon, J. (Dec 6, 2013) Love Is War: Post-Infidelity Stress Disorder, York University Trauma Blog

Ge, T., Guo, S., Kendrick, K.M., Tao, H., Xue, Z., et al., (Oct, 2011) Brain Uncouples Brain Hate Circuit. Molecular Psychiatry, 18, 101-111

Geraskov, E. A. (1994) The Internal Contradiction and the Unconscious Sources of Activity. The Journal of Psychology, 128(6), 625

Giaconia, R., Reinherz, H., Silvernam, A., Pakiz, B, Frost, A., Cohen E. (1995) Traumas and Posttraumatic Stress Disorder In A Community Population of Older Adolescents.Journal of the American Academy of Child and Adolescent Psychiatry, 34 1369-1380

Gilles, C. (1999) Style of Anger Expression: Relation to Expressivity, Personality, and Health, Personal Social Psychology Bulletin, Oct 1999, 25:1196-1207

Ginzberg, J. (1991) In Search of a Voice: Working with Homeless Men, American Journal of Dance Therapy, Spr-Sum Vol 13(1) 33-48

Godbey, G. (2009) Outdoor Recreation, Health, and Wellness: Understanding and Enhancing the Relationship. Resources for the Future, Washington DC

Goncu, A., Sumer, N. (2011) Rejection Sensitivity, Self-Esteem, Instability, and Relationship Outcomes. European Psychologist, Vol 16(4) 303-313

Graham, J. E., Lobel, M., Glass, P., & Lokshina, I. (2008). Effects of Written Anger Expression In Chronic Pain Patients: Making Meaning From Pain. Journal of Behavioral Medicine, 31(3), 201-12

Griffin, K. (Aug 8, 2011) A Buddhist Approach to Recovery: Step Four – Searching and Fearless. Huffington Post

Gross, J. (2015) Handbook of Emotion Regulation. Guilford Press, New York, NY

Gross, J.J. (Dec 2001) Emotion Regulation in Adulthood: Timing Is Everything. Current Directions in Psychological Science 10.6 : 214-219

Gross, J.J. (2014) Emotion Regulation: Conceptual and Empirical Foundations. In J.J. Gross (Ed.), Handbook of Emotion Regulation (2nd ed.) (pp. 3-20). Guilford, New York, NY

Grumet, G.W. (Dec 1989) Laughter: Nature's Epileptoid Catharsis, Psychological Reports, Vol 65 (3, Pt 2)

Guo, G., Harris, K.M. (Nov, 2000) The Mechanisms Mediating The Effects of Poverty On Children's Intellectual Development, Demography, 37(4)

Hagenaars, M.A., Brewin, C.R., Van Minnen, A., Holmes, E.A., & Hoogduin, K.A.L. (2010) Intrusive Images and Intrusive Thoughts As Different Phenomena: Two Experimental Studies. Memory, 18 (1), 76-84

Hallinan, J.T. (May 7, 2014) The Remarkable Power of Hope, Psychology Today

Hanh, T.H. (2002) Anger –Wisdom to Cool the Flames, Riverhead Books, New York, NY

Harkness, K.L., Sabbagh, M.A., Jacobson, J.A., Chowdrey, N.K., Chen, T. (2005) Enhanced Accuracy of Mental State Decoding In Dysphoric College Students. Cognition and Emotion, 19 (7) 999-1025

Harte, J. (1991) Psychoneuroendocrine Concomitants of the Emotional Experience Associated with Running and Meditation, in Behavior and Immunity, edited by Husband. A.J., CRC Press

Heber, L. (1993) Dance Movement: A therapeutic program for Psychiatric clients. Perspectives in Psychiatric Care; Apr-Jun Vol 29(2) 22-29

Heller K. (1979) The Effects of Social Support: Prevention and Treatment Implications, in Goldstein A.P., Kanfer F.H., (eds), Maximizing Treatment Gains: Transfer Enhancement in Psychotherapy. Academic Press New York, NY

Hellman, C. M., & Mcmillin, W. L. (1997) The Relationship Between Psychological Reactance and Self-Esteem. The Journal of Social Psychology, 137(1), 135-138

Herman, J.L., Perry, J.C., and Bessel A. van der Kolk, B.A. (April 1989) Childhood Trauma in Borderline Personality Disorder, American Journal of Psychiatry

Hierholzer, R., Trivedi, M. H., Rush, A. J., Fava, M., & Wisniewski, S. R. (2006) Remission Rates for Depression in STAR*D Study/Dr. Trivedi and Colleagues Reply. The American Journal of Psychiatry, 163(7), 1293-1294

Hietanen, J.K., Surakka, V., Linnankoski, I. (Sept 1998) Facial electromyographic responses to vocal affect expressions. Psychophysiology. 35(5):530-536

Holiday, R. (May 2014) The Surprising Value of Negative Thinking, Psychology Today

Holland, J. (1973) Making Vocational Choices: A Theory of Careers. Prentice-Hall, Upper Saddle River, NJ

Hollingsworth, D. (April 1, 2016) I Left Alcoholics Anonymous because I Wanted to Maintain My Sobriety. Elephant Journal

Holmes, E., (2010) The Science of Mind: The Complete Edition, Tarcher, New York, NY

Howe, L., Dweck, C. (2016) Changes In Self-Definition Impede Recovery From Rejection. Personality and Social Psychology Bulletin. 42, 54-71

Hudson, N. Fraley, R. (Sept 2015) Volitional Personality Trait Change: Can People Choose to Change Their Personality Traits? Journal of Personality and Social Psychology. 109(3):490-507

Indigo, R. (May 6, 2014) Neuroscience Proves That Meditation Works, Huffington Post

Jack, D.C. (1991) Silencing the Self – Women and Depression, Harvard University Press, Cambridge, MA

Jackins, H. (1982) Fundamentals of Co-counseling Manual, Personal Counselors Inc., Rational Island Publishers, Seattle, WA

Jaffe, E. (Feb 2013) Why Love Literally Hurts - Association for Psychological Science Observer. Vol. 26, No.2

Jaffee, S. R., Moffitt, T. E., Caspi, A., Fombonne, E., & Al (2002). Differences in Early Childhood Risk Factors for Juvenile-Onset and Adult-Onset Depression. Archives of General Psychiatry, 59(3), 215-22

Janet, P. (1889) L'automatisme psychologique, Paris

Johnson, L. (1990) Creative Therapies in the Treatment of Addictions: The Art of Transforming Shame, Arts in Psychotherapy, Win Vol 17(4) 299-308

Johnson, M.D., Galambos, N.L. Krahn, H.J. (Apr 2014) Depression and Anger Across 25 Years. Changing Vulnerabilities In The VSA Model. Journal of Family Psychology, Vol 28(2) 225-235

Kardash, T. (June 1998) Taoism - The Wu-Wei Principle, Part 4. JadeDragon.com

Kashdam T., Biswas-Diener, R. (Oct 20, 2014) The Upside of Your Dark Side: Why Being Your Whole Self-Not Just Your Good Self –Drives Success and Fulfillment. Hudson Street Press, New York, NY

Kassel, J. D., Wagner E. F. (1993) Processes of Change in Alcoholics Anonymous: A Review of Possible Mechanisms, Psychotherapy, Vol 30 (2), 1993

Kaye, A., Matchan, D.C. (1978) Mirror of the Body, Strawberry Hill Press, San Francisco, CA

Kessler, R. (2000) Posttraumatic Stress Disorder: The Burden to The Individual and to Society. Journal of Clinical Psychiatry 61 (Suppl 5). 4-14

Kilpatrick D., Ruggiero, K, Acierno, B., Saunders, B., Resnick, H, Best, C. (2003) Violence and Risk of PTSD: Major Depression, Substance Abuse/Dependence, and Comorbidity: Results from The National Survey of Adolescents. Journal of Consulting and Clinical Psychology. 71(4) 692-700

King, R. (2008) Healing Rage: Women Make Inner Peace Possible. Gotham Publishing, New York, NY

Kirk, B. A., Schutte, N. S., Hine, D. W. (2011) The Effect of an Expressive-Writing Intervention for Employees on Emotional Self-Efficacy, Emotional Intelligence, Affect, and Workplace Incivility. Journal of Applied Social Psychology, 41(1), 179-195

Kernis, M., Grannemann, B., Barclay, L. (1989) Stability and Level of Self-Esteem as Predictors of Anger Arousal and Hostility. Journal of Personality and Social Psychology 1989 Vol 56, No 6 1013-1022

Kernis, M., Grannemann, B., Barclay, L. (1991) Stability of Self-Esteem as a Moderator of the Relation Between the level of Self-Esteem and Depression. Journal of Personality and Social Psychology 1991 Vol 62 No 1 80-84

Klein, K., Boals, A. (Sep 2001) Expressive Writing Can Increase Working Memory Capacity. Journal of Experimental Psychology, Vol. 130 Issue 3, p 520

Klep, A., Wisse, B., Van, D. F. (2011) Interactive Affective Sharing Versus Non-Interactive Affective Sharing in Work Groups: Comparative Effects of

Group Affect on Work Group Performance and Dynamics. European Journal of Social Psychology, 41(3), 312

Koenen, K. C., Moffitt, T. E., Caspi, A., Taylor, A., Purcell, S. (2003) Domestic Violence Is Associated With Environmental Suppression of IQ In Young Children. Development and Psychopathology, 15(2), 297-311

Kristiansen, C. Felton, K., Hovdestad, W., Allard, C. (1995) Ottawa Survivor's Study: A Summary of Findings, Carleton University, Ottawa, ON

Kross, E., Berman, M. G., Mischel, W., Smith, E. E., & Wager, T. D. (2011) Social Rejection Shares Somatosensory Representations With Physical Pain. Proceedings of The National Academy of Sciences, USA, 108, 6270–6275

Krznaric, R., (Nov 27, 2012) Six Habits of Highly Empathic People, Greater Good, Berkely University, Berkeley, CA

Kubarych, T.S., Prom-Wormley, E.C., Franz, C.E., Panizzon, M.S., Dale, A.M., Fischl, B., Eyler, L.T., Fennema-Notestine, C., Grant, M.D., Hauger, R.L., Hellhammer, D.H., Jak, A.J., Jernigan, T.L., Lupien, S.J., Lyons, M.J., Mendoza, S.P., Neale, M.C., Seidman, L.J., Tsuang, M.T., Kremen, W.S. (July 2012) A Multivariate Twin Study of Hippocampal Volume, Self-Esteem and Well-being in Middle-aged Men. Genes Brain and Behavior. 11(5):539-44

Lambert, N, Stillman, T. F., Hicks, J. A., Kamble, S., Baumeiter, R. F., Fincham, F. D. (2013) Belong Is To Matter: Sense of Belonging Enhances Meaning in Life. Personality and Social Psychology Bulletin, 39, 1418-1427

Lawler, K.A., Younger, J.W., Piferi, R.L., Jobe, R.L., Edmondson, K.A., Jones, W.H. (Apr 2005) The Unique Effects of Forgiveness On Health: An Exploration of Pathways. Journal of Behavioral Medicine.;28(2):157-67

Lawler-Row, K.A., Karremans, J.C., Scott, C., Edlis-Matityahou, M., Edwards, L. (Apr 2008) Forgiveness, Physiological Reactivity, and Health: The Role of Anger. International Journal of Psychophysiology. 68(1):51-8

Layous, K., Chancellor, J., Lyubomirsky, S., Wang, L., Doraiswamy, M. (2011) Delivering Happiness: Translating Positive Psychology Intervention Research for Treating Major and Minor Depressive Disorders The Journal of Alternative and Complementary Medicine. Volume 17, Number 8, Pp. 675–68

Lazar, S.W., Kerr, C.E., Fischl, B. (2005) Meditation Experience Is Associated With Increased Cortical Thickness Neuroreport. Nov 28, 2005; 16(17): 1893–1897

Lee, J., Tsunetsugu, Y. Takayama, N. Park, B., Li, Q., Song, C. Komatsu, M., Ikei, H., Tyrvainen, L., Kagawa, L., Miyazaki, Y. (2014) Influence of Forest

Therapy on Cardiovascular Relaxation in Young Adults. Hindawi Publishing Corporation. Evidence-Based Complementary and Alternative Medicine.

Leman, K., Carlson, R. (1989) Unlocking the Secrets of Your Childhood Memories. Thomas Nelson Publishers. Nashville, TN

Lewis, C., Lovatt, P. (2013) Breaking Away From Set Patterns of Thinking: Improvisation and Divergent Thinking. Thinking Skills and Creativity, 9, 46-58

Li, Q., Morimoto, K., Kpbayahsi, M., Inagaka, H., Katsumata, M., Hirata, Y., Hirata, K., Shimizu, T., Li, Y.K., Wakayama, Y., Kawada, T., Ohira, T., Takayama, N., Kagawa, T., Miyazaki, Y. (2008) Forest Bathing Trip Increases Human Natural Killer Activity and Expression of Anti-Cancer Proteins in Female Subjects. Journal of Biological Regulators and Homeostatic Agents. Vol 22, No 1. 45-55

Li, Q., Otsuka, T., Kobayashi, M., Wakayama, Y., Inagaki, H., Katsumata, M., Hirata, Y., Li, Y., Hirata, K., Shimizu, T., Suzuki, H., Kawada, T., Kagawa, T. (2011) Acute Effects of Walking in Forest Environments on Cardiovascular and Metabolic Parameters, European Journal of Applied Physiology 111:2845–2853

Li, X., Wei, L., & Soman, D. (2010) Sealing the Emotions Genie: The Effects of Physical Enclosure on Psychological Closure. Psychological Science, 21(8), 1047.

Lin, Y. (1998) The Importance of Living, Foreign Language Teaching and Research Press, China

Lipschitz, D., Rasmusson, A., Anyan, W., Comwell, P., Southwick, S. (2000) Clinical and Functional Correlates of Posttraumatic Stress Disorder In Urban Adolescent Girls At A Primary Care Clinic. Journal of the American Academy of Child and Adolescent Psychiatry, 39, 1104-1111

Little, B.R. (2014) Well-Doing: Personal Projects and the Quality of Lives. Theory and Research In Education. Vol 12(3) 329-346

Lo, H.M., Ng, S. M., Chan, C.L., Lam, K.F., Lau, B. H. (Aug 2013) The Chinese Medicine Construct "Stagnation" In Mind-Body Connection Mediates the Effects of Mindfulness Training On Depression and Anxiety. Complementary Therapies in Medicine Vol 21 (4) 348-57

Lohnes, K.L., and Kalter, N., (1994) Preventive Intervention Groups for Parentally Bereaved Children. American Journal of Orthopsychiatry. 64(4):594-603

Lovatt, P. (2013) Dance Psychology: The Power of Dance Across Behavior and Thinking. Psychology Review, 19 (1), 18-21

Lynch, J.J. (1990) The Broken Heart: The Psychobiology of Human Contact, In The Healing Brain - A Scientific Reader, Edited by Robert Ornstein and Charles Swencionis, Guilford Press, New York, NY

Maltz, M. (1960) Psyco-cybernetics, Simon and Shuster. New York, NY

Mantyla, T., & Sgaramella, T. (1997) Interrupting Intentions: Zeigarnik-Like Effects in Prospective Memory. Psychological Research, 60(3), 192-199

Marigold, D. C.; Cavallo, J. V.; Holmes, J. G.; Wood, J.V. (Jul 2014) You Can't Always Give What You Want: The Challenge of Providing Social Support to Low Self-Esteem Individuals. Journal of Personality and Social Psychology, Vol 107(1), 56-80

Mascolo, M., (2015) Culture Goes All The Way Down What the West Can Learn from Asia About Learning. Journal of Applied Developmental Psychology, 34,253-255

Masicampo, E. J., & Baumeister, R. F. (2011) Consider It Done! Plan Making Can Eliminate The Cognitive Effects of Unfulfilled Goals. Journal of Personality and Social Psychology, 101(4), 667

Mattisson, C., Bogren, M., Horstmann, V., Munk-Jörgensen, P., & Nettelbladt, P. (2007). The long-term course of depressive disorders in the Lundby Study. *Psychological Medicine, 37*(6), 883-891.

Mayberg, H.S., Liotti, M., Brannan, S.K., McGinnis, S., Mahurin, R.K., Jerabek, P.A., Silva, J.A., Tekell, J.L., Martin, C.C., Lancaster, J.L., Fox, P.T. (May 1999) Reciprocal Limbic-Cortical Function and Negative Mood: Converging PET Findings in Depression and Normal Sadness, American Journal of Psychiatry. 156: 675-682

Mayer, E.A. (July 13, 2011) Gut Feelings: The Emerging Biology of Gut-Brain Communication. National Review of Neuroscience, 12(8) 453-466

Mccoll-Kennedy, J., Patterson, P. G., Smith, A. K., & Brady, M. K. (2009) Customer Rage Episodes: Emotions, Expressions and Behaviors. Journal of Retailing, 85(2), 222-237

McCormick, R., (1994) The Facilitation of Healing Among First Nations People of British Columbia, Doctoral Dissertation, University of British Columbia, 1994

McCullough, M. E. (2000) Forgiveness As Human Strength: Theory, Measurement, and Links to Well-Being. Journal of Social and Clinical Psychology, 19(1), 43-55

McGregor, J., McGregor T. (Oct 30, 2013) Empathic People Are Natural Targets for Sociopaths - Protect Yourself. Addiction Today

McGuire L, Kiecolt-Glaser J.K., Glaser R. (Feb 2002) Depressive symptoms and lymphocyte proliferation in older adults. Journal of Abnormal Psychology. 111(1):192-197

Mechanic D. (1974) Social structure and personal adaptation: Some neglected dimensions, in Coelho, G.U., Hamburg D.A., Adam J.E. (eds), Coping and Adaptation. Basic Books. New York, NY

Miles, H.J., & Gross, J.J. (1999) Emotion suppression. In D. Levinson, J. Ponzetti, & P. F. Jorgensen (Eds.), Encyclopedia of Human Emotions (pp. 237-241). Macmillan, New York, NY

Miller, M. (2006) Letting Go and Letting Your Brain Make The Decision. Belvoir Media Group

Mischel, W. Ayduk, O. (2002) Self-Regulation in a Cognitive-Affective Personality System: Attentional Control in the Service of the Self. Self and Identity, 1: 113– 120

Miu, A, Yeager, D. (Sept 2014) Preventing Symptoms of Depression by Teaching Adolescents That People Can Change: Effects of a Brief Incremental Theory of Personality Intervention at 9-Month Follow Up. Clinical Psychological Science. vol. 3 no. 5 726-743

Mongrain, M., Chin, J. M., & Shapira, L. B. (2011) Practicing Compassion Increases Happiness and Self-Esteem. Journal of Happiness Studies, 12(6), 963-981

Monroe, J. (Feb 18, 2014) Poverty Can Happen to Anyone. The Guardian

Moon, B. B., Rhee, Y. (2012) Message Strategies and Forgiveness During Crises: Effects of Causal Attributions and Apology Appeal Types On Forgiveness. Journalism and Mass Communication Quarterly, 89(4), 677-694

Moore, T. (1992) Care of The Soul: A guide for cultivating depth and sacredness in everyday life, Harper-Collins Publishers, New York, NY

Mullet, E., Houdbine, A., Laumonier, S., Girard, M. (Dec 1998) "Forgivingness" Factor Structure in Sample of Young, Middle-Aged, and Elderly Adults, European Psychologist, Vol 3, No 4, 289-297

Mumme, D.L., Fernald, A. (2003) The Infant as Onlooker: Learning From Emotional Reactions Observed in a Television Scenario. Child Development, Jan/ Feb, Vol. 74 Issue 1, p221

Myles, A. (Aug 26, 2015) Ending The Rollercoaster of Drama With A Narcissist Or Sociopath, Elephant Journal

Nachmann, R. (1996) The Empty Chair: Finding Hope and Joy. Jewish Lights Publishing, Woodstock, VT

National Public Radio (2011) Strangers Can Spot Genetic Disposition for Empathy Washington, DC

Neff, K. (June 26, 2011) Why Self-Compassion Is Healthier Than Self-Esteem. Psychology Today

Ng, W., Diener, E. (2013) Daily Use of Reappraisal Decreases Negative Emotions Toward Daily Unpleasant Events. Journal of Social and Clinical Psychology, 32(5), 530-545

Nimoy, L. (1995) I Am Spock, Hyperion, New York, NY

Nisbett, R. (2004) The Geography of Thought: How Asians and Westerners Think Differently...and Why. Free Press, New York, NY

Noelker, L.S. (Nov 6, 2013) How The Arts Can Improve Your Health. Huffington Post

Noreen, S., Bierman, R.N., & Macleod, M.D. (2014) Forgiving You Is Hard, But Forgetting Seems Easy: Can Forgiveness Facilitate Forgetting? Psychological Science, 25(7), 1295

Olivia, G. (Nov 1998) A dialogue of touchstones, Dissertation Abstracts, (59-5-B) 2428

O'Reilly, J., Robinson, S.L., Berdahl, J.L., Banki, S. (April 4, 2014) Is Negative Attention Better Than No Attention? The Comparative Effects of Ostracism and Harassment at Work. Organizational Science, 26 (3) 774-793

Ornstein, R. Sobel, D.S. (1990) The Brain as a Health Maintenance Organization, The Healing Brain - A Scientific Reader, Edited by Robert Ornstein, R., Swencionis, C. (eds) Guilford Press, New York, NY

Ornstein, R., Sobel, D. (1989) Healthy Pleasures, Addison-Wesley Publishing, Boston, MA

Ortman, D.C. (2009) Transcending Post-Infidelity Stress Disorder (PISD): The Six Stages of Healing, Celestial Arts, Berkeley, CA

Otten, M. & Jonas K.J. (2014) Humiliation As An Intense Emotional Experience: Evidence From The Electro-Encephalogram. Social Neuroscience, 9(1), 23-25

Oxman, D.K. (Nov 1995) Principle Meditative Projects in Theravada Buddhist thought and their psychotherapeutic implications as experienced in the California Bay Area. Dissertation Abstracts. Vol 56(5-B) 2879

Ozyesil, Z. (2012) Five Factor Personality Trait As Predictor of Trait Anger and Anger Expression. Egitim Ve Bilim, 37 (163), 322-N/A

Park, B., Tsunetsugu, Y., Kasetani, T., Hirano, H., Kagawa, T., Sato, M., Miyazak, Y. (2007) Physiological Effects of Shinrin-yoku (Taking in the

Atmosphere of the Forest)–Using Salivary Cortisol and Cerebral Activity as Indicators Journal of Physiological Anthropology. Mar 26(2):135-42

Parrott, D. J., Zeichner, A., Evces, M. (2005). Effect of Trait Anger on Cognitive Processing of Emotional Stimuli. The Journal of General Psychology, 132(1), 67-80

Peale, N.V. (1952) The Power of Positive Thinking, Fawcett Publications Inc. Greenwich, CN

Pennebaker, J. (May 1997) Writing About Emotional Experiences As A Therapeutic Process. Psychological Science. vol. 8 no. 3 162-166

Perilloux, C., Buss, D. M. (2008) Breaking up romantic relationships: Costs experienced and coping strategies deployed. Evolutionary Psychology, 6(1)

Perls, F.S. (1969) Gestalt Theory Verbatim, Real People Press, Lafayette, CA

Phimister, E. G., Harkin, A. (2014) Muscling In On Depression. The New England Journal of Medicine, 371(24), 2333-2334

Pilyoung, K. (Nov 12, 2013) Effects of Childhood Poverty and Chronic Stress on Emotion Regulatory Brain Function in Adulthood. Proceedings of the National Academy of Social Sciences, Vol. 110 No. 46

Pinti, R. A. (2003) The Relationship Between Social Information-Processing Anger and Aggression In Delinquent Adolescent Black Males. Hofstra University. Dissertations and Theses, 107-107

Polusny, M., Follette, V. (1995) Long-Term Correlates of Child Sexual Abuse: Theory and Review of the Empirical Literature. Applied and Preventive Psychology: Current Scientific Perspectives, 4, 143-166

Post, S. G., (2005) Altruism, Happiness, and Health: It's Good to Be Good. International Journal of Behavioral Medicine, 12(2), 66-77

Pritzker, S. (2003) The Role of Metaphor in Culture, Consciousness, and Medicine: A preliminary inquiry into the metaphors of depression in Chinese and Western medical and common languages. Clinical Acupuncture & Oriental Medicine, Volume 4, No. 1, pp. 11-28

Pruessner J.C., Baldwin M.W., Dedovic K., Renwick R., Mahani N.K., Lord C., Meaney M., Lupien S. (Dec 2005) Self-esteem, locus of control, hippocampal volume, and cortisol regulation in young and old adulthood. Neuroimage. 28 (4):815-26

Purdon, C., Clark, D. A. (2000) White Bears and Other Elusive Intrusions: Assessing the Relevance of Thought Suppression for Obsessional Phenomena. Behavior Modification, 24(3), 425-453

Quoidbach, J., Dunn, E. W. (2010) Personality Neglect: The Unforeseen Impact of Personal Dispositions on Emotional Life. Psychological Science, 21(12), 1783

Quoidbach, J., Gilbert, D. T., & Wilson, T. D. (2013) The End of History Illusion. Science, 339(6115), 96-98

Ratner, K., Mendle, J., Burrow, A., Thoemmes, F. (April 2019) Depression and Derailment: A Cyclical Model of Mental Illness and Perceived Identity Change. Clinical Psychological Science.

Reference and Research Book News (May 2009) Wired to Care: How Companies Prosper When They Create Widespread Empathy. Financial Times 24(2), Prentice Hall, Upper Saddle River, NJ

Repetti, R. (1997) The Effects of Daily Job Stress on Parent Behaviour with Preadolescents, Paper presented at the Biennial Meeting of the Society for Research in Child Development

Reynolds, G. (Aug 15, 2010) Can Exercise Moderate Anger? New York Times Magazine, 21

Reynolds, M. (July 24, 2014) You Can Be Nice and Still Get Angry, Psychology Today

Rice, M., Howell, C. (2006) Differences In Trait Anger Among Children With Varying Levels of Anger Expression Patterns. Journal of Child and Adolescent Psychiatric Nursing, 19(2), 51-61

Richards, T. J., Hamilton, S. F. (2012). Obesity and Hyperbolic Discounting: An Experimental Analysis. Journal of Agricultural and Resource Economics, 37(2), 181-198

Rijavec, M., Jurcec, L., Mijocevic, I. (2010) Gender Differences in the Relationship Between Forgiveness and Depression/Happiness. Psychological Topics, 19(1), 189-202

Risen, J. (Oct 19, 2015) Believing What We Do Not Believe: Acquiescence to Superstitious Beliefs and Other Powerful Intuitions. Psychological Review

Romero-Canyas, R., Downey, G. (2013) What I See When I Think It's About Me: People Low In Rejection-Sensitivity Downplay Cues of Rejection in Self-Relevant Interpersonal Situations. Emotion, Vol 13, No 1 104-117

Ronson, J. (April 16, 2016) Monica Lewinsky: 'The shame sticks to you like tar' The Guardian

Rottenberg, J., Devendorf, A. R., Kashdan, T. B., & Disabato, D. J. (2018). The Curious Neglect of High Functioning After Psychopathology: The Case of Depression. Perspectives on Psychological Science, 13(5), 549–566.

Rozin, P., Millman, L., Nemeroff, C. (Apr 1986) Operation of The Laws of Sympathetic Magic In Disgust and Other Domains. Journal of Personality and Social Psychology, Vol 50(4), 703-712

Rubenstein, C., Shaver, P. (1982) In Search of Intimacy. Delacourt, New York, NY

Ruggieri, V., Sabatini, N., Muglia, G. (Feb 1985) Relationship between emotions and muscle tension in oro-alimentary behaviour. Perception and Motor Skills. 60(1):75-79

Runions, K. C. (2013) Toward a Conceptual Model of Motive and Self-Control In Cyber-Aggression: Rage, Revenge, Reward, and Recreation. Journal of Youth and Adolescence, 42(5), 751-71

Ryff, C., Singer, B. (2008) Know Thyself and Become What You Are: A Eudaimonic Approach to Psychological Well-Being. Journal of Happiness Studies 9:13-39

Saarni, C. (Apr 1999) A Skill Based Model of Emotional Competence: A Developmental Perspective. Paper presented at the Biennial Meeting of the Society for Research in Child Development, Albuquerque, NM

Saffrey, C., Summerville, A., Roese, N. J. (2008) Praise for Regret: People Value Regret Above Other Negative Emotions. Motivation and Emotion, 32(1), 46-54

Salter, A. (1949) Conditioned Reflex Therapy: The Direct Approach to the Reconstruction of Personality, Creative Age Press, New York, NY

Sandstrom, G. M., Dunn, E. W. (2014) Social Interactions and Well-Being: The Surprising Power of Weak Ties. Personality and Social Psychology Bulletin, 40(7), 910

Sbarra, D. A., Smith, H. L., Mehl, M. R. (2012) When Leaving Your Ex, Love Yourself: Observational Ratings of Self-compassion Predict the Course of Emotional Recovery Following Marital Separation. Psychological Science, 23(3), 261-269

Schachter, H. (Oct 15, 2013) Finding Your Passion, After Hours. The Globe and Mail

Scheff, T.J. (1979) Catharsis in Healing, Ritual and Drama, University of California Press, Berkeley and Los Angeles, CA

Schumann, K., Dweck, C. (Dec 2014) Who Accepts Responsibility for Their Transgressions? Personal Social Psychology Bulletin; 40(12):1598-610

Schwartz, D., Proctor, L. (2000) Community Violence Exposure and Children's Social Adjustment In The School Peer Groups: The Mediating Roles of Emotion Regulation and Social Cognition. Journal of Consulting and Clinical Psychology, 68 670-683

Seemann, E. A., Carroll, S. J., Woodard, A., Mueller, M. L. (2008) The Type of Threat Matters: Differences In Similar Magnitude Threats Elicit Differing Magnitudes of Psychological Reactance. North American Journal of Psychology, 10(3), 583-594

Seery, M., Blascovich, J., Weisbuch, M., Vick, S. (2004) The Relationship Between Self-Esteem, Self-Esteem Stability, and Cardiovascular Reactions to Performance Feedback. Journal of Personality and Social Psychology. Vol 87, 133-145

Shalev, I., Moffitt, T. E., Caspi, A. (2013) Stress-Related Disorders and Leukocyte Telomere Length: A Prospective Longitudinal Study of Four Decades. Comprehensive Psychiatry, 54(8)

Shalev, I., Moffitt, T.E., Sugden, K., Williams, B., Houts, R.M., Danese, A., Mill, J., Arseneault, L., Caspi, A. (May 2013) Exposure to Violence During Childhood Is Associated With Telomere Erosion From 5 to 10 Years of Age: A Longitudinal Study. Molecular Psychiatry 18, 576-581

Shea, G.F. (1984) Managing a Difficult or Hostile Audience, Prentice-Hall, Englwood Cliffs, NJ

Sheldon, K. M., Lyubomirsky, S. (April 2006) How to Increase and Sustain Positive Emotion: The Effects of Expressing Gratitude and Visualizing Best Possible Selves. Journal of Positive Psychology. 1(2) 73-82

Sheldon, K.M., Lyumbomirsky, S. (May 2012) The Challenge of Staying Happier: Testing the Hedonic Adaptation Prevention (HAP) Model. Personal Social Psychology Bulletin, Vol. 38 no. 5 670-680

Shen, D., Mao, W., Liu, T., Lin, Q., Lu, X., Wang, Q., Lin, F., Ekelund, U., Wijndaele, K. (Aug 25, 2014) Sedentary Behavior and Incident Cancer: A Meta-Analysis of Prospective Studies. Plos One. 9(8):E105709

Shields, A., Cicchetti, D. (1998) Reactive Aggression Among Maltreated Children: The Contributions of Attention and Emotion Dysregulation. Journal of Clinical Child Psychology, 27, 381-395

Shipman, K. Zeman, J., Penza, S., Champion, K. (2000) Emotion Management Skills In Sexually Maltreated and Non-Maltreated Girls: A Developmental Psychopathology Perspective. Developmental Psychopathology 12, 47-62

Slaby, A. (1989) Aftershock: Surviving the Delayed Effects of Trauma, Crisis and Loss, Villard Press, New York, NY

Smith, J., Rhodes, J. (June 2015) Being Depleted and Being Shaken: An Interpretative Phenomenological Analysis of The Experiential Features of A First Episode of Depression. Psychology and Psychotherapy: Theory, Research and Practice. Volume 88, Issue 2, 197–209

Spaccarelli, S. (1994) Stress, Appraisal, and Coping In Child Sexual Abuse: A Theoretical and Empirical Review. Psychological Bulletin, 116. 340-362

Spera, S., Morin, D., Buhrfeind, E., Pennebaker, J. (1994) Expressive Writing ad Coping with Job Loss. Academy of Management Journal, Vol 37, No 3 722-733

Spielmann, S. S., MacDonald, G., Joel, S., Impett, E. A. (2015) Longing for Ex-Partners out of Fear of Being Single. Journal of Personality

Spielmann, S., Joel, S., MacDonald, G., Kogan, A. (2013) Ex appeal current relationship quality and emotional attachment to ex-partners. Social Psychological and Personality Science, 4(2), 175-180

Sponagle, M. (April 2011) The Complete Guide to Your Hormones. Chatelaine, 98-105

Stackhouse, M., Ross, R., Boon, S. (Feb, 2016) The Devil in the Details: Individual Differences in Unforgiveness and Health Correlates. Personality and Individual Differences. (94) 337-341

Stacy, R., Brittain, K., Kerr, S. (2002) Singing for Health: An Exploration of The Issues. Health Education, 102(4), 156

Stanton, A.L., Danoff-Burg, S., Cameron, C.L., Bishop, M., Collins, C.A., Kirk, S.B., Sworowski, L.A., (2000) Emotionally Expressive Coping Predicts Psychological and Physical Adjustment to Breast Cancer, Journal of Consulting and Clinical Psych., Vol. 68, No 5

Strigo I.A., Simmons A.N., Matthews S.C., Craig A.D., Paulus M.P. (2008) Major Depressive Disorder Is Associated With Altered Functional Brain Response During Anticipation and Processing of Heat Pain. Archives of General Psychiatry 65(11):1275-84

Sunday Review (Aug 4, 2012) The Power of Negative Thinking, New York Times, New York, NY

Sutter, M., Yilmaz, L., Oberauer, M. (Aug 2015) Delay of Gratification and the Role of Defaults: An Experiment With Kindergarten Children. IZA Discussion Paper

Swami Prabhavanada (Translator), Manchester, F. (2002) The Upanishads: Breath from the Eternal. Signet Classics, Penguin Group, New York, NY

Szalavitz, M. (July 13, 2013) How Writing Heals Wounds – of Both The Mind and Body, Time.Com

Taquet, M., Quoidbach, J., De Montjoye, Y., Desseilles, M. (2014) Mapping Collective Emotions to Make Sense of Collective Behavior. Behavioral and Brain Sciences, 37(1), 102-3

Tavacioglu, L., Kora, O. K., Yilmaz, E., Hergüner, E. (2012) Evaluation of Anxiety Levels and Anger Styles of University Students. Psychology, 3(9), 737-741

Terr, L. (1994) Unchained Memories: True Stories of Traumatic Memories, Lost and Found, Basic Books, New York, NY

Thogersen-Ntoumani, C., Loughren, E. A., Kinnafick, F.-E., Taylor, I. M., Duda, J. L., Fox, K. R. (2015) Changes in work affect in response to lunchtime walking in previously physically inactive employees: A randomized trial. Scandinavian Journal of Medicine & Science in Sports

Thogersen-Ntoumani, C., Loughren, E. A., Taylor, I. M., Duda, J. L., Fox, K. R. (2014) A step in the right direction? Change in mental well-being and self-reported work performance among physically inactive university employees during a walking intervention. Mental Health and Physical Activity, 7(2), 89-94

Thomas, Roy Wallace (1937) We Pray Thee, Lord., Cokesbury Press

Tibubos, A. N., Schnell, K., Rohrmann, S. (2013) Anger Makes You Feel Stronger: The Positive Influence of Trait Anger In A Real-Life Experiment. Polish Psychological Bulletin, 44(2), 147

Tugade, M., Fredrickson, B. (Feb 2004) Resilient Individuals Use Positive Emotions to Bounce Back From Negative Emotional Experiences. Journal of Personal Social Psychology; 86(2): 320–333

University Wire (Oct 29, 2013). Avoiding Cognitive Bias. University Wire

Van der Kolk, B.A. (1994) The Body Keeps the Score: Memory and the Evolving Psychobiology of Posttraumatic Stress. Harvard Review of Psychiatry, Vol 1 No 5, 253-265

Van der Kolk, B.A., Fisler, R. (Oct 1995) Dissociation and the Fragmentary Nature of Traumatic Memories: Overview and Exploratory Study, Journal of Trauma and Stress. 8(4):505-25

Van Der Zee, S. Anderson, R., Poppe, R. (June 2, 2016) When Lying Feels the Right Thing to Do. Frontiers of Psychology

Van Derbur, Marilyn (2003) Miss America by Day: Lessons Learned from Ultimate Betrayals and Unconditional Love. Oak Hill Ridge Press

Vincent, N. Denson, L., Ward, L. (May 8, 2015) Triggers, Timing, and Type: Exploring Developmental Readiness and the Experience of Consciousness Transformation in Graduates of Australian Community Leadership Programs. Journal of Adult Development

Vingerhoets, A. J., Cornelius, R. R., Van Heck, G. L., Becht, M. C. (2000) Adult Crying: A Model and Review of the Literature. Review of General Psychology, 4(4), 354-377

Weng, H. Y., Fox, A. S., Shackman, A. J., Stodola, D. E., Caldwell, J. Z. K., Olson, M. C., Davidson, R. J. (2013) Compassion Training Alters Altruism and Neural Responses to Suffering. Psychological Science, 24(7), 1171

Whitaker, R. (2011) Anatomy of An Epidemic: Magic Bullets, Psychiatric Drugs and the Astonishing Rise of Mental Illness In America, Broadway Books, New York, NY

Williams, D. G., Morris, G. H. (Aug 1996) Crying weeping or tearfulness in British and Israeli adults, Journal of Psych., Vol 87(3): 479-505

Williams, J. M. G., Crane, C., Barnhofer, T., Brennan, K., Duggan, D. S., Fennell, M. J. V., Hackmann, A., Krusche, A., Muse, K., Von Rohr, I. R., Shah, D., Crane, R. S., Eames, C., Jones, M., Radford, S., Silverton, S., Sun, Y., Weatherley-Jones, E., Whitaker, C. J., Russell, D., & Russell, I. T. (2013) Mindfulness-Based Cognitive Therapy for Preventing Relapse in Recurrent Depression: A Randomized Dismantling Trial. Journal of Consulting and Clinical Psychology

Wilson, T.D., Gilbert, D.T. (2003) Affective Forecasting, Advances In Experimental Social Psychology, Vol 35 345-353

Wiseman, R. (Nov 8, 2004) Think Yourself Lucky. New Statesman 17,1

Wittstein, I. S., Thiemann, D. R., Lima, J. A., Baughman, K. L., Schulman, S. P., Gerstenblith, G., Wu, K. C., Rae, J. J., Bivalacqua, T. J., Champion, H. C. (2005) Neurohumoral Features of Myocardial Stunning Due to Sudden Emotional Stress. New England Journal of Medicine, 352, 539–548

Wolf, K. Foshee, V.A. (2005) Family Violence, Anger Expression Styles, and Adolescent Dating Violence. Journal of Family Violence, Vol 18, No 6

Wong, D. (Dec 12, 2012) Six Harsh Truths That Will Make You A Better Person. Cracked.Com

Wood, J., Perunovic, W., Lee, J. (2009) Positive Self-Statements: Power for Some, Peril for Others, Psychological Science Vol 20 No 7. 860-866

Wood, A.M., Joseph, S., Lloyd, J., Atkins, S. (2009) Gratitude Influences Sleep Through the Mechanism of Pre-Sleep Cognitions. Journal of Psychosomatic Research. 66 43-48

Worthington, E. (2005) Hope-Focused Marriage Counseling: A Guide to Brief Therapy. Intervarsity Academic Press, Downers Grove, IL

Yerkes R.M., Dodson J.D. (1908) The Relation of Strength of Stimulus to Rapidity of Habit-formation. Journal of Comparative Neurology and Psychology 18: 459–482

Yeshe, T. (1999) Making Your Mind An Ocean, Lama Yeshe Wisdom Archive

Zhai, L., Zhang, Y., Zhang, D. (Sept 2, 2014) Sedentary Behavior and the Risk of Depression: A Meta-Analysis. British Journal of Sports Medicine

Zweig, C. & Abrams, J. (1991) Meeting the Shadow: The Hidden Power of the Dark Side of Human Nature. Tarcher, NY.

Check out these other inspirational books
by Mark Linden O'Meara

Prayers and Meditations for Daily Inspiration

Kitten and Bear and the Big Tree

Let's Let Go: The Raindrop's Journey

Toxic Positivity

And listen to his music on all major platforms

Renewal

Run Like the Wind

Manufactured by Amazon.ca
Acheson, AB